TEACHER EDUCATION IN TIMES OF CHANGE

Responding to challenges across the UK and Ireland

The Teacher Education Group

Gary Beauchamp   Aileen Kennedy   Trevor Mutton
Linda Clarke   Geraldine Magennis   Teresa O'Doherty
Moira Hulme   Ian Menter   Gillian Peiser
Martin Jephcote Jean Murray

With a foreword by Marilyn Cochran-Smith

First published in Great Britain in 2016 by

Policy Press
University of Bristol
1-9 Old Park Hill
Bristol
BS2 8BB
UK
t: +44 (0)117 954 5940
pp-info@bristol.ac.uk
www.policypress.co.uk

North America office:
Policy Press
c/o The University of Chicago Press
1427 East 60th Street
Chicago, IL 60637, USA
t: +1 773 702 7700
f: +1 773-702-9756
sales@press.uchicago.edu
www.press.uchicago.edu

© Policy Press 2016

British Library Cataloguing in Publication Data
A catalogue record for this book is available from the British Library

Library of Congress Cataloging-in-Publication Data
A catalog record for this book has been requested

ISBN 978-1-4473-1854-5 paperback
ISBN 978-1-4473-1853-8 hardback
ISBN 978-1-4473-1857-6 ePub
ISBN 978-1-4473-1858-3 Kindle

The right of the Teacher Education Group to be identified as authors of this work has been asserted by them in accordance with the Copyright, Designs and Patents Act 1988.

All rights reserved: no part of this publication may be reproduced, stored in a retrieval system, or transmitted in any form or by any means, electronic, mechanical, photocopying, recording, or otherwise without the prior permission of Policy Press.

The statements and opinions contained within this publication are solely those of the authors and not of the University of Bristol or Policy Press. The University of Bristol and Policy Press disclaim responsibility for any injury to persons or property resulting from any material published in this publication.

Policy Press works to counter discrimination on grounds of gender, race, disability, age and sexuality.

Cover design by Liam Roberts
Printed and bound in Great Britain by CMP, Poole
Policy Press uses environmentally responsible print partners

Contents

List of authors		v
List of abbreviations		vii
Foreword by Marilyn Cochran-Smith		x

Part One: Setting the scene: context and methods — 1

one   Introduction   3
Ian Menter

two   UK and Irish teacher education in a time of change   19
Ian Menter

three   Analysing teacher education policy: comparative and historical approaches   37
Moira Hulme

Part Two: Teacher education policy in the five nations — 55

four   Teacher education in England: change in abundance, continuities in question   57
Jean Murray and Trevor Mutton

five   Teacher education policy in Northern Ireland: impediments, initiatives and influences   75
Linda Clarke and Geraldine Magennis

six   Teacher education in Scotland: consensus politics and 'the Scottish policy style'   91
Moira Hulme and Aileen Kennedy

seven   Teacher education in Wales: towards an enduring legacy?   109
Gary Beauchamp and Martin Jephcote

eight   Teacher education in the Republic of Ireland: a challenging and changing landscape   125
Teresa O'Doherty

Part Three: Critical issues in teacher education policy: home international analyses — 141

nine   Standards and accountability in teacher education   143
Aileen Kennedy

ten   The place of research in teacher education   161
Gillian Peiser

eleven   Teacher education and higher education   179
Jean Murray

twelve   Partnership in teacher education   201
Trevor Mutton

Part Four: Conclusion	**217**
thirteen Insights from the five nations and implications for the future	219
Moira Hulme, Ian Menter, Jean Murray and Teresa O'Doherty	
References	235
Index	279

List of authors

Gary Beauchamp is Professor of Education and Associate Dean (Research) in the School of Education at Cardiff Metropolitan University.

Linda Clarke is a Professor of Education at Ulster University in Northern Ireland.

Moira Hulme is Senior Lecturer in Educational Research at the Robert Owen Centre for Educational Change, University of Glasgow, UK.

Martin Jephcote is Professor of Education, Director of Teaching and Learning, at the School of Social Sciences, Cardiff University.

Aileen Kennedy is a Senior Lecturer in Primary Education, University of Edinburgh (from May 2015)

Geraldine Magennis lectures in Education and Literacy in St Mary's University College, Belfast. Her interests include Early Years Education.

Ian Menter is the former Professor of Teacher Education and Director of Professional Programmes at the University of Oxford and was also President of the British Educational Research Association from 2013 to 2015.

Jean Murray is Professor of Education and Research Leader in the Cass School, University of East London. Her research focuses on international teacher education.

Trevor Mutton is an Associate Professor at the Department of Education, University of Oxford, and is currently PGCE Course Director.

Teresa O'Doherty is Dean of Education at Mary Immaculate College, Limerick, and former Southern Chair of the Standing Conference of Teacher Educators, North and South (SCoTENS).

Gillian Peiser is a Senior Lecturer at Liverpool John Moores University. She teaches beginning and in-service teachers and supervises doctoral students.

List of abbreviations

AACTE	American Association of Colleges for Teacher Education
ADES	Association of Directors of Education
AERS	Applied Educational Research Scheme
BA	Bachelor of Arts
BEd	Bachelor of Education
BERA	British Educational Research Association
BSc	Bachelor of Science
CASS	Curriculum Advisory and Support Service
CATE	Council for Accreditation of Teacher Education
CDA	critical discourse analysis
CICE	Church of Ireland College of Education
CNAA	Council for National Academic Awards
COSLA	Convention of Scottish Local Authorities
CPD	continuing professional development
DCU	Dublin City University
DE	Department of Education [Northern Ireland]
DEL	Department for Employment and Learning [Northern Ireland]
DES	Department of Education and Skills [Republic of Ireland]
DfE	Department for Education [England]
EBITT	employment-based initial teacher training
EBT	evidence-based teaching
EIS	Educational Institute of Scotland
ELB	Education and Library Board
ESRC	Economic and Social Research Council
ETI	Education and Training Inspectorate [Northern Ireland]
GDP	Gross Domestic Product
GERM	global educational reform movement
GIRFEC	Getting it Right for Every Child
GTCNI	General Teaching Council for Northern Ireland
GTCS	General Teaching Council for Scotland
GTCW	General Teaching Council for Wales
GTS	General Teaching Council
HE	higher education
HEA	Higher Education Authority [Republic of Ireland]
HEFCW	Higher Education Funding Council for Wales

HEI	higher education institution
HMI	Her Majesty's Inspectorate
HMIE	Her Majesty's Inspectorate of Education
IME	Irish-medium education
ITE	initial teacher education
ITT	initial teacher training
LTS	Learning and Teaching Scotland
MA	Master of Arts
MDI	Mater Dei Institute
MEP	Masters in Educational Practice
MOOC	Massive Open Online Course
MOTE	Modes of Teacher Education
NCTL	National College for Teaching and Leadership
NEC	National Education Convention
NISE	National Institute for Studies in Education
NMWCTE	North and Mid Wales Centre of Teacher Education
NPP	National Partnership Project
NQT	newly qualified teacher
OECD	Organisation for Economic Co-operation and Development
PCK	pedagogical content knowledge
PGCE	Post Graduate Certificate of Education
PGDE	Professional Graduate Diploma in Education
PISA	Programme for International Student Assessment
PRSD	performance review and staff development
QTLS	qualified teacher learning and skills [status]
QTS	Qualified Teacher Status
QUB	Queen's University, Belfast
RAE	Research Assessment Exercise
RCT	randomised controlled trial
REF	Research Excellence Framework
RoI	Republic of Ireland
RSA	Royal Society of Arts
SCCC	Scottish Consultative Council on the Curriculum
SCET	Scottish Council for Educational Technology
SCITT	school-centred initial teacher training
SCLPL	Standard for Career-Long Professional Learning
SCoTENS	Standing Conference on Teacher Education, North and South
SENCo	Special Educational Needs Coordinator
SEWCTET	South East Wales Centre for Teacher Education and Training

List of abbreviations

SfLs	Standards for Leadership
SfRs	Standards for Registration
SIG	Special Interest Group
SNP	Scottish National Party
SPD	St Patrick's College Drumcondra
SQA	Scottish Qualifications Authority
STEAC	Scottish Tertiary Education Advisory Council
SWWCTE	South West Wales Centre of Teacher Education
TALIS	Teaching and Learning International Survey
TIS	Teacher Induction Scheme
TLRP	Teaching and Learning Research Programme
TTA	Teacher Training Agency
UCET	Universities' Council for the Education of Teachers
UGC	University Grants Committee
UK	United Kingdom
UNESCO	United Nations Educational, Scientific and Cultural Organisation
US	United States
WERN	Welsh Educational Research Network
WISERD	Welsh Institute for Social and Economic Research, Data and Methods

Foreword

Marilyn Cochran-Smith

This is a provocative, important and, to my knowledge, unique book about initial teacher education within and across five national contexts – each of the jurisdictions of the United Kingdom (UK) (England, Northern Ireland, Scotland, and Wales) and the Republic of Ireland (RoI). Of course there are now many books, reports and special issues of journals that provide an international look at teacher education or compare the goals, approaches and outcomes of initial teacher preparation in two or more countries. Some of these are intended to highlight policies and practices to be imitated or borrowed from 'high-performing' countries; others provide case studies or empirical analyses of particular teacher education policies and practices in a selection of countries and then consider cross-cutting trends and policy implications. While this book joins the ranks of these extant volumes in certain ways, it is unique in others.

The book is a product of the Teacher Education Group (TEG) in collaboration with education researchers from the RoI. The decade-long agenda of TEG is inquiry into learning to teach across the four jurisdictions of the UK. As this book demonstrates, the 'home-international' approach taken up by the group is remarkably productive in revealing both continuities/discontinuities and convergences/divergences in teacher education policy since 1984 within one relatively small geographic area that has complex historical and geopolitical connections to Europe, Australasia and the Americas. In fact, I think that one of the major contributions of the book is its juxtapositioning of trenchant intra-national analyses of teacher education policy and practice in each of the five jurisdictions (Chapters Four to Eight, which describe teacher education policy in England, Northern Ireland, Scotland, Wales and the RoI, respectively) with analyses of cross-national trends and supranational discourses (Chapters Nine to Twelve, which take up broader issues, namely standards/accountability, research, higher education and partnerships, respectively). Together with three introductory chapters that lay out the book's comparative approach, the country and cross-country analyses confirm that teacher education policies – like other education and social policies – are actively translated, mediated and contested (rather than passively transferred or passed along) within and across particular national contexts. As importantly, though, the book also shows how and to what extent these processes of active transformation occur – who the players are, what historical and socioeconomic factors facilitate or impede mediation, how culturally and institutionally shaped practices influence local instantiations, and how there can be simultaneously such striking similarities but also deep divisions in teacher education policy among the very close neighbours that inhabit the islands of the UK and RoI.

My charge in this foreword was to consider how the five cases in this book relate to trends and developments in teacher education policy in the 'rest of the world'. This is, of course, a daunting and ultimately undoable task, given – as the book so skilfully shows – that nuanced variations in the historical, socioeconomic, cultural, linguistic, institutional and geopolitical characteristics of particular nations interact with one another and with larger social forces to mediate even those policies that appear on the surface to be very much the same. Much more modestly, then, in this foreword, I have selected five aspects or 'turns' in teacher education policy that are central to the discussions in this book – the policy turn, the accountability turn, the practice turn, the university/research turn and the equity turn. I comment briefly on these five in terms of broader trends and in relation to teacher education policy in the United States (US).

The policy turn

A decade ago, as this book acknowledges, I suggested that in the US, the enterprise of teacher education was increasingly conceptualised and acted upon as 'a policy problem' (Cochran-Smith, 2005b; Cochran-Smith and Fries, 2008). What I meant was that more and more often it was assumed that a key strategy for solving 'the problem' of teacher education was determining which of the broad structural arrangements and regulations of teacher education that could be manipulated by policy makers was most likely to have a positive impact on desired school outcomes, usually defined as student achievement, measured by tests. I also pointed out that at the same time that the policy turn zeroed in on outcomes-based accountability, it also marginalised other important outcomes related to students' learning and life chances, including social, emotional and moral development, civic engagement, and preparedness to participate in a democratic society.

This book focuses on the policy turn in teacher education. As importantly, the book explains why studying teacher education policy is significant politically, sociologically and educationally. As Menter proposes in Chapter One, teacher education policy reflects both the dominant (and contested) values of a particular nation, revealing how those in power desire to shape the education of those who shape the lives of society's future citizens and participants. In many countries, including the five in this book, the policy turn reflects the shift to a global and competitive knowledge society, which has also been a shift to neoliberal economics wherein individualism, free markets and private good(s) have taken precedence over other goals. In the US and in some other places, including England, neoliberal perspectives have become nearly imperceptible as ideology and are more likely to be understood as common sense (Apple, 2005; Ball, 2012). As many scholars have argued, the shift to a knowledge economy has brought unparalleled attention to the quality of education systems, and in particular to teacher education providers and teachers, who are presumed to be the generators of knowledge workers for the new economy.

The accountability turn

Unprecedented attention to teacher quality has consistently been coupled with new standards for teaching and teacher education and with outcomes-based educational accountability. All five of the countries described in this book (and many others) now have professional teaching standards that are the basis of candidate, programme and/or institutional evaluation. Although most comprise some combination of the knowledge, skills and dispositions deemed necessary by a particular governing or professional group for entry-level and/or continued teaching, they range, as the country chapters in this book aptly illustrate, from those that are more values-oriented to those that are more technically oriented, thus reflecting strikingly different ideas about the activity of teaching and the nature of teacher professionalism. As the book shows, to a great extent the different approaches depend on shifts in the power structures of educational policy making that have occurred in many countries over the last 30 years as neoliberal governments came into power, and they also depend on the degree to which teaching standards have been imposed upon, rather than emergent from, the profession.

The extreme case here may be the US where 'inputs-based' teacher education evaluation (eg, according to programme mission, faculty qualifications, resources, and curriculum alignment with professional standards) has repeatedly been deemed inferior to outcomes-based accountability by critics of university teacher education. With the latter, teacher education programmes are to be held accountable for their graduates' effectiveness, determined through value-added and other assessments that link student achievement data with teacher and preparation programme data. A case in point is the Obama administration's 2014 proposed – and very controversial – teacher education regulations that would require all states to report yearly to the federal government their ratings of all teacher education programmes according to four performance standards (from exceptional to low-performing) based on the achievement of the students of a programme's graduates, the employment outcomes of programme graduates, programme graduates' and their employers' perceptions of preparation programme quality, and state/national accreditation. Low performers that do not show improvement would be subject to loss of state approval, state funding and federal student aid (US Department of Education, 2014).

The practice turn

Across the chapters in this book, several authors describe 'the practice turn' in teacher education, also referred to as the 'practicum turn' and the 'practical turn', although these have different meanings, as Murray points out in Chapter Eleven. The practice turn has emerged internationally in the face of mounting claims that college and university preparation programmes have failed to produce effective teachers in part because of the long-perceived 'gap' between theory and practice. The notion of a 'theory–practice gap' is based on the perceived failure of the university model of teacher education, which presumably emphasises theory, values and beliefs at the expense of actual teaching practice, thus leaving new teachers on their own to implement or translate (university-produced) theory into (classroom-ready) practice. This book draws on several useful frameworks (eg, Sachs, 2001; Whitty, 2008; Furlong and Lawn, 2010) for making sense of the practice turn in the five countries of interest here as well as internationally, including unpacking the markedly different notions of practice and teacher professionalism at their core.

In the US, the turn towards practice is strong, although it has many competing manifestations, including: fast-track entry routes featuring 'on-the-job' training; state requirements that teacher candidates pass a uniform teacher performance assessment for initial licensure; school-based residency models of teacher preparation; new 'graduate schools of education', unaffiliated with universities, where the curriculum emphasises teaching the techniques of 'successful' teachers; university programmes that revolve around 'high-leverage' classroom practices;

professional requirements that stipulate that more of the overall hours of teacher preparation be spent in clinical practica; and new kinds of partnerships with communities and schools. All of these reforms take a turn towards practice, but they are dramatically different from one another in terms of their underlying views of teaching (Cochran-Smith, in press). Some are driven by a technical view, assuming that good teaching depends on management techniques, understood as explicit, highly uniform, predictable sequences of teacher behaviours. Others reflect a more complicated view, assuming that core teaching practices must be decomposed into their many parts, which have highly stable and predictable relationships, and that the parts can be taught and rehearsed separately and then recomposed in the act of teaching. Still others are based on a complex view, assuming that teaching is a more holistic activity, which is not equal to the sum of its interacting parts, given their non-linear and not fully predictable relationships. Although all of the practice turns mentioned above purportedly reject the theory–practice binary, some may actually exacerbate it by reinforcing the idea that practice is inherently non-theoretical and theory is inherently non-practical (Carr, 1987).

The university/research turn

One of the fascinating aspects of teacher education policy in four of the five countries described in this book is the emergence of the practice turn, above, and, simultaneously, the consolidation and strengthening of the place of the university in initial teacher education. These policy developments are articulated across the country chapters and also synthesised in Murray's perceptive chapter on higher education (Chapter Eleven). However, the consolidation of the university role in teacher education is instantiated very differently across the RoI, Northern Ireland, Scotland and Wales, where it is variously reflected in efforts to relocate all initial teacher education in universities, to merge or amalgamate teacher colleges with universities, to extend the length of undergraduate and/or graduate degrees, or to strengthen the role of research in and on initial teacher education.

Although the authors of several of the chapters in this book are rightly cautious not to characterise uncritically England's 'exceptionalism', it may well be that England is indeed an outlier in terms of the university turn, given its stipulations regarding the maximum number of days that teacher candidates may spend in universities, its School Direct provisions and its expansion of alternate routes into teaching. In this regard, the US is more like England than the other four countries under examination and, like England, less consistent with European trends regarding teacher preparation. In fact, if the focus of this book were on policy similarities between England and the US, one might well conclude that the words in the book's title and subtitle – teacher education in 'times of change' and 'responding to challenges' – drastically understate the tenuous future of university teacher education and fail to capture the extremity of the current policy and political situation. Analysts in the US and England – and in some other parts of the world, including Australia – have characterised teacher education's current situation with considerably more urgency and sense of crisis, using words such as tumultuous and dangerous to refer to 'the times' and words such as rupture, dislocate, deform, distort, disrupt and deride to refer to the sharp impact of the neoliberal reform movement, which has severely diminished the role of universities in teacher education and marginalised the importance and credibility of university research in and on teacher preparation.

The equity turn

Internationally, many current policies related to teacher education are based on the assumption that the existing arrangements of teacher education are not producing teachers who meet the expectation of ensuring both excellence and equity for all students. This is explicit in many national and international reports, including the often-quoted 2005 report from the Organisation for Economic Co-operation and Development (OECD, 2005) about the importance of teachers: 'Improving the efficiency and equity of schooling depends, in large measure on ensuring that competent people want to work as teachers, their teaching is of high quality and that all students have access to high quality teaching' (2005, p 1). As this book about the UK and RoI makes clear, however, although the goal of equity is reflected in the standards of all five countries, what it means to prepare teachers to teach for 'equity' ranges from a technical rational view to one that focuses more on the morality and ethics of teaching. This is especially clear in Hulme and Kennedy's chapter (Chapter Six), which points out that Scotland's teacher education standards maintain a focus on equity and social justice within a larger frame of social democracy, more so than the other four countries considered.

In the US, 'equity' is the intended outcome of many policies aimed at reforming teacher education, as reflected in what we have called the 'teacher quality gap' discourse, which uses the rhetoric and logic of civil rights to ally itself with the long struggle against injustice in the form of discrimination and exclusion of diverse and minority groups (Cochran-Smith and Fries, 2011). This discourse emphasises that all students have the right to equal educational opportunities and, presumably as a result, equal educational outcomes. However, this dominant view in US teacher education policy of 'equity as access' to teacher quality and to high standards does not address the societal structures and systems that reproduce inequalities and inequity of access in the first place. Underlying the 'equity as access' discourse is the assumption that poor and minority students, who enter school 'behind', need high-quality teachers to raise their achievement levels within the existing accountability regime. From this perspective, diversity is seen as a risk and a deficit, and it is assumed that what is needed is to ensure that all students have access to the existing curriculum, standards and knowledge canons of the current system. In stark contrast, from a social justice perspective, each of these assumptions is regarded as deeply flawed and not simply untenable, but destructive in that they actually perpetuate longstanding inequities and work against new conceptualisations. What this means is that in the US, the dominant equity turn is broadly consistent and often braided together with the policy turn of the neoliberal reform agenda, a powerful combination that ultimately serves to help reproduce school and social inequalities.

Teacher education in times of change: Responding to challenges across the UK and Ireland is a unique volume that weaves trenchant country-specific descriptions of teacher education policy in England, Scotland, Wales, Northern Ireland and the RoI, together with cross-cutting analyses of historical, geopolitical, economic and institutional trends that both unite and divide these nations, which share a relatively small geographic area. The book raises many critical questions about the past, present and future of initial teacher education during a period of enormous change in national, international and global policy and politics. It is well worth the read.

Marilyn Cochran-Smith
Cawthorne Professor of Teacher Education for Urban Schools
at the Lynch School of Education, Boston College
September 2015

Part One:
Setting the scene: context and methods

ONE

Introduction

Ian Menter

Why is teacher education policy significant – politically, sociologically and educationally? While the significance of practice in teacher education has long been recognised, influencing as it does the practice of teachers in schools and colleges and thereby having a strong effect on the quality of educational experiences for learners, the significance of policy in teacher education has only been fully appreciated in the more recent past.

It is our contention, in writing this book, that an analysis of teacher education policy in any state system is deeply revealing of the currently dominant values within that society. Through defining how and where teachers should be prepared for their work and sometimes through prescribing exactly what it is they should know and be able to do, we see how those in power in society are seeking to shape the world for future citizens. However, these values and commitments are not necessarily simply enacted within society. There may well be considerable resistances, adaptations and 'accommodations' that are made as policy processes are played out. Indeed, our further line of argument is that these contestations themselves are highly significant sociologically and are frequently indicative of deep underlying conflicts within society. It is for reasons such as this that the study of teacher education policy is of enormous interest, not only to educationalists but also to sociologists and political scientists.

Teacher education became a particular focus for political intervention in the United Kingdom (UK), the Republic of Ireland (RoI) and across the developed world during the 1980s, which was a time of enormous political and cultural change. Under the influence of neoliberal governments, cultures of accountability and control developed rapidly, leading to the emergence of teacher education systems dominated by standards frameworks, which set out explicitly what it was that teachers should be able to do and setting conditions for the provision of teacher education. There was also heightened contestation about the location of teacher education. What were the respective contributions of colleges, universities, schools, local authorities and central government, for example? And what were the governance arrangements, including the responsibilities of local and central government, teaching councils and other bodies?

This book draws predominantly on the experience of the contributors of working in and researching teacher education in the four jurisdictions of the UK and the RoI over many years. However, the perspectives taken are not inward looking and at all times we seek to relate developments in the UK and RoI to developments in Europe, North America and Australasia in particular, but also to the changing global dynamics of education more generally. Nevertheless, the insights to be gained from 'home international' investigation (Raffe et al, 1999) within what some have described as a 'natural experimental laboratory' are extremely rich. The methodological issues that arise from such a comparative approach are explored in considerably more detail in Chapter Three.

Later in this introduction, following exploration of some of the main themes of the book, the rationale for and the creation of the Teacher Education Group, its support by a number of educational organisations and its links with international networks will be explained. The chapter concludes by setting out the structure of the book.

The significance of policy in teacher education

The historic origins of teacher education systems around the world are closely associated with the emergence of the provision of public schooling. Details of the arrangements for public schooling vary enormously internationally and there is also considerable variation in the details of the provision of teacher education. Nevertheless, a number of themes have been consistently at the centre of developments in most parts of the world, including:

- the respective contributions of educational theory, educational research and practical experience;
- the respective contributions of serving teachers, other professional educators and educationalists (theorists and researchers);
- the best sites for learning for beginning teachers – the school, the educational laboratory, the college or the university.

Although these developments can be traced back well into the 19th century, one key starting point for this book is the 1980s. In particular, a key text published in 1984, with the title *Change in teacher education* (Alexander et al, 1984a), captures the dynamic upheavals and transformations that were starting to occur during that period (see Chapter Four for a fuller discussion). And although that book focused mainly on England and Wales, there were resonances of similar changes elsewhere in the UK and beyond.

The 1980s was the decade in which the full 'economisation' of state education started to take hold, as neoliberal Thatcherite policies across all of the public services were being developed. (Equivalent approaches under 'Reaganomics' in the United States [US] were soon to follow.) This was an era of the 'marketisation' of educational provision, with ideas about the use of vouchers for the procurement of schooling being floated by right-wing think tanks and 'parental choice' in schooling being promoted. Education increasingly came to be seen as a consumer good that should be subject to 'the logic of the market place' (Ball, 2003, p 8).

As will become clear later in this volume, the trajectory of such neoliberal thinking was far from consistently developed across the UK and RoI, with the RoI and Scotland each taking rather different approaches to 'reform' of both schooling and teacher education. Indeed, there was considerable resistance to neoliberal policies in Scotland and, although the Westminster-based UK government at that time had full legal authority over Scottish education, because it was administered separately through the Scottish Office, the policy community in Scotland was able to resist the policies with considerable success (Paterson, 2003). In the RoI, policy was much more influenced by developments in Europe than by those in the UK.

Furthermore, again as we shall see later, following the changed arrangements for intra-UK governance that followed from the election of a 'New Labour' government at Westminster in 1997, we saw full responsibility for education policy being devolved to new political institutions in Scotland, Wales and Northern Ireland. This led to even more distinctive trajectories than had previously been the case, with increased divergence in some key aspects of education policy (Jones, 2003; Menter et al, 2006).

But before looking at the impact of these changes post-1984 and post-1997, we should first give greater consideration to the arrangements for teacher education that had developed across the UK and RoI during the 19th and 20th centuries. The histories of teacher education have been written elsewhere (eg Cruickshank, 1970; Dent, 1977; Coolahan, 2004a) but could be summarised as follows.

The preparation of teachers for younger children had tended to be distinct from that of older children and indeed it was the development of elementary schooling that had originally led to the development of institutionalised approaches to teacher preparation. This was initially through strongly apprenticeship-based approaches, such as pupil–teacher schemes and then 'normal schools', leading eventually to the establishment of teacher training colleges or colleges of education, most of which specialised in provision for early years and primary school-aged children. The 20th century saw the steady extension of the duration of compulsory schooling – the recurrent raising of the school leaving age. This led from a time when many teachers in secondary schools were employed without a teaching qualification – usually basing their expertise on a university degree in the subject that they taught – through to a situation where a number of universities created departments of education (sometimes based on day training colleges), which could offer teaching certificates.

By the 1970s, teaching was moving towards becoming an all-graduate profession, which led to the rapid expansion of colleges of education and university departments, with many of the degrees awarded by colleges being validated by universities.

The development of education studies as a major area of academic work was associated with this expansion, with new specialist fields – sometimes known as the 'disciplines of education' (history, philosophy, psychology and sociology) – emerging (Furlong, 2013a). So it was that across the UK and RoI, by the 1980s it was common for all teachers to have a teaching qualification, either a degree such as the Bachelor of Education (BEd) (taken over three or four years) or a Post Graduate Certificate of Education (PGCE), usually a one-year programme of study following a three-year (or in Scotland a four-year) first degree.

The 1980s was a period of economic recession following the sudden rise in oil prices during the mid-1970s. There were enormous pressures on public spending and this was one of the key factors that led to the 'rationalisation' of teacher education provision in the UK, with the closure and/or amalgamation of many colleges of education (Hencke, 1978). Furthermore, many of these independent 'monotechnics' became part of multidisciplinary polytechnics or colleges of advanced technology, so bringing teacher education increasingly into the wider provision of higher education. During the 1990s, a further significant step was taken when the 'binary line' between vocational and non-vocational higher education institutions was abolished. A process began whereby almost all of the higher education institutions in the UK would become universities – or sometimes university colleges (as for example was the case for two colleges in Northern Ireland).

This, then, was the backdrop against which direct political interest in the processes of teacher education began to take a grip – especially in

England and Wales. Indeed, we tend to draw examples in what follows especially from the English context because these examples provide the clearest exemplification of the trends that are being described. Some of the examples are then discussed again, albeit in more detail, in Chapter Four, which focuses directly on England.

Political intervention in teacher education in the UK and RoI

The paradoxes inherent in neoliberal intervention in education policies have been well explored by scholars such as Ball (1994), Tomlinson (2001), Chitty (2014) and others. As Whitty and Menter (1989) put it, in an early analysis of the impact of the Education Reform Act 1988 in England and Wales, these policies demonstrate a curious combination of the moral authoritarianism demonstrated in the imposition of a prescribed curriculum and new systems of testing, on the one hand, and the economic libertarianism of new modes of governance, on the other, including such policies at that time as 'open enrolment into schools' and the 'local management of schools' (LMS).

The ideology of parental choice as the 'driver' of educational improvement could only be justified if parents (consumers) had access to information upon which to come to a decision about which school to send their child to. In this move to what LeGrand and others called 'quasi-marketisation' (LeGrand and Bartlett, 1993; LeGrand, 2007), we saw increased competitiveness between schools and new accountability measures, not least the development of school 'league tables' and the publication of school inspection outcomes under the auspices of Ofsted (the Office for Standards in Education), which replaced inspections by Her Majesty's Inspectorate in 1992.

If much of the rationale for this marketisation was provided by public concern about educational standards (sometimes seen as a media-driven 'moral panic') and about the alleged informality and progressive ideologies that were influencing teaching in many schools, then it is perhaps not surprising that attention should very soon pass to teachers and to their education and training. In England, the first very clear policy intervention in this respect came through a government White Paper entitled *Teaching quality* (DES, 1983), which was produced while Sir Keith (later Lord) Joseph was the-then Prime Minister Margaret Thatcher's Secretary of State for Education. Joseph was a key neoliberal thinker in the Conservative government, strongly influenced by neoliberal economists Friedman and von Hayek and himself strongly influencing Thatcher's economic policy. The White

Paper explicitly expressed concern about the quality of teaching in England and Wales and drew attention to the wide range of practices in teacher preparation. Emerging from this White Paper the following year was the first national body to introduce national regulations into the provision of teacher education – the Council for Accreditation of Teacher Education (CATE). These regulations were set out in a government circular (known as '3/84') entitled *Initial teacher training* (DES, 1984) and included stipulations about the balance between student teachers' study of subject matter – including the requirement of a specialist subject – and their examination of 'educational and professional studies'. They also set out a minimum amount of time to be spent in a school setting in each initial teacher education programme. Furthermore, on the basis that many 'education lecturers' in colleges and universities were deemed to be out of touch with current practices in schools, a requirement was introduced that such staff should have regular periods of 'renewal of professional experience'.

It is important to point out that much of the thinking behind these proposals and their successors – there was a succession of similar circulars that continued well into the 1990s – had been influenced by a succession of pamphlets and media stories generated by right-wing think tanks, including the Adam Smith Institute, the Centre for Policy Studies and the Hillgate Group (see Furlong et al, 2000; Chapter Three, this volume). The allegations in these publications were that teacher training colleges had been dominated by members of 'the loony left' who were preaching anti-racism, anti-sexism or even 'class warfare' to student teachers and were inculcating them with 'barmy educational theory'. These pamphleteers and their colleagues took the alternative view that good teaching was a simple matter of love for a subject and an ability to communicate that subject in a classroom. Indeed, when Kenneth Clarke succeeded as Secretary of State for Education in the early 1990s, his main platform in this area was to argue that new teachers would learn best from working alongside existing teachers (even though those teachers themselves had been subject to the alleged biased approaches of the colleges of education!). He therefore called for three quarters of the PGCE training year to be based in schools. By the time this was implemented, the proportion was reduced to two thirds, a proportion that in essence prevails in England to this day.

Thus began a process of increasingly centralised control of initial teacher education in England that was only partially mirrored elsewhere in the UK, or indeed in the RoI and Europe. The 1980s was a period of considerable tension for teachers, with a number of disputes about pay and conditions as well as them being increasingly subjected – especially then in the 1990s – to a 'discourse of derision' (Ball, 1990), with the teaching profession being portrayed as a significant part of 'the problem' of education. When the New Labour government was elected at Westminster in 1997, one of its first education publications was a Green Paper entitled *Teachers: Meeting the challenge of change* (DfEE, 1988; see also Graham, 1999). This in itself did not propose many changes in initial teacher education (other than the introduction of 'skills tests' for beginning teachers); however, it did signal the introduction of 'performance management' into teaching and the introduction of new performance-related payments, with the establishment of a pay threshold. In order to progress over the threshold, teachers had to be assessed against a series of standards.

Indeed, 'competences' and then 'standards' had been introduced just a few months earlier into initial teacher education through circular 9/97 (DfEE, 1997) – a New Labour document that set out 'observable behaviours' that beginning teachers would have to demonstrate before they could qualify. In due course, the government also introduced a national curriculum for initial teacher training and subsequently very prescriptive measures about the teaching of literacy, including the requirement to teach a particular approach to learning to read – 'systematic synthetic phonics'.

This tendency for prescription in the organisation and management of teacher education – as with the twin approaches of neoliberalism noted above in relation to schools – was complemented by a process of 'diversification' of entry routes into teaching. It is worthy of note, however, that such diversification has not occurred in Scotland and is far less prevalent in Wales. Northern Ireland has maintained its commitment to university-based partnerships, while in the RoI a distance learning provider – Hibernia – has been very active in offering 'alternative' provision. In England, though, since 1988, when employment-based routes were first introduced, there has been an increasing range of entry routes. Following the increasing emphasis on 'school-based training', England has seen the introduction of:

- school-centred initial teacher training (SCITT) schemes;
- Teach First – an employment-based route for 'bright' graduates who might not otherwise enter the teaching profession (based on Teach for America in the US);
- a range of other employment-based routes.

The most recent innovation of this kind is the introduction of 'School Direct' under the former coalition government. Michael Gove, who was

Secretary of State for Education for the first four years of the coalition government (2010–14), published a White Paper in 2010 entitled *The importance of teaching* (DfE, 2010), a title used apparently without irony, in which he called for more teacher education to be school-led, rather than university-led. There were various contradictory statements from the government about the role of universities in the provision of teacher education but Gove did make it explicit in the White Paper that his aim was that half of all provision should be school-led by the time of the ensuing General Election in 2015 (see Childs and Menter, 2013).

During the same period that the Westminster government was promoting school-led teacher education, the Scottish Government was implementing the recommendations of the 2010 Donaldson Report, entitled *Teaching Scotland's future* (Donaldson, 2011), which called for a consolidation of the contribution of universities to teacher education, with greater emphasis on university-based subject knowledge. Indeed, Donaldson apparently understood the nature of teaching in a manner that was in direct contrast to the way in which Gove understood it. Gove talked of a craft to be learned through an apprenticeship model, whereas Donaldson talked of a complex and intellectual profession to be learned over the course of a teacher's career and to be informed by a high level of research and scholarship (Hulme and Menter, 2011).

More details on all of these developments are provided in subsequent chapters. The key point for consideration here though is how it can be that policy developments have taken such different directions in two distinct parts of the UK. What is it that is driving these different policy trajectories? Is it politics, prejudice, culture or ideology – or a combination of these? Or is it the careful use of research evidence or comparative international analysis – or a combination of these? There is no doubt that across the UK, the RoI and the wider world, teacher education has become deeply politicised. It is a matter that is widely commented on in the media and by politicians. The influence of international and transnational reports and surveys about the quality of teaching (eg TALIS – the Teaching and Learning International Survey: see www.oecd.org/edu/school/talis.htm) and about the relative performance of school students (such as PISA – the Programme for International Student Assessment: see www.oecd.org/pisa/aboutpisa/) have undoubtedly played a part. But this still begs a big question about how policy on teaching can respond to these international developments in such different ways. While England may not be a total 'outlier' internationally, such a claim would certainly seem to be a reasonable assertion within the UK and RoI. No other jurisdiction appears to be taking such a restricted view of teacher professionalism, at least so far as initial teacher education is concerned. However, some of the same tendencies may be detected in the US and, more recently, in Australia and New Zealand (see Chapter Three, this volume).

For researchers, one of the big questions must be about the nature of the correspondence between policy statements made by politicians with the lived practices 'on the ground'. Just because the current English government holds a restricted view of teaching, in the way described, this should not lead us to immediately assume that practices in school classrooms or indeed practices in initial teacher education programmes are fundamentally very different from those in other parts of the UK or elsewhere. In other words, there may be a strong cultural continuity across the teaching profession in the UK, and indeed internationally, that is not reflected in the differences of political rhetoric in individual jurisdictions.

The global dimension

But if we find that trajectories are diverging within the UK and RoI, what of the wider world? Certainly, the political interest in teacher education has been almost universal, as recent collections by Townsend (2011a) and Darling-Hammond and Lieberman (2012) demonstrate. Furthermore, many researchers have commented in recent years on the increasing globalisation of education policy (eg Rizvi and Lingard, 2010; Stronach, 2010). To what extent has globalisation influenced teacher education? We look at this in more detail in Chapter Three but here we would like to draw attention to some of the key themes that seem to be emerging from such work.

One common theme is that of increasing pressure on teaching as a profession. This was detected towards the end of the 20th century by scholars in Australasia (Harris, 1982; Smyth et al, 1999), the US (Apple, 1986) and Europe (Robertson, 2000). There was some reference to the 'proletarianisation' of teachers as the occupation became increasingly deskilled. The 'reform' movement so clearly manifested in England during the 1980s and early 1990s was also felt in many other countries, as Tatto's (2007) collection of papers from 2007 demonstrates. From China to Bulgaria, from Chile and Mexico to Japan and the Philippines, we see how teaching and teachers have been systematically reconstructed. Tatto and Plank (2007, p 276) conclude from these cases that, in spite of the way in which governments around the world have focused on 'policies aimed at improving the instruction that students receive … [i]n the persistent absence of solid evidence about the attributes of good teachers or the character of effective teaching ... the reforms launched by various governments continue to display significant diversity'.

Indeed, one of the leading international scholars in teacher education, Marilyn Cochran-Smith, has pointed out that teacher education has itself become increasingly defined as a policy problem – as opposed to being a curriculum, training or learning problem. Cochran-Smith and Fries (2008), writing in the Association of Teacher Educators' handbook of research on teacher education in the US, state:

> The essence of studying teacher education as a policy problem is to identify which broad parameters of teacher education policy that can be controlled by policy makers are most likely to lead to desirable student outcomes ... it is worth noting that when teacher education is constructed as a policy problem, the focus is almost always on pupil achievement, defined as test scores, as the most important educational outcome. While this is important, it is not the only goal of preparation programs. Such outcomes as pupils' social and emotional growth and their preparedness to live in a democratic society and engage in civic discourse are also important as are goals such as teacher placement and retention in hard-to-staff schools and as advocates for educational equity. (Cochran-Smith and Fries, 2008, p 1085)

So, if the redefinition of teacher education as a policy problem is the most significant overarching concern, what are some of the elements within that broad concern? Many of the key themes have already been mentioned and Darling-Hammond and Lieberman (2012, pp 167-168) helpfully identify policies and approaches that seem to make a positive contribution to the development of effective teacher development:

- recruiting highly able candidates;
- connecting theory and practice through integrated clinical work;
- using professional teaching standards to focus attention on learning and evaluation;
- creating teacher performance assessments;
- establishing teacher induction models;
- supporting thoughtful professional development;
- establishing clear career ladders;
- profession-wide capacity building for sharing research and developing practice

Many of these themes have been elements of recent developments in each of the five nations comprising the UK and RoI, which we will examine in this book, but their introduction has not always been linked to positive outcomes. Townsend (2011b), in reviewing the set of papers that he edited, comes to the conclusion that there is enormous variation in the level of trust afforded to teachers by politicians and communities.

Some approaches such as these may well be picked up in new contexts and indeed there are some other elements where 'policy borrowing' is very explicit and direct (see also Chapter Three). The Teach for America phenomenon is perhaps the most obvious case. This has been presented as a scheme that can add dynamism and excellence in any national context. So, from its origins in the US, it soon became important as Teach First in England and Wales (although it has so far been resisted in Scotland and Northern Ireland), as well as Australia, Austria, India and about 30 other countries. What makes it so pervasive? Well, in part, the answer must lie in its sponsorship by transnational corporate entities such as McKinsey & Co. McKinsey has played a big part in promoting global awareness of the importance of the quality of teaching, not least through the so-called McKinsey reports (eg Barber and Mourshed, 2007). The 'Teach for...' brand has been adapted by corporate sponsors to suit national contexts and to be offered as an enrichment to national education services, in a way that has both an educational effect and an ideological effect, demonstrating the power of the private sector to intervene 'positively' in national education systems (see Ball and Junemann, 2012).

But other less 'branded' initiatives and themes have also emerged as global phenomena, for example:

- standards in teaching;
- high-stakes accountability mechanisms;
- tighter control of teacher certification.

Indeed, developments in teacher education across the globe fit very well within what the Finnish educationalist Pasi Sahlberg (2011a) has called the global educational reform movement (GERM). He suggests that this has five distinctive characteristics:

- standardisation;
- increased focus on core subjects;
- a prescribed curriculum;

- transfer of models from the corporate world;
- high-stakes accountability policies.

Sahlberg suggests that GERM has spread around the world like a global epidemic. It can certainly be detected in many teacher education systems. However, as we indicated earlier, there are different enactments in different contexts, including different parts of the UK and RoI. Lingard (2000) has referred to this phenomenon as 'glocalisation'.

The development of the Teacher Education Group

It was in the context of recognising that there was considerable potential in researching teacher education policy and practice across the four jurisdictions of the UK that the Teacher Education Group was established in the mid-2000s. Encouraged by the Economic and Social Research Council's Teaching and Learning Research Programme to investigate 'learning to teach across the UK', the group initially undertook a review of policies in teacher education across the four countries (Hulme and Menter, 2008a). The insights gained from intra-UK research proved to be very rich and the 'home international' comparative approach (Raffe et al, 1999) has been wholeheartedly adopted.

The group expanded to include more researchers and went on to undertake a review of UK teacher education research published between 2000 and 2008. This resulted in an analysis that was published in a Swiss education journal (Menter, Hulme and Murray, 2011; see also Wall et al, 2011) and demonstrated that there had been remarkably little large-scale research into teacher education in the UK in the period under review. The great majority of research carried out was small-scale, mainly into the researchers' own practices.

Two particular organisations have been influential and supportive in developing the work of the Teacher Education Group, namely the British Educational Research Association (BERA) and the Universities' Council for the Education of Teachers (UCET). BERA has existed for more than 40 years but it was only in 2004 that it established a Special Interest Group (SIG) on Teacher Education and Development. This quickly became one of the most active of BERA's SIGs and plays a major part in the annual BERA conference. As a matter of principle, this SIG has (at least) four convenors, drawn from all of the jurisdictions of the UK.

UCET is another UK-wide organisation that seeks to promote the role of higher education within teacher education.

Introduction

The Teacher Education Group continues to meet as a research group at least three times a year, coming together to discuss developments and to write and comment on each other's work. About three years ago, as the group was developing plans for this book, it was suggested that a fifth major jurisdiction should be included – the RoI. Colleagues in Northern Ireland were already working closely in a 'cross-border' collaboration known as the Standing Conference on Teacher Education, North and South (SCoTENS) and, for them, this collaboration was professionally and politically very important. The expansion to include the RoI has proved an important development as the group has been able to learn a great deal from looking at developments in this non-UK but English-speaking and European context.

It was a collaboration between BERA and UCET that gave rise to a report in 2012 looking at the impact of government policy on teacher education across the UK (Whitty et al, 2012). One recommendation from that report was that there should be a major inquiry into the relationship between teacher education and education research. This relationship was something that perhaps many of us in the Teacher Education Group had taken for granted for many years, but seemed not to be taken for granted by the wider political or indeed professional community. So it was that during 2013/14, BERA, in partnership with the Royal Society of Arts (RSA), carried out a major inquiry into these matters, which led to the publication of two reports (BERA and RSA, 2014a, 2014b). These reports and the contributions to them are referred to at various points in this book as several of the book's authors made significant contributions to the inquiry.

It is fascinating to us that in all five of the jurisdictions there has been major change in teacher education during the recent past. Indeed, we have seen major reviews of initial teacher education in all five countries. Earlier in this chapter we referred to the Donaldson Report in Scotland, published in 2011. In Wales, a process was started in the mid-2000s by the Welsh Assembly Government, which commissioned a review by John Furlong and colleagues (Furlong et al, 2006a), with a further review then carried out by Ralph Tabberer (2013). We are now seeing a new implementation process, again led by Furlong. Furlong has also been involved recently in Northern Ireland, where a process of review has been under way for many years now and may actually lead to some significant change there (DEL, 2014). In the RoI, the government commissioned Sahlberg and others to review initial teacher education in 2012 (Sahlberg et al, 2012) and the outcome of that review was implemented while we were writing this book. Last, but perhaps not least, during 2014, Michael Gove, in one of his last acts as Secretary of State for Education, commissioned a primary school headteacher, Sir Andrew Carter, to carry out a review of the effectiveness of initial teacher training in England. The review report was published in January 2015 (DfE, 2015) and it has been deeply fascinating to Teacher Education Group members and to the wider professional community to see how it compares with the others mentioned.

More detail on all of these matters can be found in Part Two of this book.

The structure of the book

The rest of Part One sets out the contextual and conceptual underpinnings of the approach taken in this book. Chapter Two sets our work in an historical context, dealing with matters in much more detail than we have gone into above. Chapter Three concerns the methodological thinking behind our investigation. We stress the importance of culture and history in making sense of teacher education policy and practice and we also discuss the challenges of comparative analysis in a fast-changing world.

In Part Two (Chapters Four to Eight), we highlight the particularities of each of the five contexts, pointing to some of the similarities and differences and relating these to political and cultural aspects of each jurisdiction. The authors of each of these five chapters have taken their own approach, reflecting some of the different concerns in each setting and drawing attention to the nature of the policy community there. This means that the chapters do not all follow the same pattern – we decided not to use a common template as that would be too restrictive and reduce the sense of difference and diversity.

In Part Three (Chapters Nine to Twelve), cross-country analysis is undertaken in a more systematic way. It offers a review and synthesis of what has emerged across the five nations. It is structured around four specific issues in teacher education, each of which is an enduring theme of relevance to teacher education internationally and is discussed in the light of the experiences in the five nations. The themes are standards and accountability (Chapter Nine), the place of research in teacher education (Chapter Ten), the relationship between teacher education and higher education (Chapter Eleven) and partnership in teacher education (Chapter Twelve).

Part Four consists of the concluding chapter (Chapter Thirteen). In this chapter we review what has emerged from the work and discuss this in the wider context of globalisation, citizenship and democracy.

We also offer a reflection on some of the implications for the future of teacher education, not just in the five countries but also in a global context.

TWO

UK and Irish teacher education in a time of change

Ian Menter

Introduction

There is growing international concern about all aspects of teacher education and its links with teacher professionalism, school improvement and pupil outcomes. In association with the increasing marketisation of education via parental choice mechanisms, standardised assessment techniques, national league tables and local management of schools, a significant shift has taken place in the way teachers are perceived and the way they perceive themselves as professionals. Teachers are no longer regarded as members of a self-regulated, autonomous profession, but have become subject to rigorous public scrutiny and accountability regimes. Although the concept of 'reflective practice' features prominently in this 'new' teacher professionalism, it is difficult to reconcile with government discourses that locate teaching and learning within a paradigm of technical rationality. The relentless pressure on teachers and schools to position themselves favourably in national and international performance league tables, rigorous inspection against externally determined professional standards and performance management have created 'a culture of compliance'. At the same time as teachers' space for critically reflective practice has become increasingly restricted, the demand for engaging in cross-professional and multi-agency work has become a feature of the 'new' professionalism and raises questions about the location of teachers' professional knowledge and learning and the role of the academy within the wider teacher education continuum from initial teacher education, through induction to continuing professional development.

However, universities themselves within the United Kingdom (UK) and Republic of Ireland (RoI) have not shared a coherent understanding of their potential role in teacher development on a mass scale. For example, the challenge for universities of agreeing what a 'masters' profession would consist of (Jackson and Eady, 2012) is indicative of the need for further conceptualisation of what constitutes a valid knowledge base for professional development. Debate around the short-lived Masters in Teaching and Learning in England (2010–13) indicated the need for universities to re-evaluate their own gatekeeping mechanisms and regulation of teacher participation in the academy. None of this has been resolved in the disengagement of current policy in England from these issues. In Wales, the first steps towards national-scale Masters-level professional learning for early career teachers have been closely tied to technology-supported self-directed study and the importance of working with external mentors on the Masters in Educational Practice. Here the role of the university has been conceptualised as one of designing professional learning opportunities and facilitating appropriate forms of enquiry, to be undertaken without direct face-to-face contact with higher education staff. Online learning plays a core role. Multiple interpretations of this development are possible – and probably all apply.

In this chapter we explore the tensions and paradoxes that emerge from a study of current trends in teacher education in the UK and RoI, seeking to relate them to an international context, which as we saw in Chapter One, is volatile and is itself subject to many transnational influences. The processes of policy borrowing and policy exchange are then explored in more detail in Chapter Three.

The regulation of teaching and teacher education

We noted in Chapter One how the very idea of 'teacher education' or 'teacher training' emerged out of the growth of state schooling (eg see Dent, 1977). If the purpose of state schooling was to create a literate and moral ('god-fearing') population, then it was clear that those entering the profession should not only be literate and of appropriate moral standing themselves but also be helped to develop the necessary skills to pass on those qualities to their pupils. Schools themselves, through pupil–teacher schemes, as well as colleges of education, were Christian organisations in which knowledge of the Bible and basic literacy, numeracy and general knowledge was essential. Once local education authorities and universities became more involved in the selection and preparation of teachers, the strict religious requirements were not applied so universally, but unsurprisingly the requirements for a basic level of literacy and numeracy continued to prevail. Similarly, as elementary schooling developed and was replaced in different ways in different jurisdictions by separate phases of education (nursery, infant, junior, secondary, etc), so training for each sector became more differentiated and specialised.

Nevertheless, throughout this period it remained the case that it was perfectly possible to teach outside the state sector without any formal teaching qualification. Indeed, it was not always a requirement to have a teaching qualification within the state sector, especially for example in secondary education, in the immediate aftermath of the Second World War. And even if training was required, some of this was deemed to be 'emergency training' and thus very brief in duration.

The steady move towards all-graduate status proceeded through the second half of the 20th century so that by the late 1970s it was fair to say that anyone wishing to teach in the state sector of education was required to go through some kind of formal training in order to obtain a teaching qualification (Alexander, 1984). However, it is also fair to say that, right up until the 1990s, the determination of the nature of these qualifications, particularly in terms of the particular knowledge, skills or dispositions required, was largely left to the judgement of professional institutions and academic bodies. There were processes of validation that were associated with particular awards that attracted the status of a teaching qualification, and during the 1980s we saw the introduction of certain regulations affecting the design of courses, but the actual definition of the distinctive features of what it is to be a qualified teacher was not centrally prescribed.

However, the drive for accountability in public services and the moves towards performance management during the 1990s led to increasing pressure for the creation of a clear definition of what it is that beginning teachers should be capable of doing in order to be awarded a teaching qualification. Initially this discourse was framed in terms of 'competences' – qualities that should be observable and/ or testable. In England and Scotland, for example, during this period, lists of teaching competences were published that became the basis of judgement for assessing the performance of beginning teachers (Hulme and Menter, 2008a).

However, during the same decade, the discourse moved from 'competences' to 'standards' and England led the way' here, with the Teacher Training Agency (TTA) – an English quango created in 1994 – developing a standard for 'qualified teacher status' (QTS). The process of this development was studied by Mahony and Hextall (2000) and was found to be very much steered by officials within the TTA, with many aspects of the input from external voices, including those of teachers, teacher educators and teachers' unions, being over-ridden or ignored.

Although developments were happening in parallel across the UK, a four nations study, which compared the standards documents that emerged in each country in the wake of the devolution of education policy making to the four jurisdictions, found that there appeared to be significant differences in the respective articulation of standards (Hulme and Menter, 2008a). Indeed, it was suggested that there appeared to be a spectrum of approaches to the definition of teaching standards, with one end of the spectrum taking essentially a moral stance and the other end taking an essentially technical rational stance (Hulme and Menter, 2008b). There were also significant differences in the framing of social justice issues and in articulating the relationship between teachers and educational research and enquiry.

In each jurisdiction, the lists of standards have been the subject of continuing review and development. Furthermore, the relationship between an initial standard for entry into the profession and subsequent standards (such as for full registration, advanced teacher, chartered teacher or headship) differ (and will be referred to in the chapters in Part Two of this book). Nevertheless, there has been a common realisation that even if there are to be different standards applied for different phases of a teacher's career, there are likely to be common areas under which standards can be grouped. Most commonly – and the model adopted in Scotland offers a very clear articulation of this – it seems appropriate to distinguish between dispositions, knowledge and skills. Some might say that *dispositions*, which may be seen to relate to 'values' (a very abstract and perhaps personal matter), constitute the starting point. A statement of dispositions or values is a way of setting out what kind of people might be suited to teaching. So we see in the most recent English standards a statement about teachers being able to demonstrate that they are not undermining 'fundamental British values'. Or perhaps less contentiously, in Scotland we see a requirement of a commitment to justice and equality and respect for learners.

In relation to the *knowledge* that is appropriate for teachers to have, this has commonly been broken into subsets, such as:

- subject knowledge;
- general professional knowledge;
- pedagogical content knowledge.

General professional knowledge is non-subject-specific knowledge about learning and teaching, including for example the curriculum and assessment theory. The term 'pedagogical content knowledge' was developed notably by Shulman (1987), who defined it (as summarised by Philpott, 2014, p 16) as 'that special amalgam of content and pedagogy that is uniquely the province of teachers, their own special form of professional understanding'. *Skills*, on the other hand, are what teachers need to be able to do rather than need to know, although the two are clearly closely related. So teachers need to know how to communicate, how to organise teaching and learning, how to assess students' progress and so on.

Every set of standards in the UK, RoI and indeed internationally, includes elements of all three areas. What was so distinctive about the way in which they developed in the late 20th century was that they did not emerge from within the profession but, rather, appeared to have been imposed by politicians and their policy makers – although this is more the case in some contexts than in others.

While a widely held view has developed that the adoption of such standards has led to an improvement in the quality of teaching, as called for by international bodies such as the Organisation for Economic Co-operation and Development, it has also been argued that the nature of the policy process has had the effect of undermining the self-confidence of the teaching profession. The extent of this may well vary between jurisdictions, but the general case can be made that the reformulation of teaching as a standards-based occupation reflected a great lack of trust in teachers. Indeed, we should ask why it is that teachers were not capable of developing such a common framework for themselves, as appears to have happened in many other professions, including medicine and law.

In reviewing a collection of papers on teacher education from 10 different countries, Townsend (2011b, p 497) came to the following conclusion:

> [P]oliticians in a number of countries do not trust the people they employ to do the job they employ them to do. They do not trust teacher educators to provide their students with the skills and attitudes required to do the task of teaching.... They do not trust teachers or school leaders either.'

The longstanding existence of the General Teaching Council for Scotland (GTCS) – since the mid-1960s – has undoubtedly influenced the process of standards development in Scotland very significantly (see Christie, 2008; Kennedy, 2013). In the other three countries of the UK, General Teaching Councils were created around 2000 but then the English one was abolished in 2010. In these three jurisdictions, therefore, the respective General Teaching Council has only had recent influence or virtually none in the case of England. The Teaching Council in the RoI was established as recently as 2005 but already plays a very significant role in policy developments of this kind (see Chapter Eight).

The final point to be made about the regulation and governance of teachers and their education is to remind ourselves that underlying all of these matters are the economics of teacher recruitment, retention and supply. Whenever there are severe shortages of teachers, we tend to find regulation being loosened, facilitating more flexible entry to the profession.

Competing models of teaching

In the previous section we referred to differing views of standards for teaching. In Chapter One we also made reference to differing conceptions of teaching. The ways in which teaching is understood are clearly going to have a very influential effect on the patterns of provision for initial teacher education. The starkest contrast among the five nations is the definition of teaching espoused by the former Secretary of State for Education in England, Michael Gove, and that espoused by the former Chief Inspector of Education in Scotland, Graham Donaldson.

Their different conceptions can be demonstrated simply by the following extracts from a key document produced by each of them. In the English White Paper entitled *The importance of teaching* (DfE, 2010, pp 19-20), Gove wrote:

> We know that teachers learn best from other professionals and that an 'open classroom' culture is vital: observing teaching and being observed, having the opportunity to plan, prepare, reflect and teach with other teachers ... we will ... reform initial teacher training so that more training is on the job, and it focuses on key teaching skills including teaching early reading and mathematics, managing behaviour and responding to pupils' Special Educational Needs.

Donaldson (2011, p 15), on the other hand, in his report *Teaching Scotland's future*, outlines a model of a teacher who:

is the kind of professional who is highly proficient in the classroom and who is also reflective and enquiring not only about teaching and learning, but also about those wider issues which set the context for what should be taught and why.... This concept of professionalism takes each individual teacher's responsibility beyond the individual classroom outwards into the school, to teacher education and the profession as a whole.

However, such stark differences of view on the nature of teaching and teacher education are not new. Throughout the development of formal teacher preparation there have been strong differences – again, these were alluded to in Chapter One. The influence of educational theory on teacher preparation only really got under way during the 20th century. In the 1920s, the work of John Dewey in the United States (US), with his laboratory schools, became influential. In England and Scotland, the influence of notable European educators such as Froebel, Montessori and Pestalozzi began to be felt (Cruickshank, 1970; Dent, 1977; Alexander, 1984). Educational sciences developed as a very formal area of study in mainland Europe with the creation of didactics as a field and of concepts such as '*bildung*' (a phrase that does not translate easily into English but which relates to education and the formation of the whole self) within German-speaking contexts. During the 1970s, psychology became very influential in the UK and RoI. Most notable among those whose work influenced teaching practices, was Jean Piaget, who actually described himself as a genetic epistemologist and who carried out clinical work in laboratories investigating how children learn. A much more social and linguistic view of children's learning emerged from the Soviet Union, led in particular by Lev Vygotsky.

So it was that Piagetian and then Vygotskian theory came to play a significant part in the curricula of teacher education programmes in the UK and RoI, but also in the US (although the Soviet influence was much weaker there), and learning theorists such as Jerome Bruner (1963, 1968) sought to integrate the knowledge gained from this scientific work into curriculum and pedagogical theory.

But psychology and 'learning sciences' were not the only influences on teacher education curricula. There was increasing awareness of the sociological dimensions of schooling and learning. The strong associations between social background and educational success led many to question the way in which schooling was structured in a supposedly meritocratic society. During the 1970s, focus started to turn from the structures of schooling to the processes going on in classrooms, with the development of the 'new sociology of education' (Young, 1971). Both old (pre-1970) and new (post-1970) sociologies played their part in drawing attention to questions of equality and justice in education. The possibility of schooling playing a part, not just in transforming individuals' lives, but also in bringing about broader social development, became popular. A wave of 'progressive' educational writing during the 1960s and 1970s sought to emphasise the social mission of teaching. There were examples of 'free schools' in disadvantaged urban areas in the US, there were accounts of learning for empowerment in British state schools (eg Berg, 1969; Mackenzie, 1970) and there were neo-Freudian texts such as those emerging from Summerhill School in the UK (a school where children played a large part in the decision-making) (Neill, 1962) and from New Zealand (Ashton-Warner, 1980), which emphasised the need to liberate children from institutional constraints. However, the most well-theorised and longlasting manifestation of this sort was the neo-Marxist writing of the Brazilian educator Paulo Freire (1971), which sought to use education to bring about social and political transformation. Whether educational theory was psychological or sociological, nevertheless it was seen as important in contributing to the preparation of teachers for their work. However, the attack on educational theory that was waged in the 1970s and 1980s succeeded in denigrating the contribution of such work as 'barmy' and/or subversive. So it was that the use of such work rapidly receded during the 1980s and 1990s and was steadily replaced by an emphasis on competences and then standards, referred to earlier, which made little or no reference to theory or research.

This coincided with the rise of the school effectiveness movement, again part of the accountability drive that increasingly focused on pupil outcomes as the most important measure of educational success. In a review of literature on teacher education in the 21st century, Menter et al (2010a) suggested that, in studying what had been written about teacher professionalism over the recent past, it was possible to discern four particular models of professionalism, each with particular origins and different contemporary proponents. Each of the models reflects a different balance of understanding between the theoretical and the practical, perhaps echoing to some extent the differences referred to above, between Michael Gove's understanding of teaching as a craft, best learned through an apprenticeship, and Donaldson's view of teaching as a profession, learned through a process of inquiry and intellectual development, as well as practical experience. They are as follows.

The effective teacher: standards and competences

This model has emerged as the dominant one in much official government discourse across the developed world over the last 30 years. It is closely associated with the economically led view of education that stresses the need for teachers to prepare pupils to take part in making their respective nations' economies a success. The emphases are on technical accomplishment and on measurement. It is the model for an age of accountability and performativity (Mahony and Hextall, 2000). From a political perspective, it is difficult to reject this model because it prioritises value for money for taxpayers and emphasises the opportunity for all pupils to achieve to their best potential and subsequently to contribute to the economy and society.

In contrast to the more politically driven effective teacher model, a common factor in respect of the other three paradigms is that they are models that have emerged much more from within the teaching profession and sites of teacher education.

The reflective teacher

The notion of teaching as a reflective activity emerged strongly in the UK, partly in response to the growing influence of the effective teacher model, which was seen by some as restricting teacher professionalism, rather than enhancing it (Hartley, 2002; Stronach et al, 2002). The philosophical roots of the reflective teaching model lie in the work of the American educator John Dewey. Early in the 20th century, he developed an approach to teaching based on teachers becoming active decision makers [see Pring, 2007]. Similar ideas were later developed by Schön (1983), who wrote about *The reflective practitioner* (1983), stressing the significance of values and of theory informing decision making.

At the centre of this model is a cyclical approach to planning, making provision, acting, collecting data, analysing the data, evaluating and reflecting and then planning the next step.

Built into such a model is a commitment to personal professional development through practice. It is a model that took a firm hold in teacher education institutions across the UK during the latter parts of the 20th century. The largest-scale study of initial teacher education undertaken in England by Furlong et al (2000) found that about 70% of teacher education programmes led from universities and colleges were informed by some version of 'reflective teaching' (see also Griffiths, 2000).

The enquiring teacher

Reflective teaching does not in itself imply a research orientation on the part of the teacher, although the model may be strongly influenced by a set of ideas that does promote just that conception (Forde et al, 2006). In the UK, the origins of the notion of 'teacher as researcher' is usually associated with the groundbreaking work of Stenhouse (1975), who argued that teachers should indeed take a research approach to their work. He described this as a form of curriculum development. In this model, teachers are encouraged to undertake systematic enquiry in their own classrooms, develop their practice and share their insights with other professionals. Such ideas have been taken up, developed and enhanced through a range of subsequent initiatives, often associated with university staff working in partnership with teachers and lecturers in schools and colleges.

Some of the most developed approaches to teacher as researcher or the enquiring teacher have been developed in Europe (eg Altrichter et al, 2006), North America (Cochran-Smith and Lytle, 1993, 2009) and Australia (Groundwater-Smith, 2006).

The transformative teacher

The final model to be put forward incorporates and builds upon elements of the previous two. However, its key defining feature is that it brings an 'activist' dimension into the approach to teaching. If the prevalent view of the teacher is someone whose contribution to society is to transmit knowledge and prepare pupils for the existing world, the view here is that teachers' responsibilities go beyond that – they should be contributing to social change and be preparing their pupils to contribute to change in society.

The most recent and cogent articulation of this model is that set out by the Australian teacher educator, Judyth Sachs (2003b), who talks of 'teaching as an activist profession'. Those who advocate teaching as a transformative activity will suggest that some challenge to the status quo is not only to be expected but is also a necessary part of bringing about a more just education system, where inequalities in society begin to be addressed and where progressive social change can be stimulated (Cochran-Smith, 2004; Zeichner, 2009).

Source: Selection of quotes from Menter et al, 2010a, pp 21–4

Professionalism and teacher identity

Differing conceptions of professionalism such as these may also relate to different ways in which teacher identity is understood. The teacher who sees themselves as aiming to be effective, may have quite a different professional identity to one who sees themselves as transformative. The wider questions of teacher identity and its connections with professionalism have been studied by scholars in many parts of the world (eg Huberman, 1993; Goodson, 2003; Day and Gu, 2010) and some of the psychic dissonance that has been revealed among teachers in recent years may well be accounted for by teachers experiencing challenges from policy or management sources to their established identity with which they feel uncomfortable (Menter et al, 1997; see also Gewirtz et al, 2009). We know, for example, that in England there was considerable resistance to the advent of Ofsted inspections (Jeffrey and Woods, 1998; Cullingford, 1999) and also to the introduction of performance threshold assessment (Mahony et al, 2004).

It is questionable how much simultaneous moves towards the integration of children's services have really impacted on teachers (Forbes and Watson, 2012). There has certainly been a greater awareness of the contribution of social workers and healthcare professionals in schools. There has also been a significant increase in the number of ancillary staff in schools working directly with children, such as teaching assistants and learning support assistants. However, the extent to which these developments have impacted directly on teachers is not clear and some attempts to draw training for different professional groups together have not progressed very far. It seems to be at the higher management levels that such integration has had most impact with the creation of children's services departments and the appointment of directors of children's services within local authorities.

There have been many predictions about the radical impact that new technologies will have on teachers, teaching and teacher education. There is no question that classroom teaching and the preparation and selection of teaching resources have changed considerably through the deployment of electronic technologies. Furthermore, teachers themselves are making increasing use of social media to facilitate some aspects of their professional development. However, it does not appear at this stage that such technologies are leading to fundamental changes in the processes of learning to be a teacher.

The role of the university

One of the most significant issues during the history of teacher education has been the role of higher education and the contribution of the university (and this is dealt with in much more detail in Chapter Eleven). During the 20th century, not only did higher education and university involvement in teacher education steadily increase, we also saw the development of education as a recognised field of study, albeit a multidisciplinary field. The emergence of education studies was closely associated with the drawing together of scholars from a range of traditional disciplines – notably psychology, sociology, history and philosophy – applying their expertise to the study of education.

If the 'academicisation' was one part of the university contribution, the other was the certification of awards. The processes of validation and accreditation were strongly steered by the universities and by national accreditation bodies such as the Council for National Academic Awards (CNAA). It was these processes that gave legitimacy to teaching qualifications but also were instrumental in moving teaching towards being an all-graduate profession.

The development of education studies also went hand in hand with the development of educational research. The British Educational Research Association (BERA) was founded in 1974, a time around which many UK educational research journals were also launched. Educational research ranged from classroom-based studies, intensive studies of teaching practice and longitudinal studies of pupil performance through to sociological studies of the relationship between education, social class and achievement. Interest in other aspects of inequality in education – including a focus on gender, race and ethnicity, disability and 'special educational needs' – also arose through the 1970s and 1980s (see BERA, 2014).

However, the relevance of much educational research was called into question by luminaries such as David Hargreaves (an academic as well as a senior policy official at various times) and Chris Woodhead (the highly outspoken Chief Inspector of Schools in England during a period in the 1990s). These attacks suggested that such was the esoteric and obscure nature of much research and such was the way it was typically being published in journals, 'gathering dust on library shelves', that it made very little contribution towards practice or even to policy (see Hammersley, 2007).

Such was the background against which the very involvement of the university in teacher education came to be questioned during the 1990s and then very directly in England in the second decade of the

21st century. The rapid erosion of educational studies from teacher education programmes was associated with what some have called 'the practical turn' (see Lawn and Furlong, 2011) and was soon also associated with the proposition not only that teaching was essentially a practical matter, but also that it was best learned from current teachers. While this position was developed in its most extreme form in England, similar views were also being propounded elsewhere in the world and in some other parts of the UK.

It was against this backdrop that the inquiry by BERA and the Royal Society of Arts (RSA), referred to in Chapter One, was set up. BERA was deeply concerned that such developments in teacher education might completely undermine the educational research infrastructure comprised of university departments of education, many of which had become very dependent on the income they received from major involvement in initial teacher education. The inquiry commissioned a series of review papers to see what evidence existed of links between educational research and teacher education.

One of the commissioned papers was concerned with research-based clinical practice in initial teacher education (Burn and Mutton, 2013). It had become apparent that there were programmes of study in initial teacher education that accepted to a large degree that the key site of learning was indeed the school and its classrooms. However, such clinical models also promoted careful engagement in evidence gathering and analysis of experience in a clinical fashion. This could lead to what Donald McIntyre and others had come to describe as 'practical theorising' – and 'theorising practice' (Hagger and McIntyre, 2006). McIntyre had been closely involved in developing such approaches at the Universities of Oxford and Cambridge, in departments that were also well known for the high quality of their educational research. While these initial teacher education programmes could confidently be labelled as 'school-based', nevertheless the university played a critical and integral role in the education of the beginning teachers (see Benton, 1990, for an early evaluation of the Oxford 'internship' scheme; see also Furlong et al, 1988).

Clinical practice models of different kinds were also being developed elsewhere in the UK as well as in parts of the US and Australia (see Burn and Mutton, 2013). In many ways, the approaches echoed some of the practice that had been developing in Finland, where university training schools had played a key role in teacher education for a number of years and were part of the development of Masters-level entry into teaching (Sahlberg, 2011a).

The conclusion that the BERA–RSA inquiry arrived at was that the very best practices in initial teacher education demonstrated a full integration of theory and practice and showed a strong enquiry orientation in the ways in which the learning of beginning teachers was organised. Such an approach, while not by definition requiring a university contribution, was nevertheless likely to be strongly enhanced by such involvement (BERA and RSA, 2014b).

The continuum of professional learning

Another continuing challenge that has faced the development of teacher education across the UK and RoI has been ensuring that teacher learning and professional development continues throughout a teacher's career – that there is a 'seamless web'. Almost every report on teacher development, whether from professional or political sources, at least since the James Report of 1972 in the UK (James, 1972), has argued for the importance of this. In the 1980s, a working party on teacher education in Northern Ireland coined the term 'the three Is' to represent Initial teacher education, Induction and In-service, which it was argued need to be connected and to lead from one to the next (see Chapter Five, this volume). Some policy steps were taken to achieve this.

In Scotland, the 2010 Donaldson Report (Donaldson, 2011) made very strong play of the idea of career-long development. Indeed, Scottish policy had been seen to be leading the way in this respect through the introduction early in the 21st century of the Teacher Induction Scheme (TIS) and the chartered teacher (see Chapter Six). The TIS provided a structured period of support for the first year of teaching, which was critically associated with a guaranteed first-year of employment on completion of the Standard for Initial Teacher Education. Successful completion of induction, a year during which the teaching commitment was only 70% of the timetable (later increased to 90%), would lead to achievement of the Standard for Full Registration.

Scotland also saw in this period the introduction of a route towards the achievement of the Standard for Chartered Teacher. Admittedly, this did leave a gap in professional development support during the early part of a teacher's career from year two to year six (which was the qualifying period for the chartered teacher scheme), but it did mean a three-stage set of standards for classroom teachers. However, the chartered teacher scheme was dropped after a few years (see Chapter Six).

In England, various post-qualifying standards were introduced, including the Standards respectively for Advance Skills Teacher, for Expert Teacher and for Special Educational Needs Coordinator (SENCo).

However, across the five jurisdictions, the current position is that we do not really see that seamless web of continuing professional learning and development, in spite of much research showing how important it is that teachers receive appropriate support at each of the phases of their career (Day, 1999; Day et al, 2007).

Earlier on we mentioned the move towards a Masters-level entry, already achieved in Finland. When Donaldson was carrying out his review in Scotland, there was some speculation that his report would recommend a move in this direction. In the end, while he did not argue against it, he chose not to make it a formal recommendation. In England in the run-up to the 2010 General Election, it had appeared that a Masters in Teaching and Learning would be introduced across the country. This would not have been compulsory nor would it have been an entry-level qualification. However, it was designed to support the development of classroom practice to Masters level for recently qualified teachers. In 2010, the incoming coalition government withdrew funding for it as one of its immediate 'savings' and so there is now no national scheme of this sort in England. The most successful introduction of a scheme of this kind now appears to be in Wales, with the development of a Masters in Educational Practice (MEP), which is available to all newly qualified teachers and has had reasonable success in recruitment since its initiation in 2012 (see Chapter Seven for more details on the MEP).

The issue of university involvement in post-initial teacher education is again important, with it usually being assumed that any Masters award would need to be associated with higher education in some form. However, it would be fair to say that across the UK and RoI the involvement of universities in any provision that takes place following the initial qualification is very variable and cannot be assumed to be present.

What is the 'new professionalism' in teaching?

What we have described in this chapter so far is a very variegated picture of provision for the professional learning of teachers. Provision has been influenced strongly by wider pressures in society, especially those connected to public services. The drives for accountability, value for money, consumer responsiveness and the like, have led to a reshaping of the culture of teaching and teacher education. In one sense, this can be summarised as the impact of a new form of managerialism – sometimes called New Public Management (NPM) (Newman, 2000). But in another sense, the ways in which teachers and the teaching profession have responded to these forces can be seen to have led to the emergence of what we might call 'a new professionalism' among teachers.

How might this 'new professionalism' be characterised? What are some of its distinctive features? They would certainly include the greater use of 'data' by teachers. This is indubitably one aspect in which new technologies have had a major impact on teachers and their schools. Most schools are now heavily 'data-rich' environments. The data available include attendance data for pupils, attainment data, performance measures of teaching (whether for pay purposes or as part of Ofsted inspections) and much else besides. Data are seen as 'evidence' that can be used to assist in the processes of the improvement of teaching and thereby of school improvement.

Indeed, we have seen much commitment in a number of quarters to the development of teaching as an evidence-based profession – evidence-based teaching (EBT). This term has been adopted very wholeheartedly in England by the Department for Education and its National College for Teaching and Leadership (NCTL). However, the extent to which it matches up with the ideas of teacher as researcher that we outlined earlier in this chapter is debatable. EBT is not always seen as being about questioning underlying values, purposes and motives and may actually be seen as a means of becoming 'more effective' – that is, it is a way of improving 'the effective teacher'. In one of the BERA–RSA review papers, Winch et al (2103) set out three models of teaching, using philosophical arguments alone. Their 'technical' model, which is a relatively restricted form of professionalism, could be well supported by the EBT view.

So there continues to be debate, not only in England, but across all of our jurisdictions about the extent, the scope and the warrant of the evidence and research that teachers may draw upon and indeed the extent to which they themselves should be encouraged to become researchers as part of their work. The BERA and RSA (2014b) report came to the conclusion that while all teachers should have the *capacity* to engage in research and enquiry, research and enquiry should not necessarily be part of their daily routine. However, the report did come to the conclusion that research literacy should be a fundamental part of every teacher's professional 'apparatus'. All teachers should be equipped with the ability to identify and evaluate relevant educational research and respond in their professional practice. This disposition does appear to be an established commitment through the standards in most of the jurisdictions we are concerned with and hopefully will soon be fully endorsed in all of them. General Teaching Councils appear fully to support this approach and if a College of Teaching is indeed established in England, as is currently being proposed, it too would appear to be assuming that research literacy is a fundamental aspect of teachers' working life.

Leadership in schools has also become increasingly significant and has been applied across all levels of the profession. Educational leadership now is seen as applicable from classroom level upwards – it may take different forms for promoted staff but, like general teacher development, it involves a series of skills that need to be developed throughout a teacher's career. The National College for School Leadership was established in England under the New Labour government of the late 1990s but has had an influence across the five nations under study here. In Scotland, while there is no physical college, there is a virtual college that the Scottish Government has supported since 2012 – the Scottish College for Educational Leadership (SCEL) (see www.scelscotland. org.uk/about/).

As we have seen, there are many ways in which teachers and the teaching profession are being given encouragement to have greater self-determination, whether it be through, for example, teaching schools, general teaching councils or a 'school-led system'. This indicates a profession that is going through a significant process of change. All of these developments must be considered carefully and critically – and that is what we seek to do in this book. A great deal of what we have been discussing and reviewing in this chapter is caught in the phrase adopted by Hargreaves and Fullan (2012) – 'professional capital'. In their 2012 volume with that title, they call for teachers to be treated with respect and 'empowered' to deploy their expertise in a collegial and critical manner, so that pupils in schools are taught by confident and skilled staff. They call for governments to invest in professional capital and state:

> A big part of this investment is in high-quality teachers and teaching. In this view getting good teaching for all learners requires teachers to be highly committed, thoroughly prepared, continuously developed, properly paid, well networked with each other to maximise their own improvement, and able to make effective judgements

using all their capabilities and experience. (Hargreaves and Fullan, 2012, p 3)

Conclusion

In this chapter we have reviewed some of the key debates and changes that have influenced the nature of teachers' work and therefore shaped the pattern of teacher education. We have seen how the late 20th and early 21st centuries have been a period of some turbulence and of increasing influence of both global forces and national governments in determining what goes on in schools and in teacher education.

In the next chapter we turn to look more directly at how a careful appraisal of similarities and differences, and how an awareness of cultural and historical developments, can deepen our understandings of policy and practice in teacher education.

THREE

Analysing teacher education policy: comparative and historical approaches

Moira Hulme

Introduction

In the past decade, as we have seen in the previous two chapters, teacher education has assumed greater significance in global education policy (OECD, 2011a, 2011b; Asia Society, 2013; World Bank, 2013). Strategies to improve education outcomes have increasingly focused on improving teachers' learning, leading to national reviews of teacher education. A repertoire of global reforms has sought to increase control over teachers' work and performance while simultaneously emphasising teachers' knowledge and discretion (Tatto, 2007). International organisations and global policy entrepreneurs have promoted a degree of convergence around certain core themes:

- the quality of entrants;
- practicum enhancement;
- the imperative of career-long teacher learning;
- school leadership;
- the use of evidence, including research, to inform improvement.

Critical scrutiny of teacher education is not new. Recent debate connects with longstanding deliberation on the knowledge bases, content and control of teacher education, the location of professional preparation and the status of personnel involved in this complex enterprise.

It is important to establish the provenance of policy ideas in education and how they are transformed as they migrate. Moving beyond a 'transfer' paradigm, an alternative approach invites interrogation of the 'homeless terms' that populate global education policy (Popkewitz, 2013a, p 6). Thus, for example, we see how critical analysis of policy requires interrogation of seemingly transcendent and ahistorical ideas that are presented as lessons derived from comparison. Procedures for competitive comparison are supported by a renewed enthusiasm for evidence-based education and what some have called 'improvement science'. Supranational policy texts work to universalise (and normalise) particular readings of the qualities and characteristics of the 'effective teacher' and models of teacher education that 'work'. Working against the grain requires reflexive engagement with the analytical categories and units of comparison deployed in research for policy (Sobe, 2013a). It is important to ask how policy moves make possible particular understandings of 'teacher quality', and how these are linked with constructions of the future citizen, the educated person and a just society.

Throughout this book we consider how 'travelling policy' is re-contextualised within local sites of influence (Jones and Alexiadou, 2001; Seddon and Levin, 2013). Through an examination of national case studies in Part Two (England, Northern Ireland, Scotland, Wales and the Republic of Ireland [RoI]) and the identification of cross-cutting themes in Part Three (standards, research, higher education and partnership), we explore how possibilities for convergence or creative adaptation of globally mobile ideas are influenced by:

- particular institutional structures;
- the national guiding principles of education;
- the range and power of domestic 'veto players' that operate in different jurisdictions. (Martens et al, 2010)

In this chapter we draw attention to the 'troubling history' of education as a university subject in and beyond the United Kingdom (UK) (Lagemann, 2000) and the hybrid or 'pluridisciplinary' nature of educational studies (Hofstetter, 2012). Drawing on Abbott's (1988, 2005) influential contribution to the sociology of the professions, we suggest that the diverse 'academic sub-tribes' of teacher education (Menter, 2011b) face a considerable challenge in building alliances and formulating a collective response to jurisdictional challenge. The chapter is structured into three main sections, which offer comparative, historical and ecological perspectives on teacher education, respectively. The overall intention of this chapter is to introduce a set of methodological lenses that may assist in making sense of the dynamic policy contexts that we are exploring in this book.

Travelling policy: a comparative perspective

A substantial body of literature has developed over the past two decades on the movement of ideas, policies and practices in education. This literature suggests that 'cross-national attraction' (Phillips, 2006) encourages:

- policy borrowing (Steiner-Khamsi and Florian, 2012);
- policy transfer (Dolowitz et al, 2000);
- policy innovation diffusion (Cohen-Vogel and Ingle, 2007); and less often
- policy learning (Raffe, 2011).

Borrowing produces varying degrees of convergence and is motivated by a desire to attain distinction or parity among competing jurisdictions. Looking elsewhere has been used to 'glorify' (Steiner-Khamsi, 2004, p 207) and to 'scandalise' in order to 'trigger' action (Ochs, 2006, p 602). Comparative references are frequently deployed selectively to provide support for preferred (and possible) local choices (Alexander, 2012). Evidence from comparing is deployed as 'weapon' or 'warrant' (Cochran-Smith, 2002a), supported by the commissioning of reform-oriented 'useful' research.

Policy makers are attracted to reviews that claim to draw on lessons from around the world (Schleicher, 2012) to establish how the world's most improved school systems keep getting better (Mourshed et al, 2010). 'High performing education systems' (World Bank, 2013), identified as 'strong performers and successful reformers' (OECD, 2011b), become reference societies. International organisations such as the Organisation for Economic Co-operation and Development (OECD), the United Nations Educational, Scientific and Cultural Organisation (UNESCO), the World Health Organization and the World Bank are 'entrepreneurs of convergence' that use soft governance mechanisms to influence national education policies (Martens et al, 2010, p 18). A degree of dissonance between international models and domestic guiding principles creates pressure for change. Where there is significant 'misfit' between preferred models and local realities, and where there is consensus on the need for change, the rate of adaptation is faster. International organisations lend external legitimacy to directions of reform desired internally that have otherwise proven difficult to advance. Epistemic communities of experts exert influence through consulting services. Opinion formation and coordinating activities are powerful tools of soft governance (Windzio et al, 2010).

Pressure to conform to regional, national or transnational standards is particularly evident in the movement to 'govern by numbers' (Ozga et al, 2011), as demonstrated in the response of nation states to performance rankings in the OECD Programme for International Student Assessment (PISA) (Ozga, 2012; Lingard et al, 2013; Meyer and Benavot, 2013). Benchmarking has become a preferred model for comparison in a global educational reform movement (GERM) that promotes test-based accountability systems (Sahlberg, 2012). Adopting the business lexicon of 'good to great', education systems use performance indicators to mobilise reform efforts. In Wales, the-then Minister for Children, Education and Lifelong Learning, Leighton Andrews, argued in 2011: 'Ours is not a good system aiming to become great. Ours is a fair system aiming to become good' (Andrews, 2011, p 11). Scotland asserts an aspiration to move 'from good to great' (Russell, 2013). Fullan (2013) raises the bar as Ontario transitions from 'great to excellent'. Paine and Zeichner (2012, p 573) have noted how global education reform 'puts teachers at the center – at least as a policy focus if not as policy actors'. Assessments of effectiveness are informed by and fuel drives for enhanced public accountability. The 2013 OECD International Summit on the Teaching Profession aligned teacher quality with demands for improved evaluation and teacher appraisal (Asia Society, 2013). Attention turns inwards and downwards. Education is positioned as a source of economic growth, and a means for individuals to overcome disadvantage. Teachers are positioned as a source of salvation and blame (Weisburg et al, 2009), as 'heroes and villains' (Robertson, 2013, p 78). In the past decade, education effectiveness research has extended its reach from school effectiveness (between schools) to teacher effectiveness (variance between classrooms). The quality question is now focused on teaching quality and (individual) teacher quality using the proxy measure of pupil performance. A neoliberal educational project is evident in the growth of education economics directed to 'service delivery failure' arising from the 'failure of input-based policies' (Bruns et al, 2011, pp 3, 5). For example, an explicit economic rationale informs recent research efforts to measure teacher effectiveness in the United States (US) (Bill and Melinda Gates Foundation, 2010).

Post-devolution UK and the RoI offer a 'natural laboratory' for exploring the mediation of globally mobile policy ideas at close quarters. The education systems of 'the Celtic isles' are linked (through the cross-border flow of ideas and personnel) but are shaped by differences in history, politics, governance and culture. Recognition of high levels of 'entanglement' (Sobe, 2013a) challenges overly tidy bilateral and diachronic models of policy transfer. In a critique of nation-state-centred approaches, Sobe (2013a, p 96) argues that 'transfer paradigms have particular difficulty recognising and analysing "crisscrossing": the reciprocal, reversible and multiple vectors of movement and exchange.' Deliberation on policy needs to reflect broader changes in the relationship between national and international, public and private actors in education policy networks over the last 30 years (Nagel, 2010; Lingard and Rawolle, 2011; Ball, 2012). The nation state now manages 'transnational politics within national borders' (Appadurai, 2003, p 5). Jessop (1999, p 387) has described the 'hollowing out' or 'denationalisation of the state' as capacities are transferred to local, regional or international bodies. Recent policy moves reflect the interaction of globalisation and localisation, and are marked by a move from government to systems of networked governance.

A brief examination of national responses to PISA outcomes is instructive in illustrating both the pervasiveness of travelling discourse and how similar performance is received, translated and mediated differently in different contexts. Translations are contingent on a range of political, historical and socioeconomic factors. The outcomes of PISA 2012 were similar across the four nations of the UK and RoI, with outcomes for Wales dipping more sharply. However, the public response differed markedly. Katja Hall, the Confederation of British Industry's (CBI) chief policy director, offered the broad criticism that 'UK schools are treading water when we know that matching the very best could boost the growth rate by one percentage point every year' (Adams, 2013). In the devolved context of Scotland, *The Scotsman* sounded an optimistic note: 'Scotland "standing still" in schools league table but still beats the rest of UK' (Marshall, 2013). Significant progress, especially in science, was reported by the *Irish Times* in subdued tones: 'Satisfactory progress but could do better' (Ahlstrom, 2013). Ireland had responded sharply to a 'PISA shock' in 2009 (Conway and Murphy, 2013; Chapter Eight, this volume). Relief at 'recovery' in Ireland was not repeated elsewhere. In Wales, following a poor performance in 2009, a 20-point action plan for improved attainment was instigated by the-then Minister Leighton Andrews, who argued that 'PISA is a wake-up call to a complacent system. There are no alibis and no excuses. It is evidence of systemic failure' (Andrews, 2011, p 4). The Welsh Assembly Government developed a 50-page guidance pack for teachers, followed by a 'PISA INSET Training Pack' for teachers.[1] In December 2013, Huw Lewis, Welsh Minister for Education and Skills, reflected once more that 'The PISA results are stark and the message is very clear, we must improve educational attainment and standards right across the board.' Poor performance allowed the-then English Education Secretary, Michael Gove, to describe Wales as 'a country going backward' that was paying the price for abandoning performance tables and external accountability (Adams, 2013). Reversals of earlier policy direction ensued (see Chapter Seven, this volume). The 2013 *Review of initial teacher training in Wales* identified 'problems in recruitment, quality and consistency', declaring: 'The current quality of ITT in Wales is adequate and no better.... The evidence from inspection and self-evaluation shows that ITT provision in Wales is not meeting the standards set by the highest performers globally' (Tabberer, 2013, pp 14-15).

In contrast to linear models of policy 'borrowing', policy sociology emphasises the social embeddedness of policy formation. That teacher education reforms are enacted in diverse cultural, historical and geopolitical contexts is obvious when one considers the reference societies of Shanghai-China, Ontario, Finland and Singapore. Systems and models of teacher education are heterogeneous both between and within national jurisdictions. Inconsistencies are common in claims to policy learning ostensibly based on reviews of international practice. Education reform movements that appear similar can be informed by quite different rationales, enacted in different ways at different times, within as well as between national and cultural borders. There may be convergence towards common policy goals but also strong path dependency. Rust (2000, p 16) notes how processes of policy formation entail 'culturally conditioned judgments and culturally shaped constructs'. The political culture of the host country (or region) remains significant in filtering and remodelling generic transnational policies. Global policy is recontextualised within local sites of influence – national, regional and institutional (Ozga and Jones, 2006). Ozga (2005, p 208) explains that '[e]mbedded policy is to be found in "local" spaces, where global policy agendas come up against existing priorities and practices'. Of particular significance is the role of the 'collective narrative' of the national policy community (Popkewitz et al, 1999).

In this reading, passive concepts of transfer and diffusion are displaced by attention to active processes of translation, transformation or mediation. Thus, for example, Sobe (2013b) asks: 'how is it that certain ideas, practices and actors take on the aura of being global' (p 42); how are educational ideas 'made mobile'? (p 47). In order to travel, ideas must be materialised or named (for example as best value or best practice). Czarniawska and Sevon (2005, p 11) have directed attention to: What is travelling? Who is doing the translating? How does it travel? Increased attention has focused on chains of translations and the role of mediating organisations and veto players that may accelerate or impede the activities of reform-minded ministers. These include national agencies and structures of democratic accountability such as local authorities, as well as general teaching councils, teacher unions, the school inspectorate, teacher education/training providers and a growing number of think tanks and foundations. Translations may imitate but are never identical to the original or universally understood. Translations are products of intercultural exchange and contestation (Beech, 2006). The activities and influence of commissioned review panels and the mobility of panel members across jurisdictions in small and closely linked systems merit further attention.

The politics of cross-national borrowing and the activities of influential 'edupreneurs' are hardly novel phenomena. Travellers' tales accompanied the development of state-aided mass instruction from the 19th century. Celebrated pioneers of comparative education include:

- Marc-Antoine Jullien and Victor Cousin in France;
- John Griscom, Horace Mann, Paul Monroe and Isaac Kandel in the US; Joseph Kay, Matthew Arnold, James Kay-Shuttleworth and Michael Sadler in England (Beech, 2011).

The first ranking of national education systems is attributed to the French statistician Pierre Émile Levasseur in 1891 (Noah and Eckstein, 1969, p 43). The first use of *policeywissenschaft* or policy science can be traced to Germany universities in 1727 (Horlacher, 2013, p 136). By 1933, Kandel, following Sadler, was to observe: 'The comparative approach demands first an appreciation of the intangible, impalpable, spiritual and cultural forces which underlie any education system: the factors and forces outside the school matter even more than what goes on inside' (cited in Blake, 1982, p 3). Critics suggest that early lessons have not been learned as politicians draw selectively from reference societies for ammunition to support ideological (as much as evidence-informed) reforms and international organisations circulate 'context-indifferent' solutions to complex and embedded educational problems (Lingard and Sellar, 2013). By historicising reform it becomes possible to see how concepts of 'effectiveness' and 'quality' in teaching and teacher education are operationalised, and the range of purposes served by the political arithmetic of the 'comparative turn' (Nóvoa and Yariv-Mashal, 2003).

Teacher education in crisis: an historical perspective

Fear and hope are the recurring motifs of education reform approached as a modern project (Popkewitz, 2013b). We need not look far to locate an insistent critique of educational research and systems of teacher education, often compounded by assessments of the performance of national systems of schooling (as mentioned earlier). A language of crisis permeates the eastward (Anglo-American) drift of ideas on teacher education. Epistemic doubt around the knowledge base of teacher education and the ambivalent position of schools of education in research-intensive universities are compounded by political narratives of crisis. Tatto and Plank (2007, p 269) describe teacher education institutions operating within an 'environment of permanent educational crisis'. International organisations have intensified debate, often presenting (over)simplified abstract solutions 'based on questions of urgent pragmatism and amelioristic action' (Beech, 2011, p 265). Darling-Hammond (2012, p ix) describes 'a tsunami of reform' around an increasingly 'limited menu of change'. In this section, we place contemporary 'discourses of derision' within a historical and transnational frame.

The 'lowly status' and 'isolation' of schools of education is an enduring theme in histories of US teacher education (Katz, 1966; Clifford and Guthrie, 1988; Lagemann, 2000; Labaree, 2004). The efficiency of the school system was challenged in the high profile publications *And madly teach* (Smith, 1949), *Educational wastelands* (Bestor, 1953) and *Why Johnny can't read* (Flesch, 1955). Cross-national comparison linked to national competitiveness resound in works such as *What Ivan knows that Johnny doesn't* (Trace, 1978). Reflecting on the universification of teacher education, Goodlad (1990, p 25) observes: 'Teacher education not only ranks low among university priorities, it is marginal in the school or college of education.' The National Council on Teacher Quality's (2013, p 1) recent review of teacher preparation programmes describes US schools of education as 'an industry of mediocrity' and laments that '[o]nce the world leader in educational attainment, the United States has slipped well into the middle of the pack. Countries that were considered little more than educational backwaters just a few years ago have leapt to the forefront of student achievement'. Extending an economised logic to the higher education market, the National Council on Teacher Quality (NCTQ, 2013, p 2) argues that 'the vast majority of teacher preparation programs do not give aspiring teachers adequate return on their investment of time and tuition dollars'.

Contest and challenge mark teacher education in England and Wales. The literature is consistent in identifying periods of turbulence as colleges and departments/schools of education contend with academic and professional demands through periods of expansion followed by severe contraction. Scotland and the RoI have not been immune to rationalisation and uncertainty around institutional allocations, but teaching and teacher education have retained public esteem; writing on teacher training in England in 1913, on the other hand, Helen Wodehouse suggests: 'No profession but that of the priesthood has rivalled us, probably, in the amount of public disapprobation that we receive' (cited in Gardner and Cunningham, 2010, p 252). In advance of the report of the inquiry into teacher training (James, 1972), Taylor (1971, p 258) noted 'hysterical denunciations' in press reports of 'badly designed courses, inexperienced lecturers, poor quality recruits, low morale, isolation, paternalism, interference with the personal lives of students, inadequate contacts with the schools and insufficient attention to basic teaching skills, and of the new BEd strangled by university academics'. The success of the Black Papers' (Cox and Dyson, 1969; Cox and Boyson, 1977) attack on progressive education for lowering standards in primary schools prepared the ground for a conservative educational strategy (Jones, 1983). In Williams' (1961) terms, the utilitarian ideology of the 'industrial trainers' gained influence over the traditional values of the 'old humanists' in shaping education policy at this juncture. Repeated public attacks on the professional education of teachers accompanied centralisation of control from the mid-1980s. The necessity of reform was supported by the polemical publications *Teachers mistaught* (Lawlor, 1990), *Who teaches the teachers?* (O'Hear, 1988) and *The wayward elite* (O'Keeffe, 1990). At the beginning of the 21st century, Robinson (2000, p 52) records a 'damaging and sensationalised climate of hostility towards teachers and their teaching methods, teacher educators, educational theories and education research'.

Against this backdrop, reform in England was rapid following the election of the Conservative–Liberal Democratic coalition government in May 2010. A sense of urgency and closure of alternative readings was expressed in the White Paper, *The importance of teaching* (DfE, 2010): 'We have no choice but to be this radical' (p 4); 'Tweaking things at the margins is not an option' (p 5); 'Reforms on this scale are absolutely essential' (p 5); 'there is a fierce urgency to our plans' (p 7). Reform is couched in a crisis narrative centred on the economic functions of education. The White Paper cites Arne Duncan, the US Secretary of Education: 'in a knowledge economy, education is the new currency by which nations maintain economic competitiveness and global prosperity' (DfE, 2010, p 17). The-then Secretary of State for Education, Michael Gove, described academics and teacher unions as 'enemies of promise' whose opposition to the conversion of local authority community schools to (independent) academy status reflects the 'bigoted backward bankrupt ideology of a left wing establishment that perpetuates division and denies opportunity' (Gove, 2012). Responding to criticism to proposed reform of the secondary school curriculum, the minister attacked academics in university departments of education as 'The Blob', a 'network of educational gurus ... in thrall to Sixties ideologies ... more interested in valuing Marxism, revering jargon and fighting excellence' (Gove, 2013). Recent reforms have promoted school-based training through School Direct and Teach First (Beauchamp et al, 2013) and pedagogical 'best practice' through trialling interventions associated with pupil gains (such as the National College for Teaching and Leadership's Test and Learn programme). Improvement science returns as a mode of legitimation and lever of change, including the gold standard of evidence – the randomised controlled trial (Goldacre, 2013).

The '(re-)turn to the practical' and concern with efficiency is not restricted to the UK. In Australia the Minister for Education, Christopher Fyne, announcing the formation of a Teacher Education Ministerial Advisory Group in February 2014, insisted that:

> Old shibboleths will be cast aside. There'll be a relentless focus on the outcomes for students, and that means the kind of training that we give to our teachers at university. I want it to be more practical. I want them to have better experiences in the classroom rather than in universities, and I want it to be less theoretical. (Fyne, 2014, unpaginated)

The ideological and discursive construction of permanent crisis in teacher education in Anglophone nations reflects a constant struggle for control. This struggle is an expression of tension between familiar poles:

- the study and practice of education;
- models of teacher education based on notions of craft apprenticeship or a learned profession;
- struggles for control between external stakeholders and higher education institutions (HEIs); and
- intra-organisational struggles within HEIs.

The most recent practicum turn in different countries is underpinned by different conceptions of professionalism in teaching; for example between the dominant actors in the policy communities of England (DfE, 2010) and Scotland (Donaldson, 2011), and perhaps between Australia (Fyne, 2014) and New Zealand (Timperley, 2013), or Sweden and Norway (Lundahl et al, 2013). This is evident in different articulations of teachers' standards in terms of the level of prescription, or the degree of visibility of the accountability purpose (see Aitken et al, 2013; Chapter Six, this volume).

Jurisdictional challenge: an ecological perspective

The establishment of a profession is always the outcome of competition between different claimants to legitimate jurisdiction, that is, the 'link between a profession and its work' (Abbott, 1988, p 20). Teacher education from its inception has been the focus of constant dispute. It is inextricably linked to state centralisation of public education and the nation-building projects of the late 19th and 20th centuries. Writing of the institutionalisation of teacher education in mid-19th-century France, Toloudis (2010, p 589) stresses that 'without a commonly agreed upon set of stories about the professionals' claim to expertise, the legitimacy of their jurisdictional claims is suspect'. For illustrative purposes, it may be instructive to draw some observations from the early decades of the 20th century and the 21st century. This is not intended as a narrative of evolution or a search for origins but an attempt to show how teacher education as a practice, as an academic field and as a policy arena, is the product of contestation. Taking a long view, archival research in Europe by Hofstetter and Schneuwly (2006, p 1) shows how '[t]he spread of education and the building of the so-called teacher State (*Etat enseignant*) were both the object and result of numerous confrontations between the many social groups involved'. Deliberation focused then, as now, on:

- the purpose of education;
- the organisation and quality of teacher preparation;
- the curriculum and content of teacher preparation courses;
- teacher selection;
- the effectiveness of education practices and systems in addressing social and economic needs.

Popkewitz (2006, p 143) reminds us that the social and education sciences were formed in 'international conversations about modernity', that is, were inherently reform-minded. He traces the transatlantic travel of a Northern European Protestant reform movement seeking to address 'the Social Question'. Aspirations for the pedagogical sciences were aligned with the pursuit of individual freedom and social progress: 'the pedagogical sciences expressed in an almost evangelical and redemptive faith that education could rectify social disorder and improve and possibly perfect society' (Popkewitz, 2006, p 143). Smeyers and Depaepe (2010) describe the rise of the 'educationalisation of social problems' or *pädagogisierung*, that is, (over)confidence in the contribution education can make to the resolution of human problems. The emerging pedagogical sciences pursued 'universal agendas with local distinctions' (Popkewitz, 2006, p 163) and were influenced by indigenous understandings of the child and the purposes of education. Taking the examples of Dewey and Freire, Popkewitz (2006) describes how the ideas of 'indigenous foreigners' are 'reassembled in different places'. For example, how child-centred education crossed ideological lines. Using the metaphor of 'travelling libraries' (amalgamated practices), an account is offered of the flow of ideas associated with Adolphe Ferrière, Édouard Claparède, Ovide Decroly and Jean Piaget and how these were amalgamated in different ways and put to work for local projects. Context matters. The underlying drivers of reform influenced take-up and produced different patterns of reception in diverse locales. Thus, for example, what became known as the Pestalozzi 'method' (associated with the ideas of the Swiss reformer Johnn Heinrich Pestalozzi) changed significantly as it migrated and was reconstituted in heterogeneous 'Pestalozzi schools' across Europe (Tröhler, 2013). Horlacher (2013, p 135) argues that 'beyond the rhetorical level these educational institutions hardly changed the locally anchored organisational and pedagogical arrangements. Standardisation, then, turns out to be rhetorical, formal and covers the organisational and pedagogical varieties below the easy-to-reach visible structures'.

The coupling of progressive education (in its various forms) and the nascent educational sciences is aptly described by Hofstetter and Schneuwly (2006) as 'the tumultuous relations of an indissociable and irreconcilable couple'. The first educationists linked experimental pedagogy with radical school reform. The New Education was characterised by 'reformist fervour and positivist convictions' (Hofstetter and Schneuwly, 2006, p 1). This movement is discernible as the *Education nouvelle* and *Ecole active* in France, Progressive/New Education in England and *Reformpädagogik* in Germany (Boyd and Rawson, 1965; Selleck, 1968). Research institutes and university departments sought to academicise the movement; for example, in

Switzerland Claparède's *Institut Rousseau/Ecole des Sciences de l'Education*. Experimental schools sought to promote theory through practice, including the celebrated Laboratory School in Chicago, *Maison des Petits* in Geneva, the experimental schools of Zaventem, Ghent and Sofia, and *Referendenschule* in Budapest (Hofstetter and Schneuwly, 2006; Depaepe, 2012). The diverse multidisciplinary commitments of this movement in the first decades of the 20th century in the UK, Europe and US set up an ambivalence that continues to hold the field in tension. Much continues to rest on the popular legitimacy of the educational sciences and progressive education.

Abbott (2005) brings an ecological approach to the histories of the professions. His analysis brings to the fore competitive and contingent relations between actors and fields. For Abbott, 'ecological theory allows us to escape the false historiography produced by assuming immanent development. A linked ecologies argument moves beyond this by taking into account the simultaneous existence of numerous adjacent ecologies, all of whose actors seek alliances, resources, and support across ecological boundaries' (p 247). This analytical approach is particularly appropriate to the 'pluridisciplinarity' of educational studies and its application to teachers' work and school reform (Hofstetter, 2012). Licensing/registration and academic accreditation are examples of jurisdictional tactics played by the state, academy and profession. The making, un-doing and re-making of alliances are constant features in establishing and re-establishing professional authority through claims to expert knowledge.

> Professions wish to aggrandize themselves in competition, taking over this or that area of work, which they constitute into 'jurisdiction' by means of professional knowledge systems. A variety of forces - both internal and external - perpetually create potentialities for gains and losses of jurisdiction. Professions proact and react by seizing openings and reinforcing or casting off their earlier jurisdictions.
> (Abbott, 2005, p 246)

Abbott (2005) directs our attention to relations between three linked ecologies: 'the jurisdictions of the professions, the settlements of the disciplines, and the bundles of politics' (p 253). He pays particular attention to the stability and duration of settlements. Professional jurisdictions based on the principle of exclusivity are regarded as comparatively stable. Academic settlements are less exclusive, more open and can move more quickly. Political settlements are most agile and can progress at a more rapid pace. Consideration of the temporal dimension in how settlements are achieved in different spaces helps our understanding of how shifts occur at different paces within closely linked ecologies. Such an approach helps to make sense of the 'jarring discontinuity' that is often noted between university and school (Labaree, 2004, p 84) and the recurring theme of relevance and obsolescence within crisis narratives.

From this perspective, universitisation (placing teacher education under the auspices of universities) is not an inevitable evolution, but a move associated with alliances formed through a process of 'secondary disciplinarisation' (that is, growing from and with existing professional knowledge) (Hofstetter, 2012, p 325). Universitisation is a process open to revision and indeed reversal. The impetus for the academic discipline comes from the practice field (the teaching profession). A degree in education can be seen as an 'avatar' (Abbott, 2005, p 265) of the professional ecology seeking to access the university ecology. Demands for a 'separate training faculty' grow as an expanding number of faculty compete within the academic ecology for resources and status (Abbott, 2005, p 266). Specialisation and the creation of separate sub-specialities offer temporary respite from competition in the academic ecology. The bonds loosen between the practice field and academic discipline, giving rise to claims of loss of relevance and renewed external pressure for academisation.

Abbott (2005, p 267) notes a 'pattern of academicizing followed by capture from the academic side and a new academicizing from the practice side'. The development of experimental pedagogy as a field of study served to support the uncoupling of pedagogy from philosophy in the academy in the early 20th century. The (re-)turn to a stronger practical (school) orientation from the 1930s – and subsequently – gave autonomy to teacher education as an area of specialist (professional) work but weakened its authority and position in the academy. Goodchild (2006, p 71) argues that while mainland Europe sought to establish a science of pedagogy in the first decades of the 20th century, universities in the US sought to harness 'scientific professionalisation' for teachers for the expanding school system. Similarly, Aldrich argues that while Alexander Bain's *Education as a science* was published in the UK in 1879,

> Since then, less and less has been heard of this claim ... in the early decades of the twentieth century, day training colleges and university departments of education in England and Wales had great difficulty in developing a systematic

science or sciences of education, or even a coherent science of teaching. They remained subject to the traditional disdains of politicians, civil servants, the ancient universities and public schools. (Aldrich, 2004, p 629)

In the first decades of the 21st century, further weakening of the jurisdictional claims of university-based teacher educators – in England in particular – may endanger the reduced aim of 'scientific professionalisation'.

The twin poles of academisation and professionalisation are clearly connected with the crisis narrative mentioned earlier (Furlong and Lawn, 2011; Furlong, 2013a). In an edited collection of papers, published in 1963, from a symposium convened to consider 'if there is, or can be, a discipline of Education', Walton describes his introductory chapter as 'a kind of vehicle of liberation, a resolution of a dilemma, and an opportunity to redeem the study of education from a meretricious professionalism and a slavish dependence on the other academic studies' (Walton and Kuethe, 1963, p 4). Walton (1963, p 12) refers to education as 'a Diaspora in reverse', drawing contributions from the foundations/disciplines but seldom contributing to them. In the same volume the philosopher R.S. Peters (1963, p 20) derides the 'looseness, fogginess and general lack of rigour within philosophy of education, concluding: 'It is no wonder that most philosophers regard this field as a philosophical slum.' Carroll (1963, p 119) suggests that the inclusion of educational psychology in the teacher education curriculum reflects 'a mixture of pious optimism and subdued embarrassment'. The American historian Bernard Bailyn offers a rueful summary of the disassociation of the disciplines and professional education

> When education took the scholarship of its origins with it into seclusion and nurtured it in isolation, a retrogression, relative to the advances in the contributing disciplines – some kind of intellectual calcification – took place.... What had begun as an effort to achieve academic respectability and intellectual maturity through institutional autonomy, appeared to end in isolation that reduced contacts between the traditional disciplines and education, damming up the currents of intellectual life to the detriment of all. (Bailyn, 1963, pp 129-130)

The enduring isolation of educationists within many HEIs, combined with increasingly acute divisions between the 'academic sub-tribes' that comprise education faculty (Menter, 2011a; see also Chapter Eleven, this volume), reduce the possibility of building strong alliances against external incursion. From the 1990s, teacher education policy in England and Wales (especially) became more school-focused while many European countries and other nations extended the process of universitisation. Such fragmentation and diversification have increased the likelihood of a future teacher education workforce for whom 'the (disciplinary) past is another country' (Lawn and Furlong, 2011, p 1). The place of research in teacher education in the UK is ever less secure (BERA and RSA, 2014a, 2014b; see also Chapter Ten, this volume). Reflecting on the victory of American administrative progressives over pedagogical progressives in the first half of the 20th century, Labaree (2005, p 276) observes that the latter 'failed miserably in shaping what we do in schools, did at least succeed in shaping how we talk about schools'. He goes on to suggest: 'The Pyrrhic victory by the pedagogical progressives is that the airy realm of educational rhetoric has fooled participants in the debate into assuming that substantive victory on the ground in the classroom is (for one) a possibility and (for the other) a reality' (Labaree, 2005, p 288). In the English context, in particular, this Pyrrhic victory has rendered teacher education vulnerable to successive waves of conservative populism.

Reflecting on negative media portrayals of teachers and their work before the 1992 General Election, Wallace (1993, p 327) argues: 'The rhetoric of progressivism, adopted within the myth of *primaryspeak*, was taken as reality by teachers' attackers in creating a counter-myth that progressive practice had lowered standards. Teachers had unwittingly provided government ministers and the media with their ammunition.' Before the 2015 UK General Election, familiar narratives of hope and fear, risk and salvation, became enmeshed with myths that allowed the simplistic re-polarisation of theory and practice, the academic and the professional, the progressive and the traditional. The think tank Civitas picked up the mantle of the Black Papers (Peal, 2014; Young, 2014), ably aided by teacher advocates for change (Bennett, 2013; Christodoulou, 2013). The doubt that continues to surround the knowledge claims of teacher education, compounded by renewed enthusiasm for the policy technology of evidence-based education, threatens to re-ignite old paradigm wars. In the most recent 'empirical turn', teachers appear as data, or as sources for local experimentation by more knowledgeable others, rather than as knowledge (co-)producers. The repositioning of teachers and recalibration of teacher education reflect the outcome of new trials of strength among the many stakeholders.

Conclusion

In the resurrection of binary divides, two clear influences are discernible in travelling ideas on teacher education policy. The first retains links to varying degrees with the professional project; the second reflects the encroachment of market discipline in the provision of initial teacher education. Continuity with the professional project is evident in:

- support for clinical practice models of teacher education;
- the promotion of professional learning across the career course;
- cultivation of a disposition towards enquiry; knowledge of diversity and different cultural groups; the development of adaptive expertise to support curricular and pedagogical innovation.

The second approach promotes a growth in market-oriented, flexible, 'fast-track' routes to qualified teacher status (Musset, 2010). There are points of divergence between international organisations, notably between the OECD and the market philosophy of the World Bank. The former emphasises teacher engagement in reform efforts (OECD, 2011a); the latter promotes teacher incentive policies that link pay or tenure directly to performance (World Bank, 2013).

Hargreaves (2013) distinguishes between an emergent 'business capital' and 'professional capital' view of teaching. The former:

> favours a teaching force that is young, flexible, temporary, inexpensive to train at the beginning, un-pensioned at the end (except by teachers' self-investment), and replaceable where ever possible by technology. Finding and keeping good teachers then becomes seeking out and deploying (but not really developing or investing in) existing human capital – hunting for talented individuals, working them hard, and moving them on when they get restless or become spent. (Hargreaves, 2013, p 293)

As mentioned in Chapter Two, the 'professional capital' view of teaching in contrast argues that:

> getting good teaching for all learners requires teachers to be highly committed, thoroughly prepared, continuously developed, properly paid, well networked with each other to maximise their own improvement, and able to

make effective judgements using all their capabilities and experience. (Hargreaves, 2013, p 294)

Seddon and Levin (2013, p xviii) argue that 'detecting travelling reforms is relatively easy when compared to understanding them.... It is not sufficient to state that a reform in one country resembles that of another, but it is important to understand at what level, with what means and for whose benefit and at whose expense convergence occurs'. The following chapters examine some of the key differences and similarities in trajectories of reform across the five nations of the UK and RoI, and elsewhere. Home international studies have particular utility in understanding policy moves within closely linked systems. Processes of globalisation and transnationalism intersect with national education discourses to create new policy spaces within which possibilities for teacher education are formed. By drawing on the theoretical resources of the sociologies of education it is possible to move beyond 'methodological nationalist' frames of reference (Seddon, 2014, p 22) to enhance our understanding of teacher education in times of change.

Note
[1] 'PISA INSET training pack', 2012. Up-to-date information on PISA INSET training materials can be found at: http://wales.gov.uk/topics/educationandskills/schoolshome/curriculuminwales/wgpisa/pisa-inset/?lang=en

Part Two:
Teacher education in the five nations

FOUR

Teacher education in England: change in abundance, continuities in question

Jean Murray and Trevor Mutton

Introduction

Alexander, Craft and Lynch's (1984a) book *Change in teacher education* was written just before the publication of the landmark government circular 3/84 (DES, 1984) on teacher education, although its 'substantial change in the direction of travel' (Craft, 1984, p 332) was already clear. Alexander et al aimed to 'reflect upon the changes in context and provision' (Craft, 1984, p 332) that had characterised teacher education between the publication of the Robbins Report in 1963, and 1983. Their analyses identified both changes and continuities in teacher education over those 20 years, including:

- the changing role of government;
- shifts in the power of other stakeholders;
- the challenges of institutional reorganisation;
- the increasing engagement of the teaching profession in teacher education;
- the decline in the university 'monopoly'.

But, as the editors of that volume also commented, two decades of organisational change had taken place 'within a context of cultural and epistemological continuity' (Alexander et al, 1984b, p xviii) in which similar debates about forms, contents and values of pre-service education or initial teacher education (ITE) persisted.

Teacher education in England in the 30 years since 1984 has been subject to significant changes, as part of an ever-present focus on raising educational standards in schools. Successive governments – of three political hues – have used ITE to address issues around the supply of high-quality teachers able to deliver improvements in the school system.

As MacBeath (2011, p 377) has commented, because of this, teacher education has remained a 'contentious issue'.

Research on teacher education in England has been accused of ahistoricism (Dent, 1977), of failing to take the 'long view' of historical change to bear on understanding the present and anticipating the future. Addressing such critiques, Gardner (1993) offered an analysis of how the 'pendulum' of ITE has swung over time between higher education institutions (HEIs) and schooling. Drawing on that analogy, the direction of the pendulum 'swing' between 1984 and 2014 was a movement, driven in large part by central government policies, further away from the dominance of higher education (HE) in earlier parts of the 20th century and towards schools and schooling as more influential stakeholders in ITE at present. With these changes have come significant alterations in the epistemologies, cultures, governance and institutional structures of ITE in England.

It is not our intention to give a comprehensive account of events since 1984, not least because that work has already been achieved by others (see, for example, Gilroy, 1992; Furlong et al, 2000; Furlong, 2013a). The later sections of this chapter focus on four themes from Alexander et al's 1984 book and outline the related changes and continuities of the last 30 years. We begin this chapter by presenting a brief picture of ITE in England as it stands at present to give a context for our later analyses of changes and continuities since 1984. Our focus here is deliberately on ITE for the school sector rather than continuing professional development.

Towards school-led initial teacher training: 2014

The sheer scale of ITE in 2014, as in 1984, is a significant factor in determining ITE provision, with the number of student teachers (now often called 'trainees') having been projected to be around 43,500 in 2014/15 (Universities UK, 2014). With the exception of secondary shortage subjects, recruitment has been good since 2000 partly as a result of the economic downturn and consequent graduate unemployment. There are multiple 'providers' (a term that indicates organisations validated to 'train' teachers) and diverse routes into teaching, including through employment-based initial teacher training (EBITT) schemes – notably School Direct, discussed in more detail later in this chapter – and school-centred initial teacher training (SCITT) schemes. These routes exist alongside and are sometimes interwoven with traditional study for one-year Post Graduate Certificates in Education (PGCEs) or undergraduate degrees giving 'qualified teacher status' (QTS). There are also schemes aimed at particular groups such as Teach First (like the Teach for America programme on which it is modelled, which recruits only trainees with 'good' degrees) and Troops into Teaching (for ex-members of the armed forces). In 2013/14, there were more than 33,000 entrants into teacher education (Universities UK, 2014).

After the election of the coalition government in 2010, there were wide-ranging changes to schooling, with the implementation of the Free Schools initiative and the acceleration of the Academies programme.[1] Significantly for ITE, these state-funded but 'independent' schools are now permitted to recruit untrained teachers, if they so wish. There is also an 'assessment only' route by which intending teachers can apply for QTS through assessment against the eight current teacher standards (Beauchamp et al, 2015).

These changes in themselves have signalled disregard for the value of ITE, but the government has also implemented moves for 'reform' by using school-led models of training and opening up the 'market' to new providers. The main instrument here has been the School Direct programme, in which schools recruit intending teachers, provide the majority of their school experience and arrange any other necessary training towards QTS.[2] Aspects of the ideology behind School Direct echo statements from conservative educationalists of earlier eras, notably portraying teaching as the efficient transmission of personal subject knowledge to pupils, with any necessary practical skills acquired through a short period of apprenticeship to a 'master teacher' (Hillgate Group, 1986; Gove, 2010; see also Chapter Three, this volume).

First introduced as a small-scale pilot in 2011, by 2013/14, 25% of all ITE places were notionally allocated through School Direct (UCET, 2014), with 'the scale and speed of the growth' taking many in the university sector by surprise (UCET, 2014, p 2) and making the scheme already a significant route into the profession. The impact of the scheme has been compounded by a revised and more rigorous inspection framework aimed at improving the performance of providers. In a revised allocation system, universities are given some – usually reduced – student numbers, but guaranteed or 'core' places are only allocated to providers achieving 'outstanding' results in inspections carried out by Office for Standards in Education (Ofsted).[3] The result is that many universities without those results now rely on gaining 'training contracts' from schools under the School Direct scheme. The market-led model in use here may be seen as one of purchase by a customer (the school) of an ITE programme from a service provider (usually but not always a university), sometimes following a process that resembles competitive tendering. Whitty (2014, p 471) sees this situation as resulting from the 'neo-liberal combination of the strong state and the free market'. With this context for 2014 established, we now turn to our thematic analysis of changes and continuities between 1984 and 2014.

Changes and continuities: ebbs and flows in a contested field

Government intervention and the decline of the university influence

In 1984, Alexander et al (1984b, p xviii) commented on the 'pivotal but changing' role of government, particularly the 'marked centralisation' of control over teacher education between 1963 and 1983. Those earlier commentators could, of course, have had little sense of the extent of government control established by 2014. The first stage towards this was circular 3/84 (DES 1984), a 'constitutionally revolutionary circular' (Wilkin, 1991, quoted in Furlong, 1996, p 150) because it represented a new model of state intervention and became the foundation stone for building a nationwide, government-determined and accountable system. It established the Council for Accreditation of Teacher Education (CATE) to oversee all ITE courses, extending the government's control and challenging the power of the HEIs.

Since 1984, there have been numerous other items of legislation and 'guidance', together with the creation of regulatory structures and inspection regimes through Ofsted in 1994/95 and the establishment of quasi-governmental organisations charged with monitoring ITE (first CATE then – notably – the various versions of the mutating Teacher Training Agency [TTA] from 1994 to 2012 and now, in 2015, the National College for Teaching and Leadership [NCTL]). These and other changes to ITE have mirrored aspects of the 'initiativitis' (PWC and DfES, 2007, p vii) of school reforms from the late 1980s onwards.

At various points, government pronouncements have dictated many elements of ITE, including:

- governance structures;
- quality assurance mechanisms;
- partnership requirements;
- curricula and pedagogical structures;
- student teacher outcomes;
- HE staff recruitment criteria.

These pronouncements have often followed a pattern of 'introduction, intensification and instantiation', until many of them have become part of the 'public discourses' (Popkewitz, 1987) of the field.[4] This pattern has held even when specific legislation has been rescinded or has fallen into abeyance. Examples here include the trajectory of the controversial specifications of the recruitment and retention criteria in circulars 3/84 and 24/89 (DES, 1984, 1989). These emphasised the importance of all teacher educators having 'recent and relevant' knowledge of schooling, acquired through regular experience in classrooms. The introduction of this particular criterion in 1984 was regarded as inappropriate and objectionable at the time (Boxall and Burrage, 1989). But these specifications were still implemented and had a radical effect on the staffing bases of HEIs, bringing in a new generation of teacher educators straight from school teaching. The 'recent and relevant' legislation itself has long fallen into abeyance, but the need for all teacher educators to have had experience of working in schools has become part of the 'common sense' of recruitment for ITE work (Ellis et al, 2012). Furthermore, experiential knowledge of schooling and identities as 'once-a-teacher' form the foundations of pedagogy for many teacher educators (Murray, 2002).

A similar pattern can be seen in the implementation of the detailed statutory curricula for ITE in government circulars (DfEE, 1997, 1998) and the specification of pedagogical approaches issued by the TTA in 1999. Dutifully implemented by all providers at the time, the legislation and the non-statutory guidance were later rescinded, but by then the 'right' of the government and its agencies to micro-manage the ITE curriculum, in the 'common-sense' interests of ensuring that its structures, content and pedagogies related directly to the school curriculum, was well established. In 2011/12, when primary ITE courses were instructed to include the teaching of synthetic phonics into their literacy programmes, there were protests, but all HEIs duly implemented the measure. This was not least because compliance to this requirement was (and still is) monitored and regulated by responses from the newly qualified teacher (NQT) surveys and through Ofsted inspections.

But perhaps the most important example of this process of policy instantiation is that of partnership. Here circular 24/89 (DES, 1989) built on the 1984 circular's identification of partnership mechanisms between schools and universities. Partnership requirements were then further specified in circulars 9/92 and 14/93 (DfE, 1992, 1993), including structures that HEIs should implement, in partnership with schools, in terms of planning teaching and assessing (Furlong et al,

2000) and requirements for the transfer of HEI funding to schools. These two circulars accelerated the trend for ITE to become a more practical and school-focused enterprise in its curricula, practices and assumptions of professionalism (Furlong et al, 2000). For HEIs, this legislation certainly made partnerships with schools obligatory, as well as validating teachers' involvement in ITE, and moving further in the direction of reducing their autonomy (and funding). Mandated in legislation like this, partnership between schools and university providers was a 'core principle of provision' (Furlong et al, 2006b, p 33) from 1992 until 2011. Many saw partnership as a hegemonic discourse of teacher education (Crozier et al, 1990, p 44), with its associated structures and practices often going unquestioned and unchallenged, as the next section of this chapter explores.

McNamara (2010) identifies the cumulative effects of these multiple changes in ITE as:

- a drive towards political control;
- the generation of 'practical' and 'relevant' school-based teacher training routes, some with no HEI involvement;
- increased regulation and bureaucratisation, including the micro-management of the sector;
- strong systems of surveillance and control to monitor compliance.

The resulting models of ITE may be defined as existing in a 'national framework of accountability' (Furlong et al, 2000, p 15) and 'culture of compliance' (Menter et al, 2006, p 50). The government's right to micro-manage ITE has become part of the 'common sense' of the field, as has providers' adaptation to rapid changes in criteria for ensuring compliance and 'quality' provision.

But these policy changes by government have been 'decoded in complex ways (via actors, interpretation and meanings in relation to their history, experiences, skills, resources and context)' (Ball, 1994, p 16). Fundamentally, then, policies have been differentially implemented by stakeholders in varying degrees – to use Ball's terms – of compliance and resistance, accommodation and adaptation. An example is that even on PGCE routes, where little time is allowed for study on campus, most university-involved programmes have continued to combine perspectives from educational research with meeting the official imperatives of making programmes 'demanding, relevant, and practical' (Furlong, et al, 2000, p 144) and meeting the current teacher standards, which make no explicit mention of research (Beauchamp et al, 2015). The provision of research-informed ITE is, as a review by the British Educational Research Association (BERA) and the Royal Society of Arts (RSA) identifies (BERA and RSA, 2014b), of great importance in considering the quality of provision (see Chapter Ten, this volume).

With the HE sector itself also in transition across these 30 years, as we detail later in this chapter, government interventions in ITE have had the overall effect of bringing significant changes to a metamorphosing and already destabilised sector. These interventions have changed ITE fundamentally by making it a more school-focused enterprise, accelerating the 'turn to the practical' (Hoyle, quoted in Furlong and Lawn, 2011) and increasing the power of the 'discourse of relevance' (Maguire and Weiner, 1994). The epistemology of teacher education has therefore changed, with experiential, practical and contemporary knowledge of teaching becoming central. Other nations have also experienced a 'practicum turn in teacher education' (Mattsson et al, 2011, p 17) or a 'turn toward practice' (Zeichner and Bier, 2014, p 103) but in few contexts has this led to the degree of epistemological and cultural change found in ITE in England (Beauchamp et al, 2015).

Shifts in the power of stakeholders

The dominant power in ITE, then, has been increasingly in the hands of central government since 1984, with universities – and teacher educators as their agency – suffering a considerable decline in their influence. This shift has also given far more power and influence in ITE to teachers and schools. Behind these major patterns of change, however, have been other, more complex shifts in the power of the multiple stakeholders in ITE. It is the details of some of these shifts that we explore here.

In their analysis of 1919–83, Alexander et al (1984b, p xiii) describe 'the continuing shifts in the power and influence, relative to each other, of the various participants and interests – teachers, teacher educators, universities, the CNAA [Council for National Academic Awards], public sector Higher Education, local government, central government and Her Majesty's Inspectorate' (HMI). Some of the stakeholders they describe are, of course, now absent from the field or transformed within it, telling an interesting story about the pace of educational change.

Public sector HEIs, once under the control of local education authorities are now within the university sector, as we describe later in this chapter; the CNNA, a regulatory body validating academic awards for those HEIs, is long defunct; and the old HMI system has gone, with some of its functions having vanished and others having been transformed into punitive Ofsted mechanisms. The stakeholder power of the local education authorities declined sharply when the public sector institutions moved into the university sector. The partnership structures of the 1990s created some renewed opportunities for local education authority involvement through the schools in their areas, and the current school-led ITE initiatives might have offered new power bases for local education authorities, had the deregulation of schooling not already caused a steep decline in their influence. In the current educational landscape, then, local education authorities are not powerful stakeholders in ITE.

Another stakeholder, now gone from the field, was the short-lived General Teaching Council (England), established in 2000 as the professional body for teaching and operating as such until 2012, when it was abolished by the coalition government. The absence of a well-established General Teaching Council in England has meant that, unlike in Scotland, where such a national council has existed for nearly 50 years, there has been no trusted professional stakeholder able to represent and mediate the interests of both schools and HEIs for the overall benefit of the teaching profession (Gilroy, 2014).

Alexander et al (1984a) do not even mention the churches, once powerful stakeholders in ITE (Dent, 1977), thus reflecting their diminishing power even between 1963 and 1983. At present while some denominational HEIs continue to exist, their ITE provision is now part of a diversified and secularised portfolio of HE courses and denominational influences at national levels of teacher education are small.

As Alexander et al (1984b, p xiii) describe, 1963 to 1983 saw 'the increasing but belated engagement of the teaching profession in debates and decisions about its own training and continuous professional development'. As explored earlier, particularly between 1992 and 2010, the concept of 'partnership' with HEIs facilitated the engagement of schools and teachers in ITE, giving them considerable stakeholder power. As an 'integrating ideal', partnership seemed to facilitate genuine teacher involvement, to represent a consensus and to epitomise 'inherent goodness' (Crozier et al, 1990, p 44). Furlong et al (2006b) argued that there were three models of partnership in existence by the 2000s: collaborative, complementary and HEI-led. Their analysis indicated that complementary and HEI-led partnerships were more prevalent, but all models valorised professional practice in schools, involved teachers in recruitment, mentoring and assessment, and aimed to achieve mutual respect and trust between schools and HEIs (Furlong et al, 2000).

Partnership certainly spawned a new emphasis on mentors in schools, their expertise, professional development and career opportunities. For many, supporting students on practicum, teaching campus-based sessions and participating in student recruitment gave opportunities to share and develop knowledge and personal practice. As MacBeath (2011, p 380) commented, the best form of partnership was and is always 'three-way ... with the student, the teacher (or mentor) and the university teacher engaged in a form of collaborative assessment and forward planning' and making use of the varied expertise of all parties. There are many examples of individual mentors providing outstanding support for students (Jones et al, 2009; Counsell, 2013), although a Select Committee report on teacher education (House of Commons Children, Schools and Families Committee, 2010) raised concerns about inconsistency in the quality of mentoring and therefore of learning experiences in schools.

Like the dominant discourses of earlier decades, however, partnership could also hide a divergence of values and perspectives (Dhillon, 2009) and reconceptualise old binaries (Hill, 1992). But until 2011, HEI–school partnerships remained the dominant model of ITE and one that seemed to deliver high-quality provision, against the quality indicators of the time. Ofsted (2010) stated that, in 2009/10, 47% of HEI partnership provision was 'outstanding' whilst 94% was 'good or better'. Such results led to celebrations from universities and government identifying institutional successes and, nationally, proclaiming the production of 'the best trained teachers ever'. Yet, as a new government came to power in 2010, it became clear that those achievements were not validated by all stakeholders in the field.

The power of student teachers as stakeholders in ITE has, arguably, been increased through a range of measures. Growing marketisation and the variety of training routes on offer give prospective teachers greater choice about how, where and when they study, with more opportunities to match individual needs and prior experiences to the chosen pattern of training. The annual NQT survey gives new teachers a voice in commenting on the quality of the ITE programme they followed. HE quality assurances mechanisms also value 'student voice', routinely including student participation in evaluations, course committees and similar structures. Other factors, particularly the introduction of fees of up to £9,000 for a PGCE year, have also accelerated the importance of 'student voice' and made many students more demanding and critical consumers of HE than previously.

Yet, alternative perspectives might argue that the NQT survey permits responses only to a range of centrally determined questions and is better seen as part of the regulatory structures driving ITE than as a genuine 'student voice' mechanism. The same accusations might be levelled at university quality assurance structures. Choice of routes has been an important factor in the past in bringing a more diverse workforce into teaching, but there is anecdotal evidence that the number of choices now available is confusing rather than empowering potential teachers.

Most seriously, there is little evidence that choice and marketisation are offering consistent improvements in the *quality* of student learning on offer. Indeed, there are worrying patterns emerging in some programmes where workplace learning is central. These patterns include:

- erosions in the recognition of the status of students as learners (ATL, 2013);
- tendencies for the replication of practice observed in particular schools (McNamara et al, 2013);
- erosions of the time and space allocated for learning (ATL, 2014, p 10);
- the provision of only limited workplace learning opportunities (ATL, 2014, p 11).

Student voice and choice are both important, but genuine increases in power for this vital stakeholder group can only be achieved when improving the *quality* of learning for *all* is the major driver for change.

A further important group of stakeholders – pupils in schools – is often cited, especially in policy documents, as the beneficiary of improvements in teacher education, but rarely consulted or considered directly.

The balance of power among the stakeholders in teacher education has, then, shifted greatly since 1984, with the state assuming explicit control of more areas of the field and the school sector assuming much greater professional influence. The traditional autonomy of HEIs has been systematically challenged and undermined. Universities are no longer seen by some as being either necessary or distinctive in terms of the focus, curriculum and practices they offer. Others, of course, would assert that HEIs must still play a central role in ITE (MacBeath, 2011; BERA and RSA, 2014a, 2014b), not least in ensuring research-informed provision. Schools – and teachers within them – have gained considerable power and influence over the last 30 years, now seemingly becoming more dominant forces than HEIs. And, as a further part of its vision of a 'school-led' education system, the government has planned to set up 600 teaching schools by 2016, building networks of teaching school alliances and taking on ITE, continuing professional development and – increasingly – research roles.

Institutional changes to organisational structures and communal cultures

Alexander et al (1984b, p xviii) refer to 'the challenge of unprecedented institutional change' in ITE between 1963 and 1983, and 'its impact not only on organisational arrangements, but also at the deeper level of institutional culture'. These changes were driven by shifts in national policy for HE, initiated by the Robbins Report (Robbins, 1963), and exacerbated by economic factors and demographic shifts in pupil numbers. In the 1960s training colleges, in which the majority of ITE was then located, expanded dramatically, offering degree-level courses for the first time. In the 1970s, those colleges underwent a further series of radical changes, driven by the need for rapid contraction of ITE numbers. This triggered a huge institutional upheaval, termed 'colleges in crisis' by one analyst (Hencke, 1978). By 1981, the number of colleges was reduced dramatically, with many institutions closing down, and others merging with universities – or more commonly polytechnics – in a seemingly haphazard restructuring of the field (Hencke, 1978). A new type of institution was created (the diversified institutes of higher education [IHEs]), with subsequent cultural changes (Lynch, 1984). Many teacher educators in colleges faced redundancy; those who survived often saw established practice swept away (Bell, 1981).

While ITE in the university sector was largely protected from the effects of the rapid expansions and contractions experienced by the colleges (Plunkett, 1984), it did experience cuts (Taylor, 1984); some universities also experienced mergers with colleges (Shaw, 1984) and lived through subsequent cultural shifts; and all university schools of education continued to live with the perceived academic low status of their field (Judge et al, 1994).

During the 1980s the surviving colleges and IHEs, together with the polytechnics, formed a group of ITE providers known as the public sector institutions, on the other side of the 'binary line' from the established (or 'old') universities. The differences between provision in the two types of institutions were significant (DES, 1987). But by 1992, many of the public sector institutions had increased academic and corporate status and were given the accreditation powers necessary for gaining university status as 'new' or post-1992 universities (Pratt, 1997).

When other HEIs offering ITE attained university status between 1993 and 2013, it meant that all but a tiny fraction of HE-informed provision was in the university sector for the first time. There was considerable irony in this timing, of course, just as school-led ITE gained further ascendancy (Furlong, 2013a).

The larger, more diversified university sector of 2014 is, of course, very different from the sector as it was in 1984, and in some ways teacher education sits more easily in the current institutions at present. This is not least because many other types of vocational courses, including social work and nursing, are now located in HE, where they also face the multiple and sometimes conflicting imperatives of the university and their professional fields (Murray, 2007). This factor affects teacher education provision in all universities in the United Kingdom (UK), as do many other changes since 1984, including:

- the expansion of HE,
- the impact of neo-liberal performativity regimes and the quinquennial UK-wide research audits,
- the research funding drought since 2008/09, and
- internal and institutional volatility.

Because of this pan-UK relevance, these matters are discussed further in Chapter Eleven while in this section the focus is on the particular issues facing ITE in universities in England.

In 2015, the 70 universities offering ITE range from long-established, research-intensive institutions to newly created teaching-intensive universities. The majority of HEI places overall are in the 'new' universities (including all the primary provision at undergraduate level). Indeed, the majority of primary ITE places are in these 'new' universities. 'Old' universities offer approximately 50% of all secondary PGCE courses, although in general the numbers in each student cohort are smaller than in the 'new' universities, and some primary PGCE provision.

The recession, funding downturns and recent demographic changes, combined with the coalition government's changing ITE policies, mean that providers in the university sector have been hit hard, for reasons outlined earlier. This situation has led to course closures and redundancies in some universities, with secondary courses initially suffering more because of demographic changes in schooling. Closures have occurred in small programmes in 'old' universities, in particular, reducing the range of subject-specific secondary provision offered. Two 'old' universities and one 'new' university have to date withdrawn from ITE, and more are questioning their ongoing commitments. The combined effects of these factors have led to fears that nearly all schools of education have been destabilised and that the continued existence of teacher education within universities is threatened (Universities UK, 2014).

A further challenge for the universities is that, as schools are encouraged to take on increasingly greater levels of responsibility for ITE, some established models of school–university partnerships have been destabilised and subjected to new market-led forces. Recent studies (Brennan et al, 2014; Brown et al, 2014) indicate that at least some HE-based teacher educators have experienced considerable changes in their institutional cultures, work patterns and attitudes to work since 2012. Brennan et al's (2014) study on the effects of School Direct, for example, shows teacher educators taking on what are, in effect, sales and marketing work with schools in order to 'win' contracts for training, engaging in widespread consultancy roles and systematically transferring knowledge to schools.

However, even before the introduction of School Direct, it was clear that schools of education had already undergone considerable cultural changes. Like all in the education sector, they had learned to live with an instrumental language in which teacher education is 'training' offered by 'providers' to student teachers who are 'trainees' and taught by teacher educators who are 'trainers' 'delivering' sometimes narrow, skills-based programmes, located largely or wholly in schools. And, as we have noted earlier, in terms of its epistemology, ITE has changed profoundly since 1984.

Most seriously, in terms of cultural change, all ITE providers now have to demonstrate compliance with imposed regulatory structures and follow models of managed professionalism to meet corporate goals set by both the government and its agencies. Ranson (quoted in MacBeath, 2011, p 385) states that this has created 'a regime of performativity that works from the outside in, through regulations, controls and pressures ... disciplined by targets, indicators and measures of performance'. In other words, what counts as valid professional knowledge has been profoundly changed, not least because its generation rests, in part, on the 'organised practices through which we are governed and through which we govern ourselves' (Dean, 1999, p 28). These new types of knowledge and practice increasingly claim authority over previous modes.

New (and old) conceptualisations of theory into practice

Alexander et al (1984b, p xviii) identified the 'cultural and epistemological continuity' of ITE between 1963 and 1983. Other continuities included arguments about 'theory and practice', and the seemingly intractable disconnect between them. These arguments continue to reverberate in the English teacher education context 30 years on. Current understanding of ITE still all too frequently constructs a conceptual binary around 'theory/practice' and a related 'universities/schools' divide. These constructs, in tandem, position schools as the only places where 'practice' can be generated and universities as the sole 'providers' of 'theory', which is often viewed as irrelevant.

As outlined earlier, recent government policies have led to an increasing emphasis on the relevance and value of learning taking place in schools. This valuation of practice in schools is not new; its origins can be traced back to the emphases of the James Report (James, 1972). In the early 1980s, Craft (1984, p 338) also identified the drive towards more 'practical preparation of teachers, involving more classroom experience'.[5] A feature of legislation in the early 1990s (DfE, 1992, 1993) was the requirement for students to spend a statutory minimum number of days on practicum. Legislation (DfE, 2010) now requires that on PGCE courses lasting 36 weeks, student teachers must spend 24 weeks in schools and 12 in HEIs. On some School Direct schemes, all 'training time' may be spent working in schools, since 'most providers consider that every day on their course includes training' (NCTL, 2014b, p 2). These and similar valuations often seem to imply that more time spent learning 'on the job' and in schools will automatically lead to better student learning and more effective ITE.

Such assumptions are often grounded in outdated apprenticeship models of training where learning is perceived to happen through immersion in classrooms and the accrual of knowledge through experience alone. But research on workplace learning (see McNamara et al, 2013, for a summary) indicates that for real learning to happen 'training programmes' in school workplaces need to be carefully designed and implemented. McNamara et al (2013, p 295) state that there must be a communal learning culture within the school in which student teachers are valued and in which 'symbiotic relationships between the multiple discourses about theory and practice, teaching and learning in ITE can be facilitated'. Students need 'participation in a well-planned, rich and flexible variety of activities balanced between organisational and individual needs', with 'availability of time and space for quality learning opportunities and experiences to occur, and then further time to reflect upon them' (McNamara et al, 2013, p 295). Finally, all student teachers need colleagues who undertake supporting roles and challenge them. Above all, the workplace learning literature stresses that the student teacher's status as a learner needs to be preserved, with time for learning protected from other demands within the school. The mere *quantity* of time spent in schools, then, should not be seen as the determining factor but rather the *quality* of the learning experiences that time offers for learning to be a teacher.

The dominant, binary constructs of theory/practice as separate and distinctive, still found in many of the 'public discourses' (Popekwitz, 1987) of ITE, overlook much past work, which strove to achieve more integrated senses of knowledge. In the 1980s, the Oxford Internship Scheme (Benton, 1990) was developed around such a need, recognising the distinctive contributions of both school and university (McIntyre, 1990b). Similar work was undertaken in the 1980s at the Universities of Leicester and Sussex (Furlong et al, 1988). Hagger and McIntyre (2006) argued for a model of school-based ITE in which research-based knowledge and understandings are promoted through engagement with practice, with the university still having a distinctive role to play. Childs et al (2013, p 30) argue that in their current university–school partnership, they establish a 'multi-layered system of distributed expertise' built around research, continuing professional learning and ITE. This provides a structure that enhances ITE experiences for students, endorses teacher agency and offers professional learning for teachers and teacher educators. The BERA–RSA review (2014a, p 3) has recently recommended that all involved in teacher education 'work in partnership rather than in separate and sometimes competing universes', bringing an end to 'the false dichotomy' between HE and school-based approaches to ITE.

These dominant constructs of theory/practice and university/school also ignore international work identifying that integrated approaches are vital. The American Association of Colleges for Teacher Education (AACTE), for example, recently called for a greater emphasis on classroom experience in the United States, including a 'minimum of 450 sequential hours of closely monitored and supervised clinical experience' (AACTE, 2010, p 11). But it also recognised that this 'clinical experience' needed to involve both university- and school-based teacher educators working together. Similar ideas about integrating different sources of knowledge are widely recognised as supporting students as they learn to make constructive sense of classroom experiences. The processes by which such learning occurs have been described variously as 'judgment in practice' (Alter and Coggshall, 2009, p 3), 'clinical reasoning' (Kriewaldt and Turnidge, 2013, p 104) or 'practical theorising' (Hagger and McIntyre, 2006, p 58), with learning always dependent on close collaboration between universities and schools. A key aspect of all such partnerships has been the rejection of the theory/practice binary and of 'theory into practice' models, with the acknowledgement that de-contextualised research findings do not translate into 'recipes for practice' for any and all contexts. Instead, strong and effective models of collaborative partnership in ITE claim that the integrated nature of their programmes means that they are models of 'research-informed clinical practice' (Burn and Mutton, 2013).

As the pendulum swing of ITE moves further towards school-led models, with more time spent learning in the classroom, one of the key issues is still how any programme supports student teachers in drawing on and integrating rich and varied sources of knowledge, including relevant research, to develop their practice. In achieving this aim, an emphasis on the *quality* of student learning, rather than simple *quantity* measures, is central. That quality emphasis in turn needs to be translated into well-designed and carefully implemented learning structures and materials. Last but certainly not least, as Craft (1984, p 336) reminds us, it is also essential that ITE contributes to 'the informed scepticism of a social democracy', 'countering intellectual conformity and rigidity' in education.

Conclusion

Between 1984 and 2014, the pendulum swing of ITE in England moved further away from the dominance of the HEIs and towards schools and teachers as very influential stakeholders in the field. This change, although influenced by strong partnership schemes run by universities since 1984, was fundamentally driven by central government interventions. These have changed the governance, language, cultures, structures and institutional organisation of ITE, making it a more school-focused and instrumental enterprise, accelerating the 'turn to the practical' (Hoyle, quoted in Furlong and Lawn, 2011, p vii), and increasing the power of the 'discourse of relevance' (Maguire and Weiner, 1994) and changing the epistemologies of teacher education. The principle of HEIs making a necessary and distinctive contribution has been steadily eroded by the multiplicity of providers and routes now involved in the 'marketplace' of school-led ITE. Institutional shifts have also occurred as universities have been swept along in the fast-flowing tide of change in the HE sector. One unhelpful continuity over time has been the maintenance of theory/practice and university/school as binary constructs, despite more than 30 years of partnership and many exemplars of alternative ways of implementing ITE.

At the time of writing, degrees of instability and uncertainty continue to affect nearly all schools of education in England, a situation not helped by last-minute changes in allocation patterns in the summer of 2014 when the School Direct scheme had recruited to only 69% of its target (Universities UK, 2014). While some established models of school–university partnerships seem to be surviving the processes of marketisation and reform, others have been destabilised (Brennan et al, 2014).

The *Carter review of initial teacher training* (DfE 2015), published early in 2015, included a recommendation that student teachers should understand that they only need QTS, with a PGCE as optional. Although this controversial recommendation was not taken forward by the-then coalition government, because of differing perspectives on its wisdom, this attempt to divorce PGCE and QTS qualifications remains worrying, especially in the light of the outcome of the 2015 General Election, which has led to a majority Conservative Party government. Despite the Carter review's claims to authority, many HE educators would still agree with Gilroy's (2014, p 630) statement that the government approach to school-led ITE seems to be 'ideology heavy and evidence light'.

The question then becomes: Does 'England's teacher training system [stand] on the threshold of the biggest change in its history' (Smithers et al, 2013, p 28)? Or will the pressures of recruitment at scale, allied with the long history of HE as a stakeholder in the field, maintain some form of the status quo? (Gilroy, 2014). Furlong (2013a, p 140) concludes that 'the shape of teacher education' in England 'could be fundamentally different in five years time' with the size of the sector certainly becoming smaller. Whitty (2014, p 473), quoting Bell, discusses future options around:

- the emergence of a 'system of many small systems';
- the complete deregulation of ITE;
- the ending of 'the core national professionalism associated with the QTS award'; and
- the emergence of 'local' and 'branded' professionalisms.

The future, then, is uncertain. But whatever happens next, it is likely to involve yet another 'pretty bumpy ride' (Craft, 1984, p 340) for teacher education in England in the decade ahead.

Notes

[1] Academies are independent, state-funded schools that are managed by teams of co-sponsors. Free schools are independent, state-funded schools that can be set up by interested groups such as parents, religious groups and education charities.

[2] There are two sub-routes in School Direct: most trainees follow the basic route, as described above, but the School Direct salaried route offers older graduates the chance to work and be paid as an unqualified teacher while training.

[3] The guarantee of places for these 'grade 1' providers lasted only until the 2015 allocations round.

[4] Popkewitz (1987, p ix) talks of 'the public discourses' of the field, which dull 'sensitivity to the complexities that underlie the practices of teacher education ... [by] a filtering out of historical, social and political assumptions'.

[5] Craft (1984, p 338) nevertheless argued that 'the role of theoretical analysis in the development of critical judgement and as a training in professional adaptability is not to be minimised'.

FIVE

Teacher education policy in Northern Ireland: impediments, initiatives and influences

Linda Clarke and Geraldine Magennis

Introduction

The report on the first stage of the recent review of teacher education in Northern Ireland highlights a stark policy deficit: 'At the time of writing this report there is no agreed strategy for Teacher Education in Northern Ireland' (Grant Thornton, 2013, p 23).

This does not mean that there is no policy, nor that there has been an absence of significant policy developments. It does, however, reflect the singularly perplexing policy landscape that persists in Northern Ireland where several of the most significant policy challenges in teacher education are characterised by a remarkable longevity and seem set to endure long into the future.

This chapter begins with a contextual outline of the distinctive policy-making landscape in Northern Ireland. In examining this landscape, it is clear that both incremental progress and strategy building have often been stymied by a range of local structural and political tensions, which, particularly since the 1999 devolution process, have led to distinctive and persistent local policy impasses. By contrast, there have been many significant local initiatives and many important policy developments have occurred as a result of policy transfer, largely from elsewhere in the United Kingdom (UK). At various times, these transfers have taken the form of one or more of the elements of Dolowitz and Marsh's (2000) classification of policy transfer: copying, emulation, combinations and inspiration. It is debatable, although not for analysis here, whether some of the key local initiatives have ever been wholly independent of such transfers. In addition, both demographic and financial pressures have periodically either driven or impeded change.

In order to demonstrate the ways in which these influences have impacted on policy, some key examples of policy for schools and policy for teacher education will be outlined. Focusing largely on post-devolution changes, the core of the chapter explores how both the many reviews of teacher education and some key elements of teacher education policy (institutional arrangements, partnerships and professionalism) are influenced by the tensions between local impasses and local initiatives, demographic and economic pressures and policy transfers. The chapter concludes with an outline of some potential new directions for teacher education policy in Northern Ireland.

Key features of the policy landscape

The decades immediately following the partition of the island of Ireland in 1921 saw the creation of a school system that, although not originally envisaged as such, gradually became largely separated along denominational lines. Northern Ireland also developed a teacher education system that was partially denominational in character. These systems reflected the deep communal divides that were inherent in the new state of Northern Ireland itself. From the late 1960s, entrenched local political divisions were enacted in widespread intercommunal violence – the 'Troubles' – during which over 3,500 people were killed. Following the signing of the Good Friday Agreement in 1998, policy making took place within a new set of structures, which were divided between the devolved government of Northern Ireland and the UK government. Governance was overlain with sets of statutory arrangements, which included vetoes and checks and continues to manifest a lack of collective responsibility across the factional fault lines of a deeply divided Cabinet. The current devolved government is based on a form of consociationalism, with five parties sharing power. Education, including further and higher education, is a devolved matter. As a result of these complex arrangements, policy styles are less consensual (Birrell and Heenan, 2013) and policy making less evidence-based (Birrell, 2013) than in other jurisdictions.

Moving teacher education policy forward in Northern Ireland post-devolution is also distinctively challenged by the fact that this policy area falls under the remit of two separate departments within the Northern Ireland Assembly – the Department of Education (DE) and the Department for Employment and Learning (DEL) with two separate ministers (each from a different political party) – and is scrutinised by two separate Stormont committees. DE is responsible for the supply of teachers to the school system and DEL for funding this supply (and for the supply of teachers to the further education sector). This bifurcation of responsibilities is intrinsically impracticable and the resulting problems (such as cross-department divisions about the allocation of teacher education quotas) can be exacerbated by the political divisions between the ministers in charge of each of the two departments.

Since the signing of the Good Friday Agreement, there have been several intermittent periods of return to temporary direct rule from London, on occasions when the peace process faltered, which have produced an 'episodic experience which has hamstrung policy achievements and constrained the extent to which devolution has made a difference to the daily lives of its population' (Wilford, 2010, p 134). Montgomery and Smith (2006, p 55) describe these periods in which:

> Under direct rule, the possibilities of change are limited ... with the ... responsible ministers elected to Westminster by constituents in England, Scotland and Wales who act as 'caretakers', unaccountable to the Northern Ireland population, but unlikely to take risks with policy decisions because of their temporary tenure.

These ministers tended to rely on experienced civil servants in DE's Teacher Education Branch, who played an important role, both in maintaining 'business as usual' amidst some periods of violent upheaval on the streets, and in implementing some important transferred policies within Northern Ireland. Local civil servants convene stakeholder committees such as the Northern Ireland Teacher Education Committee (NITEC), which has been in abeyance since 2009. There are regular meetings between DE and DEL civil servants, the Education and Training Inspectorate (ETI), and the heads of each of the colleges and university schools of education, under the auspices of the Universities' Council for the Education of Teachers Northern Ireland (UCETNI).

In this context, it is worth noting the role and potential of the unique, cross-border (all-Ireland) body for teacher education, the Standing Conference on Teacher Education, North and South (SCoTENS). This body was set up following the Good Friday Agreement and is funded by both its members (including higher education institutions, teaching councils and unions) and by government departments north and south of the border. It provides seed-funding for cross-border research partnerships and organises student teacher exchanges and well-attended annual conferences. It brings together teacher educators, civil servants, government ministers and union and professional body representatives from across the island with expertise from national and international areas. In a recent evaluation, Furlong et al (2011, p 35) commend this body for 'facilitating authentic professional collaboration which has stimulated genuine professional and personal development'.

The way in which the operation of each government department can, in effect, be trammelled by both its committee and by vetoes within the Cabinet has the potential to create policy blockages within each area of government, which can act to snuff out any partisan attempts to bring about radical change. Gallagher (cited in Donnelly et al, 2006) describes and exemplifies the way in which attempts to broker the cross-community agreement that is needed to bring about key policy changes often take the form of either private debates among a Platonic elite or public disputes within Northern Ireland's highly contested civic and political arena. Both mechanisms have had their successes but both also have had their drawbacks and discontents; in particular, both have had demonstrably enormous potential to postpone and subvert policy development through protracted disagreements, as several of the following examples – first from the school sector and second from the teacher education sector – will demonstrate.

Policy for schools and policy for teacher education: some parallel progress, some parallel challenges

It is, perhaps, unsurprising that the nature and implementation of policy for schools in Northern Ireland in recent years are characterised by a combination of policy transfer from elsewhere in the UK and internally embedded impediments to change. Occasionally, however, distinctive local initiatives have emerged, informed by both local circumstances and evidence or inspiration from elsewhere. The former has produced, inter alia, successive curricular reviews, the introduction of area-based planning, and the revision of examination specifications that have been some of the main drivers for change in schools over the past 30 years. More recently, in each case, local post-devolution initiatives have brought about the creation of very distinctive local models of the curriculum, area-based planning in the form of 'area learning communities' and a review of General Certificates for Secondary Education (GCSEs) by the local exam board – the Council for the Curriculum, Examinations and Assessment (CCEA) – which means that Northern Ireland is set to have a different grading system from that in England and Wales. Meanwhile, many other local initiatives – including the integrated education movement (which seeks to educate pupils from different religious backgrounds together), the removal of DE's school league tables and the prohibition of academic selection at age 11+ (the primary–secondary transfer stage) – have looked set to bring about some far-reaching changes. However, these changes have not fully materialised in reality, at least not in the ways that were planned.

The integrated sector educates some 7% of pupils, with around 93% of pupils attending separate Catholic or state (de facto, Protestant) schools (DE, 2015). It should be noted that integrated schools in Northern Ireland are not secular but are essentially Christian in character and welcome all faiths and none (see www.nicie.org). Following protracted, bitter and entrenched public debates, the 11+ exam has been abolished, only to be replaced with two private-sector entrance exams, which are used in grammar schools in a way that is largely divided on communal grounds: a Protestant 11+ and a Catholic 11+. In recent years, however, it is demographic and financial downturns, rather than government policy, that have driven a gradual decline in academic selection, particularly in the Catholic sector where church policy has also favoured a removal of academic selection, while staunchly upholding the value of faith-based education. The elimination of school league tables, which was announced by Martin McGuinness in his final days as Education Minister in 2002, was, by contrast, welcomed by teachers across all school types. However, this development was destined to have a very limited impact due to the earlier advent of market principles, in the form of parental choice (Education Reform (NI) Order 1989), based on the Education Reform Act 1988 in England and Wales. Local newspapers regularly publish both school league tables and extensive school advertisement supplements containing lavish amounts of comparative data. The consequences of the thwarting of these plans may be seen to pale into insignificance in comparison to the blockage of attempts to reform the administrative arrangements for education. Protracted political wrangling had been largely responsible for the failure of an ambitious and radical plan to replace the five local education authorities (the Education and Library Boards, ELBs), and a wide range of other educational quangos, with a single, very large quango, the Education and Skills Authority. The Education Authority, a less ambitious amalgamation of the ELBs only, came into existence in April 2015.

There are parallel examples to change and blockage in the teacher education sector. The importance of teachers (and, by extension, teacher education) in delivering the potential benefits of innovation in schools is widely recognised, as discussed in Chapters One and Three. However, in Northern Ireland, policy development in teacher education has been much influenced by similar sets of tensions, between internal impediments, demographic changes, financial exigencies and external influences. The impact of the last of these cannot be overestimated. In teacher education policy, too, conformity with policy in the rest of the UK has been a key driver that has periodically energised some tangible changes in Northern Ireland. In some cases these have been implemented in combination with distinctive local adaptations. Most notably, the emphasis on cultures of accountability and scrutiny within the public sector have influenced the establishment and impact of the General Teaching Council for Northern Ireland (GTCNI), which was formed in 1998 and designated as a non-departmental public body in May 2012. New legislation is planned to make GTCNI fully independent of DE. GTCNI has produced, inter alia, a revised set of professional competences and an accreditation process for teacher education courses. The introduction of an innovative three-stage teacher education model – the '3 Is': Initial, Induction and In-service – (NITEC and CEPD, 1998) and the concomitant development of a distinctively voluntary school–higher education institution (HEI) partnership model also reflect unique local influences. It might be suggested, however, that, not unlike attempts to reform the Education and Library Boards, it is changes to the institutional arrangements for teacher education that continue to be seen to present the greatest (most longstanding, controversial and profound) challenges for some advocates of policy reform in teacher education in Northern Ireland.

Institutional arrangements and reviews

This section lays out the institutional arrangements for teacher education in Northern Ireland. The many reviews of teacher education are also outlined, because most of these were focused on institutional configuration. Other key issues sometimes were either not examined or were sidelined in post-review debates about institutional arrangements. Important progress in the areas of partnership and professionalism is discussed later in the chapter.

Institutional arrangements

Teacher education courses in Northern Ireland are currently approved by DE, funded by DEL, accredited by the GTCNI and inspected by the ETI. Approved student teacher quotas in 2014/15 provided for a total of 600 places, with 258 of these being in the primary sector

(190 Bachelor of Education [BEd], 68 PGCE) and 342 in the secondary sector (100 BEd, 242 PGCE) (DE, 2013).

Two universities provide full-time primary PGCE courses (University of Ulster) and post-primary PGCE courses across a range of subject specialisms (Ulster University and Queen's University, Belfast [QUB]). Two university colleges – St Mary's College (with a predominantly Catholic student teacher intake) and Stranmillis College (with a predominantly Protestant student teacher intake) – offer BEd courses along with a limited number of PGCE courses, including an Irish-medium education (IME) course at St Mary's (IME being education provided in an Irish-speaking school). IME provision for the growing Irish-medium school sector makes up 46 of the 600 places noted above. Only the universities' postgraduate courses have consistently drawn students from across the community in roughly equal numbers. In addition, only Ulster's provision is located outside Belfast, in the north west of the province, on the Coleraine Campus. The Open University has offered part-time post-primary PGCE courses (20 students in 2014/15) in selected subjects, but has withdrawn from this provision (and from initial teacher education right across the UK) since May 2014. This may have a significant impact on equality of access for those teacher education applicants who do not have the flexibility to undertake a full-time course or to leave Northern Ireland to seek part-time provision. There are no school-based or employment-based routes into teacher education in Northern Ireland. Each of these institutions provides Masters-level and short-course continuing professional development (CPD) provision, some of which is overlapping and competing.

Entrance to all of the initial teacher education courses is greatly oversubscribed, with between five and 15 well-qualified applicants for every place in many courses. These are qualities that Northern Ireland's system shares with both the Republic of Ireland (RoI) and the internationally acclaimed Finnish education system (Sahlberg, 2011a). They represent a very considerable and distinctive strength of education in Northern Ireland. Both the abundance and the high calibre of these new applicants to the profession distinguish teacher education in Northern Ireland from that in England, where there are periodic shortages of teachers, particularly at times of strong economic growth. Applicants who are not successful in obtaining a place on courses within Northern Irish institutions frequently travel to other parts of the UK to complete teacher education courses. In many cases, these young teachers return to Northern Ireland, following graduation:

> In each of the last four years over 400 individuals who trained in other parts of the UK have registered with GTCNI. (Grant Thornton, 2013, p 12)

Reviews of teacher education

A perceived oversupply of newly qualified teachers and of teacher education provision has been a persistent concern in Northern Ireland, an issue that dates back to the 1960s and episodically through the late 1970s, 1980s and 1990s and to the present day – the most recent review cites an employment rate for local teacher graduates of 18.48% in 2013 (DEL, 2014, p 20). A report by the Chilver Review Group (1980) recommended a reduction in the number of teacher education institutions to two. One centre was to remain in the north west and a second was to have been formed by the merger of the Belfast-based institutions: QUB with Stranmillis College and with the two then existing Catholic teacher education colleges (St Joseph's, male students only, and St Mary's, female students only). This was deemed to be impossible at the time, because it would not allow for specialist denominational provision. Interdenominational mergers were seen as a step too far amidst Northern Ireland's delicately balanced sectarian divide. However, by 1986, the two Catholic colleges had merged with each other, and a merger of the New University of Ulster and Ulster Polytechnic brought the configuration of local provision to four. When PGCE provision was introduced in the two universities in the late 1980s, some rationalisation of course provision was possible. Following discussion with both institutions, the only PGCE primary provision in Northern Ireland was allocated to Ulster, and, to ensure complementarity, post-primary subjects were divided among the two universities, with only PGCE English being offered in both. The colleges moved from being monotechnic institutions to offering a more diverse range of course provision alongside teacher education courses. Stranmillis now offers a BA in Early Childhood Studies as well as a BSc in Health and Leisure Education, while St Mary's offers a Liberal Arts degree pathway with subject specialisms. Fulton (cited in Osborne et al, 1993, p 232) argues that these arrangements meant that 'complementarity among the four institutions in relation to initial teacher training has largely been achieved'.

With the benefit of hindsight, it seems clear that these changes are the only significant alterations to institutional/course configurations that have occurred in the last 40 years. This is despite consternation about demographic decline and financial pressures and several further reviews with their concomitant recommendations and consultations. None of the subsequent efforts has, to date, produced any substantial changes to institutional configurations. It can be argued that this distinctive institutional configuration is appropriately reflective of Northern Ireland's school system, which is, in turn, a product of parental choice and of political will, with the largest political parties in Stormont staunchly supporting the respective college (either Stranmillis or St Mary's) on each side of the political/religious/communal divide.

A further bout of teacher education reviews, which was jointly commissioned by DE and DEL, began with the Teacher Education in a Climate of Change Conference in 2003 (DEL, 2010), and is still in progress. Initially there were five successive studies and five associated rafts of proposals. These reviews are summarised on DE's website and in the appendix of the report of the second stage of the most recent review (DEL, 2014). The DEL minister restarted the review process in 2011, commissioning a two-stage review. The first stage engaged consultants Grant Thornton to conduct a review of teacher education infrastructure, aiming to discover more exact comparative data that were not found in previous reviews. Notably, the ensuing report suggested that teacher education costs vary considerably between providers:

> QUB and UU [University of Ulster] are broadly on a par in relation to funding costs when compared with England. The two University Colleges are higher per student by £1,877 for Stranmillis and £1,508 for St Mary's due to small and specialist premia paid [to the colleges] whilst no such equivalent payments are made in England. (Grant Thornton, 2013, p 139)

The report also highlights the demographic and financial downturns of the early 21st-century, which were cited as reasons for recent reductions in student quotas. The largest of these reductions were applied only to the university courses, leaving the quotas for the two colleges unchanged.

The second stage of this review (2014) is distinctive from previous reviews in that the combined expertise of the international review team (led by Pasi Salhberg) permitted them to employ an analysis of both practice elsewhere (including the presentation of some germane case studies) and international trends in teacher education. These were used to establish principles that underpin their proposals for enhancement and to delineate and assess four proposed options for future development, which do not include a status quo option. These options are:

> enhanced collaboration between the existing institutions; a two-centre model, with one institution based in the North-West and the other in Belfast; a Northern Ireland Teacher Education Federation, in which existing institutions continue but with some ceding of responsibilities to a supra-institutional federal body; and, finally, a single Northern Ireland Institute of Education in which the distinctive missions of the current teacher education institutions would be retained. (DEL, 2014, p 2)

These options were to be the basis of discussions between the DEL minister, Dr Stephen Farry, the HEIs and other stakeholders in the autumn of 2014. This minister has succeeded in bringing to bear a combination of forensic financial analysis and wide-ranging external expertise on a set of longstanding policy dilemmas. The review had recourse to a conflation of both of the public and private approaches to the development of policies in contentious areas discussed earlier (Gallagher, cited in Donnelly et al, 2006), with articles in newspapers, for example, decrying the potential demise of Catholic teacher education, while the review group has met key representatives of each HEI in private. The minister responsible (who is a representative of one of the smaller parties in Stormont) has found it difficult to make any progress in implementing the recommendations of the latest review.

When not embroiled in protracted arguments about institutional arrangements, policy makers have periodically had the opportunity to move forward other, arguably more important, areas of teacher education policy. In two key areas there have already been significant and quite distinctive developments in policy and practice, namely partnership and professionalism. These are crucial to appreciating the more creative, positive and dynamic segments of teacher education in Northern Ireland. Both point the way towards a future in which it may be possible to prioritise the development of a system-wide vision, which looks beyond the instrumentalism that has characterised so much of the debate around teacher education to date. With little or no political overtones, it is only the current economic climate that may yet prove to be an insurmountable challenge to the further enhancement of partnerships and professionalism.

Partnerships and professionalism

Partnerships in teacher education have been constructed within an innovative '3 Is' model which is discussed below together with the key developments in relation to the local professorial body, the General Teaching Council for Northern Ireland (GTCNI), which was established in 1998.

Partnerships

The partnership model was designed around a lead partner for each stage of the '3 Is' model. HEIs were to take the lead during the Initial stage, the Education and Library Boards' (ELBs) Curriculum Advisory and Support Service (CASS) at the Induction stage and the schools at the early professional development (EPD) or In-service stage. Although the bulk of responsibility for the initial teacher education courses remained firmly with the HEIs, closer and stronger support by schools was regarded as vital. NITEC, which included key civil servants and a range of other stakeholders including HEIs, schools and the ELBs, agreed this new partnership model. The partnership is distinctive in the fact that it is voluntary and informal in nature (NITEC and CEPD, 1998) relative to the more formal arrangements elsewhere in the UK and RoI. A *Teacher education partnership handbook* (NITEC and CEPD, 1998) provided guidance to ensure a common approach to the provision of support for students and beginning and serving teachers by identifying the most appropriate aspects of learning to teach in light of the development of competences through reflective practice rather than a standards-based approach (Moran, 1998).

The language of the handbook (NITEC and CEPD, 1998) was deliberately sensitive and cautious, reflecting the distinctive voluntary nature of these new partnership arrangements, not least because schools do not receive payment for student teachers on placement. The need for such sensitivity was borne out in the fact that consultations with all the main partners in teacher education showed that some teachers expressed 'reluctance to assume more formal responsibilities for the development and assessment of student teachers' (Moran, 1998, p 456). There was recognition of the tension between ensuring that all student teachers had an equitable placement experience and a concern that 'over-formalisation might lead to situations where some of the best schools decline to accept student teachers due to the demands which more formalized arrangements impose' (Moran, 1998, p 459). Additionally, some cited a lack of equity in terms of accountability, with HEIs being obliged to lift the greater part of the load (Caul and McWilliams, 2002). As the model bedded down and the educational landscape became increasingly complex, a call for the reconceptualisation of this model was issued (Moran et al, 2009). It was thought that greater equality among the partners might be achieved through a renewed model characterised by the hallmarks of 'consistency', 'continuity' and 'community' (Moran et al, 2009, p 957).

With regard to induction, the handbook articulates the aims of induction and the effective use of a Career Entry Profile, which is intended to form a formative link between initial teacher education and induction. It is a guide to discussions with the schools' teacher tutors about support needs in the form of suitable induction programmes, accompanying action plans and any relevant courses to meet the needs of beginning teachers (NITEC and CEPD, 1998, p 40). Poor full-time, permanent employment rates for initial teacher education graduates in Northern Ireland have meant that, in the most recent version of the handbook (DE, 2010), schools are encouraged to modify their induction programme for short-term, temporary beginning teachers. The very considerable inequalities in induction experiences highlighted by Moran et al (2009) include the fact that the dearth of permanent teaching posts means that many of these teachers do not teach the subjects, or belong to the school sector, for which they were originally trained.

Moving beyond the important but limited administrative issues, a clarion call for even greater collegiality in the form of 'research-informed clinical practice' (DEL, 2014, p 11) between universities and schools is reiterated strongly in the Northern Ireland section of one of the British Educational Research Association and Royal Society of Arts inquiry reports (BERA and RSA, 2014b). Both reports also issue a summons to initial teacher education providers to become much more directly and strongly involved in continuing professional development, an area in which coherent strategy is currently virtually non-existent.

Despite being decidedly innovative at the time of its inception, the '3 Is' partnership model has lost some ground in the recent policy voids, which have permitted complex and important partnerships to be contingent on the goodwill and tenacity of overstretched staff. The CASS service has been largely dismantled in preparation for the creation of the Education and Skills Authority and reductions in teacher education intakes have led to reductions in staffing in this sector too. This has allowed strategic infrastructural affordances and initiatives to wither and wane. Such unfortunate lacunae underline the need for a professional body with the resources and authority to create the coherence and continuity that is required to build and sustain the profession.

Professionalism

A key initial achievement of the GTCNI was to produce a competence-based teacher education model identifying 92 competences regarded to be at the heart of best practice. It was tasked by DE in 2005 to undertake a review of the competence model and of CPD (GTCNI, 2005). The review was informed by the work of two advisory groups, which were populated by a wide range of stakeholders, including practising teachers. These groups proposed, inter alia, the establishment of a Professional Development Framework underpinned by the teacher competences, with two new professional milestones of chartered teacher and advanced chartered teacher. The advisory groups also recommended CPD pilots to include professional development bursaries, visits/exchanges, teacher research scholarships and teacher sabbaticals. The number of competences was reduced to 27. In the preface to the revised competences, *Teaching: The reflective profession*, GTCNI (2007) has also shown itself to be open to the influence of research-based evidence, emerging as an advocate for teachers as autonomous, reflective practitioners.

The GTCNI has piloted some of these ideas but a recent review of evaluation and assessment in Northern Ireland has highlighted a key flaw in the implementation of the competence model, which is not being used to its fullest potential:

> While the competence model appears well established in initial teacher education in Northern Ireland, challenges remain in ensuring that it is also used as a reference for other aspects of the profession, namely: registration, regular teacher appraisal through PRSD [performance review and staff development – a teacher appraisal process] and continuing professional development. (Shewbridge et al, 2014, p 92)

Since performance review and staff development (PRSD) is often strongly based on specific School Development Plan priorities, these can supersede the importance of more broadly based competences and the potential for continuity may be lost.

Northern Ireland's professional body has made important inroads into the registration of teachers and has laid down important markers in relation to teacher professionalism, but is overstretched and is not yet fully independent of government. Nonetheless, the latest review of teacher education identifies a crucially important future role for the GTCNI, proposing that 'a Partnership Concordat should be established, under the leadership of the GTCNI, to oversee partnership between universities, schools, and employers, across the whole range of professional activities, including research' (DEL, 2014, p 44).

Conclusion

This chapter has outlined and exemplified the distinctive structural and political tensions, persistent impasses, demographic and financial pressures, policy transfers and local initiatives that shape and inhabit the teacher education policy landscape in Northern Ireland. Although a perennial focus on institutional arrangements has taken most of the limelight over the years, the latest external review (DEL, 2014) also seeks to map the way forward for both partnership and professionalism. In the cogently argued report of this review, some evidence of good practice from Northern Ireland and from around the globe is marshalled to build both an identification of strengths and deficits and a sense of urgency for improvement. Recent changes to teacher education across the UK, which are outlined in other chapters of this book, are also highly visible to policy makers in Northern Ireland. The contrastingly rapid and radical developments in England (Chapter Four) are particularly obvious. So too, are the outcomes of the recent review in the RoI. This review, which was also chaired by Pasi Salhberg, highlighted distinct targets in respect of building a 'world-class' system, which are similar to those suggested for Northern Ireland (Sahlberg et al, 2012). Most strikingly, both reviews recommend a research-informed, Masters-level teacher education system. Interestingly, too, the RoI review also triggered a radical institutional reduction, including an inter-denominational colleges–university merger in north Dublin. Whether such an arrangement is either desirable or feasible in Northern Ireland is debatable.

Policy making in teacher education in Northern Ireland is not, and has not been, the protean realm of the impatient dynamo. It is not easy, not flexible, not reflexive and not well supported by political consensus. The volatility associated with the rapid recent changes to teacher education in England has led some in Northern Ireland to count the blessings of prolonged deliberation and relative stability, while simultaneously decrying the persistent dearth of continuity, missed opportunities and recurring unresponsiveness of the local system. Such is the perplexingly janiform outlook of policy makers for teacher education here in Northern Ireland that it is hardly surprising that there is no agreed strategy for teacher education.

SIX

Teacher education in Scotland: consensus politics and 'the Scottish policy style'

Moira Hulme and Aileen Kennedy

Introduction: teacher education as public policy

In order to understand teacher education policy in Scotland, it is necessary to set the wider public policy context in which teacher education sits. The first part of this chapter does that, before going on to look at teacher education as a policy field in itself. Against this background we then problematise the specifics of teacher education policy in the Scottish context, which includes an exploration of the policy community itself, processes of policy deliberation and resulting policy instruments. Our intention is not to produce a chronology of teacher education policy in Scotland – that can be found elsewhere (eg, Hulme and Menter, 2013) – but rather to consider how teacher education policy functions as a part of wider public policy making in Scotland.

Scotland has had separate education legislation from the rest of the United Kingdom (UK) since the 'Scottish Office' was first established in 1885. However, public policy in Scotland is now legislated through the Scottish Government, education being one of its devolved functions (alongside health, justice, rural affairs, housing and transport). Devolution and the (re-)establishment of the Scottish Parliament in 1999 promised new ways of working – promoting access, consultation and transparency. While the extent to which these early aspirations have been met is still debatable, the sentiment reflects the perceived will of the Scottish people and, in theory, the electoral system in Scotland does allow for this kind of approach to governance. The Scottish Government is elected through a system of proportional representation, meaning greater likelihood of a coalition government than should be the case under a 'first past the post' system (still the voting system for the UK government). Proportional representation therefore supports the greater likelihood of a consensus government; one that engages in bargaining and compromise, both within the confines of parliamentary engagement and with wider stakeholder groups. This is important in the context of teacher education policy, as consensus politics are evident in the minutiae of policy development and enactment, as will be illustrated.

However, despite the greater likelihood of a coalition government under the proportional representation system, a Scottish National Party (SNP)-led majority government was returned in 2011, following an SNP-led minority government in the 2007 General Election. The rise of the SNP in Scotland led to the establishment of a referendum on independence, held on 18 September 2014, in which independence was rejected by a slimmer majority than had previously been expected. Following a last-minute cross-party vow by the major Westminster-based parties to work towards giving Scotland more devolved powers, 55% voted against independence, and 45% for independence, with a turnout of 85%. These developments in governance have progressively focused the notion of education as a central pillar of the Scottish identity (McCrone, 1992), and therefore as an important focus in public policy making.

Devolution has meant that, as Pickard and Dobie (2003, p 3) maintain, 'for the first time there exists a group of elected national representatives for whom education is an area worth specialising in'. Education and health both became important portfolios in the-then Scottish Executive, renamed the Scottish Government in 2007 (confirmed by the Scotland Act 2012). In 2010, the Scottish Executive Education Department (SEED) was replaced in a reorganisation that replaced nine departments with six overarching directorates (finance, learning and justice, health and social care, communities, enterprise, environment and innovation, strategy and external affairs). Within the learning and justice directorate, responsibility for school-based learning is held by the learning directorate and responsibility for post-16 learning is held by the employability, skills and lifelong learning directorate. The Scottish Government currently shares the education portfolio between a Cabinet Secretary for Education and Lifelong Learning, a Minister for Children and Young People and a Minister for Learning, Science and Scotland's Languages.

There is a long tradition of pride in the distinctiveness of education in Scotland (Bryce et al, 2013; Paterson, 2003). Incursions from the UK government on domestic policy – especially those deemed to 'anglicise' – have been fiercely resisted. The so-called 'myth' of Scottish education is regularly invoked to articulate the values and priorities of Scottish education. Humes and Bryce (2013, p 139) describe this as:

> a story or 'myth', shaped by history, but not always supported by historical evidence, to the effect that Scotland is less class-conscious than England; that ability and achievement, not rank, should determine success in the world; that public (rather than private) institutions should be the means of trying to bring about the good society; and that, even where merit does justify differential rewards, there are certain basic respects – arising from the common humanity of all men and women – in which human beings deserve equal consideration and treatment.

While romantic in some respects, and located firmly in the Scottish historical context of education for all and comprehensivisation, the focus on equity and social justice continues to be seen today in the way in which the Scottish Government positions its priorities. The Scottish myth encapsulates much of what might be known today as 'social democracy', comprising of 'a commitment to social equality; a desire to humanise capitalism; and the pursuit of social liberalism' (McCrone and Keating, 2007, p 18).

In terms of public policy, it is worth noting that the public sector in Scotland accounts for a much greater proportion of expenditure, employment and other such indicators than it does in the UK as a whole (Cairney and McGarvey, 2013), thus supporting in part the commitment to public institutions expressed as part of the Scottish myth. During 2011/12, total expenditure on services per head in real terms in Scotland was £10,240 compared with £8,618 in England (HM Treasury, 2013, p 117). Despite the sharp contraction in public sector employment from 2009, in 2013 public sector employment accounted for 23% of total employment in Scotland (Scottish Government National Statistics, 2013), compared with 13% for the UK as a whole.

It seems, therefore, that both structural dimensions and historical/cultural dimensions influence what Cairney and McGarvey (2013, p 154) refer to as 'the Scottish policy style'. This is characterised by the central involvement of stakeholder, or pressure groups, dialogue with ministers and civil servants and a perception of being involved in governance processes. Keating et al (2009, p 57) assert that the Scottish Government 'relies on policy-making networks and professional groups more than the UK Government'. This network governance approach can be seen in education policy development in Scotland (Kennedy and Doherty, 2012) and is something made easier by the population and geography of Scotland (Cairney and McGarvey, 2013).

The Christie Commission on the Future Delivery of Public Services (2011, para 1.4) reasserted the popular view that there remains in Scotland a 'particular ethos – a set of guiding beliefs or principles – that should underpin the delivery of public services to the citizens of Scotland. Central to that ethos is the conviction that public services exist to support a fair and equal society, and to protect the most vulnerable'. Successive administrations have upheld such a commitment in the form of:

- free personal care for older people;
- no upfront tuition fees for resident Scottish students in post-compulsory education;
- concessionary travel;
- free eye tests;
- no prescription charges;
- retention of the Education Maintenance Allowance for post-compulsory education;
- a Council Tax freeze;
- the Scottish Social Wage (defined as a 'pact' between Government, public services and employers to ensure a living wage for all. Over 100 employers in Scotland, including the Scottish Government, are now accredited 'Living Wage employers').

In education, improved outcomes have been sought through:

- the Early Years Framework[1] launched in 2008 (Scottish Government, 2008);
- implementation of the 3–18 years *Curriculum for Excellence*[2] from 2010;
- the promotion of inter-agency working through *Getting it Right for Every Child* (GIRFEC)[3]; and
- a sustained commitment to comprehensive schooling.

Law and Mooney (2006, p 523), among others, point out that authorised versions of the 'New Scotland' tend to celebrate the tradition of the 'democratic intellect' (Davie, 1961) while remaining less vocal on 'the persistence of marked class divisions and structured inequalities within contemporary Scottish society'. Although Scotland performs well in cross-national comparisons of pupil attainment, enduring educational inequity raises questions about the rate of progress facilitated through devolution (Machin et al, 2013; Riddell et al, 2013). Needs must be met within the context of declining resources after a period of year-on-year growth: 'The real terms increase in Scottish Government spending between 1999-2000 and 2009-2010 is estimated to have been around 60 per cent (i.e. 5 per cent a year). From 2009–10 to 2016–17, the budget change is estimated to be an 18 per cent real terms cut' (CPPR, 2012, p 4). The report of the Christie Commission on the Future Delivery of Public Services (2011, p viii) argued that '[u]nless Scotland embraces a radical, new collaborative culture throughout our public services, both budgets and provision will buckle under the strain'.

Since 2007, public policy making in Scotland has adopted an outcomes-based approach, where government and public bodies are expected to work together to achieve agreed outcomes across the range of public policy fields, evidenced through the National Performance Framework. This approach brings together both structural and cultural dimensions of governance and involves national and local government, public bodies and the third sector. Reducing inequity and enhancing social justice remain strong themes in this approach across the public policy portfolio. Five central objectives have been identified, the first of which is to develop a 'wealthier and fairer' Scotland – an amalgam of competitive and welfare nationalism with a focus on enterprise, individual responsibility and social justice. Arnott and Ozga (2010, p 93) suggest that for the SNP government it is the combination of a central focus on the economy together with a 'well-established' notion of national identity that has led to the current approach to education governance. They characterise this approach as one that adopts a 'simultaneous process of "inward" referencing of ideas of fairness and equality combined with "outward referencing" which places Scotland with new comparator nations' (2010, p 96). This 'simultaneous process' can be evidenced through attempts to address inequality flagged up in reports such as the Organisation for Economic Co-operation and Development country report in 2007 (OECD, 2007), referred to frequently in education policy initiatives, together with an increased focus on the education and social welfare policies of Nordic countries.

Teacher education as a policy field

An overview of recent developments in Scottish teacher education policy can be found in a number of edited collections. These have directed attention to:

- the reshaping of teacher education (Menter and Hulme, 2008, 2011; Conroy et al, 2014);
- implications for the professional identity and work of teacher educators (Menter, 2011b; McNicholl and Blake, 2013);
- accounts of local innovation in school–university partnerships (Livingston and Colucci-Gray, 2006; Conroy et al, 2013);
- the impact of austerity measures (Menter and Hulme, 2012; Livingston and Hulme, 2014).

Analyses have been offered of the report of the most recent review of teacher education in Scotland by Donaldson (2011): *Teaching Scotland's future* (Hulme and Menter, 2011; Kennedy and Doherty, 2012); and the related review of teacher employment in Scotland by the Scottish Government (2011): *Advancing professionalism in teaching* (Kennedy et al, 2012). However, despite increased international attention on teacher quality and teacher learning, there remain few empirical studies of the processes of policy *making* in teacher education in post-devolution Scotland (although see Beck, 2013). The paucity of research *on* and *for* teacher education across the UK has been noted by Christie et al (2012), prompting the British Educational Research Association and Royal Society of Arts inquiry (BERA and RSA, 2014a, 2014b).

That teacher education before 2010 attracted comparatively little attention from those engaged in policy research reflects, in part, a degree of insulation from the legislative reach of Westminster and the mediating role of a policy community operating with established patterns of representational governance that predate devolution (Menter et al, 2004; Menter and Hulme, 2008). The sense of 'rupture' and 'shift in the value base on teacher education' experienced elsewhere in the UK (Lynch, 1979, p 1) has not been felt with equal force in Scotland. And while the Robbins Report on higher education (DES, 1963) doubled the number of universities in Scotland from four to eight in just four years, the third sector of monotechnic colleges of education endured until the 1990s. Perhaps most significant is the absence of a New Right critique from the 1980s that attacked the legitimacy of the knowledge claims of teacher education (Lawlor, 1990; O'Hear, 1998), and laid the ground for current moves in England towards a school-based and school-led system of teacher education (Taylor, 2013). There are currently no employment-based routes into teaching in Scotland and teachers qualifying by these routes are not eligible to register with the General Teaching Council for Scotland (GTCS).

Two earlier reviews of initial teacher education (ITE) produced little change (Scottish Executive, 2001, 2005). The representation of teacher education as a policy 'problem' in Scotland emerged most forcibly from 2010. Heightened attention to teacher education has been driven not as strongly by 'discourses of derision' (Ball, 1990) exacerbated by cross-national competitive comparison, but by the exigencies of teacher supply (in the context of anticipated retirals and growth in the primary school population) and the putative challenge to the teacher workforce proposed by curriculum and assessment reform. These national issues, together with growing interest in 'outward referencing' (Arnott and Ozga, 2010), have seen teacher education in Scotland being given more serious consideration as a policy problem worthy of addressing.

Processes, people and policy instruments

In contrast to elsewhere in the UK, and reflecting 'the Scottish policy style' (Cairney and McGarvey, 2013), processes of teacher education policy deliberation in Scotland have typically been consultative (Menter et al, 2004), but tensions remain between central steering and local innovation. Size matters. The small scale of provision (eight university providers of ITE accommodate 2,500 places per year), bolstered by mobility of key actors between agencies during a career in Scottish education, has traditionally created strong ties across the policy community (Humes, 1986; McPherson and Raab, 1988). The composition of review teams and engagement of relevant bodies in formal consultation procedures reveals a network of multiple affiliations and cross-cutting ties. Protracted processes of deliberation across multiple stakeholders and the strength of potential veto players, such as the GTCS and teacher unions (the largest being the Educational Institute of Scotland [EIS]) can inhibit radical change and lead to ambiguity in outcome (while avoiding stalemate).

In recent years there have been changes in the role and status of key agencies – particularly the GTCS and Education Scotland – now operating with reduced budgets (Humes, 2013). The GTCS, established in 1965, gained full independent status on 2 April 2012. It now also has responsibility for producing the *Entry requirements to programmes of initial teacher education in Scotland* and *Guidelines for initial teacher education programmes in Scotland*, documents previously produced by the Scottish Government. The remit of Education Scotland, formed in July 2011 through the merger of Learning and Teaching Scotland (LTS) and the schools inspectorate (Her Majesty's Inspectorate of Education [HMIE]), is 'to build the capacity of education providers and practitioners to improve their own performance; to provide independent evaluation on the quality of educational provision; to provide evidence-based advice to inform national policy' (Education Scotland, 2013).[4]

Scottish education policy generally, and teacher education in particular, is increasingly enacted through the exercise of 'soft power': 'a range of governing devices ... [including] networking, seminars, reviews, expert groups' (Lawn, 2006, p 272). Exemplification of this can be seen in the way that major policy initiatives have been progressed from government commissioning a review, led by a trusted member of the education establishment, resulting in a review report that is generally accepted in its entirety by government. Recent examples of this include the reform of the school curriculum, the Donaldson (2011) review of teacher education and the McCormac review of teacher employment (Scottish Government, 2011). Requisite conditions for such an approach to policy development include a commitment to consensus building through partnership working (Birrell and Heenan, 2013).

The remainder of this chapter addresses the key protagonists or partners engaged in sustained deliberation on teacher education policy – the universities, government, national agencies, local authorities and the teaching profession. Attention is directed to points of contestation, the formation of alliances and the realisation of temporary settlements. Four foci are selected for particular consideration:

- the organisation of ITE in Scotland;
- the professional accreditation and academic validation of ITE;
- partnership in teacher education;
- post-ITE.

Organisation of initial teacher education – universitisation

Despite the reaffirmation of the university basis of teacher education advanced in the recent review of teacher education – *Teaching Scotland's future* (Donaldson, 2011) – involvement in ITE was notably absent from university activity for the greater part of the 20th century. From 1920 until the 1990s (with the exception of Stirling University established in 1967), ITE was the responsibility of monotechnic colleges. Throughout the 20th century, there was little evidence of a common purpose within higher education in respect of responsibility for, and the content of, programmes of teacher preparation. Battle lines have been drawn and redrawn in regard to:

- the relative autonomy of higher education institutions from external authority;

- inter-institutional and inter-sectoral rivalry (between universities and colleges of education) and, more recently, intra-organisational competition (following university restructuring);
- occupational jurisdiction, including the 'relevance' of different forms of knowledge to professional practice (Abbott, 2005).

The last of these is encountered in recurrent fears of 'academicism', which fuel demands for a (re-)turn to the practical.

A report by the Advisory Council on Education in Scotland (1946) entitled *Training of teachers* advised against transferring responsibility for teacher education to the universities. In the late 1950s, a renewed proposal by three Scottish universities to undertake ITE was ignored (Pilley, 1958). The principals of the monotechnic colleges of education and the Scottish Education Department enjoyed a close relationship between the late 1950s and 1960s. The expansion of the college system in the 1960s to address a shortage of teachers reignited deliberation on the university role in teacher education. The siting of a new college in Hamilton in 1966 was resisted, without success, by the main teachers' union (the EIS), which lobbied for new buildings to be sited near universities to sustain the tradition of combined graduate and non-graduate teacher training (Marker, 1994, pp 24-5). Pressure for contraction was fiercely resisted (SED, 1977). However, unlike elsewhere in the UK (see Hencke, 1978), in Scotland all 10 colleges initially survived.

In contrast to strategies deployed in the 19th century and early 20th century – which saw universitisation as integral to teachers' demands for professional status – defenders of the college system cautioned against the dangers of 'academic drift'. In evidence to the Scottish Tertiary Education Advisory Council (STEAC), Kirk (2000, p 4) warned of the risks of transferring decision making to those 'who have not grasped the distinction between academic accomplishment and capacity for intelligent professional action'. In retaining the college system, teacher education remained under Scottish control. From the mid-20th century, Scotland's colleges of education were largely funded by the Scottish Office Education Department (63%) and local authorities (21%) (Paterson, 2003, p 165). University provision was largely funded through the UK University Grants Committee (UGC). The STEAC report (SED, 1985) recommended retaining the college system, despite reservations over quality and capacity. For Kirk (2000), former principal of the Moray House Institute of Education in Edinburgh, this reflected acquiescence to a powerful lobby by college principals in the face of opposition from universities, the Association of Directors of Education (ADES) and the Convention of Scottish Local Authorities (COSLA).

Pressure for change escalated in an unfavourable economic climate. In the 1980s, the college system was reduced through a series of mergers and one closure. The number of colleges fell from 10 to seven in 1981. By 1987, there were five remaining colleges (see Table 6.1). The transfer of all ITE to a university location was completed at the turn of the century. This move was precipitated by changes to the funding of higher education and the granting of degree-awarding powers to former polytechnics, which signalled the end of the Council for National Academic Awards (CNAA). The repatriation of the Scottish Universities in 1992 (Further and Higher Education (Scotland) Act 1992), introduced new funding arrangements for all higher education institutions administered by the Scottish Higher Education Funding Council. This regime was not supportive of resource-intensive courses such as teacher education. Funding concerns were exacerbated by the introduction of the Research Assessment Exercise in 1992, then the Research Excellence Framework (REF),[5] which awards additional funding for research productivity (and 'impact') (Conroy and McCreath, 1999). A report by Sutherland (1997) endorsed the integration of teacher education within universities. While premised on the academic case for merger, a hostile financial climate made universitisation inevitable.

The first decade of the 21st century witnessed further change as ITE became progressively embedded within reorganised university structures. A comparison of university structures in 2005 (Stewart et al, 2005) with current structures reveals a shift in the location of university schools of education within wider university structures. This has implications for the influence of educationists in the strategic management of education within collegiate or 'super-faculty' structures (Hulme and Menter, 2013, p 910). Of the pre-1992 institutions, only Stirling has moved from an Institute of Education within a Faculty of Human Sciences to a School of Education (with equal footing among seven academic schools). Within little more than a decade, institutions with links to the former monotechnic colleges have all transitioned from being a (new) faculty of education in a university to a school within a wider or college. And the responsibilities and influence of the monotechnic college principal (pre-1990s), dean of faculty (1990s) and head of school (from the late-1990s) are different.

The full incorporation of teacher education within universities has produced a diverse and stratified workforce. Menter (2011b) identifies four distinct 'sub-tribes' among education faculty in Scotland:

- longstanding university staff;
- former college of education staff;

Table 6.1: Teacher education institutions in Scotland

1960s monotechnic colleges	1980s rationalisation	2000 'universitisation'
Four city colleges:		
Aberdeen College of Education	Merged with Dundee College of Education to become Northern College of Education in 1987	Northern College (Aberdeen) merged with the University of Aberdeen to become the Faculty of Education in 2001
Dundee College of Education	Merged with Aberdeen College to become Northern College in 1987 but split again in 2001	Merged with the University of Dundee to become the Faculty of Education and Social Work in 2001, now School of Education, Social Work and Community Education in the College of Arts and Social Sciences
Jordanhill College, Glasgow		Became the Faculty of Education of the University of Strathclyde in 1993, now School of Education in the Faculty of Humanities and Social Sciences
Moray House, Edinburgh		Moray House Institute of Education, with Cramond Campus, became the Faculty of Education of the University of Edinburgh in 1998, now Moray House School of Education in the College of Humanities and Social Science
Six smaller colleges:		
Dunfermline College of Physical Education, Cramond, Edinburgh	Merged with Moray House College of Education in 1987	

1960s monotechnic colleges	1980s rationalisation	2000 'universitisation'
Hamilton College, Lanarkshire	Merged with Jordanhill College of Education in 1981	
Craigie College, Ayr	Merged with University of Paisley in 1993	University of Paisley merged with Bell College to become the University of the West of Scotland in 2007. Teacher education is located within the School of Education
Callendar Park College, Falkirk	Closed in 1981	
Notre Dame, Glasgow (Catholic teacher education)	Merged with Craiglockhart College to form St Andrew's College, as the national Catholic college for teacher education in 1981. Lay principal from 1987	St Andrew's College became the Faculty of Education of the University of Glasgow in 1999, now School of Education in the College of Social Sciences. The St Andrew's Foundation for Catholic Education was established in 2012
Craiglockhart, Edinburgh (Catholic teacher education)	Merged with Notre Dame to form St Andrew's College in 1981	

- newly appointed university staff;
- temporary appointees of various sorts.

Following universitisation, the relative esteem attached to teaching and research, and to different types of research (disciplinary, applied, development and evaluation, and practitioner enquiry), has been debated within and beyond the academy, nationally and internationally (Pollard and Oancea, 2010; BERA and RSA, 2014b) and continues to cause tensions.

In light of the foregoing discussion of the wider public policy context and the specific teacher education policy field in Scotland, this section now seeks to exemplify these policy processes through the identification and discussion of a number of prominent policy instruments that shape teacher education. We take the starting point as the most recent review of teacher education in Scotland – *Teaching Scotland's future*, commonly referred to as 'the Donaldson Report' (Donaldson, 2011) – which has produced or consolidated a number of what might be termed 'policy instruments'. (For further detail on and discussion of the Donaldson Report, see Kennedy and Doherty, 2012; Kennedy, 2013.) In outlining these key developments, we consider their historical development so as to illustrate the genesis of the various elements of teacher education policy over time.

Professional accreditation and academic validation of initial teacher education

One of the principal policy instruments to shape teacher education in Scotland is the accreditation of courses of ITE, a role for which the GTCS takes responsibility, in part because newly qualified teachers can only become registered with the GTCS if they have passed an approved programme of ITE. The GTCS has been in existence since 1966, as a result of the Teaching Council (Scotland) Act 1965, playing a significant role in the approval of courses of ITE, initially on behalf of the Secretary of State for Scotland and then the Scottish Government (since devolution in 1999). Since 2 April 2012, when the GTCS gained full independent status, it has taken full responsibility for this function, and the associated production of the *Guidelines for initial teacher education programmes in Scotland*.

As a policy instrument, the approval of courses of ITE has been significant in helping to ensure that ITE as a whole has been kept firmly in the university sector, particularly since teaching in Scotland became an all-degree profession in the 1980s and the universitisation of teacher education in the early 1990s. This commitment to academic quality has been intertwined with the requirements for registration with the GTCS, thereby linking these two facets of the policy instrument, requiring an element of cooperation and partnership between the GTCS and the universities providing teacher education in Scotland. This commitment to retaining central university involvement in ITE might be seen in part to be influenced by the historic academic tradition in Scotland – a central plank of the 'Scottish myth' – but might also be seen as a product of a small, typically conservative nation, which traditionally has not embraced experimentation or risk taking in its public policy making. ITE in Scotland has not embraced a range of alternative routes, instead sticking broadly to two main routes: the one-year Professional Graduate Diploma in Education (PGDE), which follows an undergraduate degree (for both primary and secondary teachers), and the four-year undergraduate route (principally for primary teachers, but also including a small number of so-called 'concurrent' routes, in which students study their own subject alongside education).

The undergraduate route – traditionally a Bachelor of Education (BEd) – has recently been subject to fairly radical change. Despite the requirement since 1984 for all ITE to be degree level, and universitisation from the late 1990s, reservations continue to be expressed with regard to the level of intellectual challenge offered by the Bed degree for prospective primary school teachers. Several submissions to the 2010 review of teacher education (Donaldson, 2011) reflected this concern, and in an opinion piece in *The Times Educational Supplement Scotland*, Lindsay Paterson, Professor of Educational Policy at the University of Edinburgh, argued that '[i]t is the civic duty of universities ... to educate prospective primary teachers with the full extent of the university's scholarly distinction, aiming to equip prospective teachers with the developed intellect through which they might comprehend what teaching is' (Paterson, 2011, p 35). The Donaldson Report (Donaldson, 2011, p 39) identified 'an over-emphasis on technical and craft skills at the expense of broader and more academically challenging areas of study' and recommended that:

> In line with emerging developments across Scotland's universities, the traditional BEd degree should be phased out and replaced with degrees which combine in-depth academic study in areas beyond education with professional studies and development. These new degrees should involve

staff and departments beyond those in schools of education
(Donaldson, 2011, p 88)

Despite contention about the extent to which the recommendation was truly evidence-based (see Smith, 2011), the various universities' responses to this recommendation have led to much greater diversity in undergraduate provision, albeit all of it approved through GTCS processes. From August 2014, successor qualifications to the BEd include Bachelor of Arts (BA), Bachelor of Science (BSc) or Master of Arts (MA) awards, involving concurrent (education alongside other subjects throughout the degree) or sequential studies (education and other subjects at different periods within the degree programme) (see Table 6.2). The new degrees are intended to strengthen the transferable skills and employability of students within and beyond education, as well as advancing 'a more academic style of professionalism' (Paterson, 2014, p 411). Some universities are offering direct entry to a fifth MA-level year following the four-year undergraduate programme. Others are offering specialist subject pathways within the primary education degree, for example languages, earth sciences, religious education and mathematics. Yet others are offering education as a subject to all humanities and social science students, with prospective teachers studying education alongside students from elsewhere in the faculty. This enforced engagement with the wider university has the potential to impact on the place of teacher education as a subject within the university sector as a whole as its deeper integration within wider university structures serves to make it less hidden and separate.

The partnership agenda

Another key policy instrument emanating from the Donaldson Report has been the mandate for greater partnership between schools, local authorities and universities in the delivery of teacher education in general, but ITE in particular. The partnership agenda is big, not only in terms of the structure of programmes of ITE but also in terms of the negotiations, decision making and sharing of resources – both human and financial. This reflects the broader direction of public policy making in Scotland, and in part can be seen as a positive, social-democratic approach to policy. However, this approach to policy making can be seen to privilege consensus over innovation and, when viewed as a form of network governance, can perhaps be seen in a less positive light (Kennedy and Doherty, 2012). The exercise of government power is much less obvious under a partnership or network approach

Table 6.2: Successor qualifications to the BEd (primary) in Scotland from 2014

University	Type	Programme	Duration	Entry tariff 2014
Aberdeen, School of Education	Pre-1992	MA (Honours) Education*	4 years	4 Highers (H) at grades BBBB
Dundee, School of Education, Social Work and Community Education	Pre-1992	MA (Honours) Education*	4 years	4H at grades ABBB
Edinburgh, Moray House School of Education	Pre-1992	MA (Honours) Education*	4 years	4H at grades BBBB
Glasgow, School of Education	Pre-1992	Masters Diploma in Education (4 years) or Master of Education (Masters degree programme with undergraduate entry, of 5 years duration)	4+1 years	4H at grades AAAB
Highlands and Islands, federation	University status awarded in 2011	No undergraduate routes (PGDE only)	n/a	n/a
Stirling, School of Education	Pre-1992	BA (Honours) Education (Primary)	4 years	4H at BBBB
Strathclyde, School of Education	Pre-1992	BA (Honours) Primary Education	4 years	4H at AAAB
West of Scotland, School of Education	Post-1992	BA (Honours) Education	4 years	4H at ABBB

* The Scottish 'MA' is an undergraduate degree awarded by the ancient Scottish universities. It is academically equivalent to a BA.

to policy development, yet the subtlety of it can serve successfully to limit contention or objection, as stakeholders do not wish to be outside the partnership, and therefore work harder to commit to consensus, albeit perhaps at a cost.

In structural terms, the partnership approach is seeing university staff spending increasing amounts of time in the school setting, and school staff being encouraged to take on greater responsibility as 'teacher educators', with recommendation 39 in the Donaldson Report stating that 'all teachers should see themselves as teacher educators and be trained in mentoring' (Donaldson, 2011, p 98). Despite these fairly wide-reaching aspirations, the partnership agenda is not supported by a specific budget, and while there is a range of types and levels of training provided by local authorities, universities and other providers, it looks unlikely at present that this aspiration will be fulfilled, despite the increased expectations being placed on school staff in relation to the support and assessment of student teachers.

Post-initial teacher education

Teacher education at the post-initial stage in Scotland has been given greater priority in recent years, notably since the 1998 consultation on a national framework for continuing professional development (SOEID, 1998). This was followed by the progressive development of what is now called the 'suite of professional standards', developed and published by the GTCS, the most recent of which is the post-Donaldson *Standard for career-long professional learning* (GTCS, 2012b). The development of professional standards as a central plank of teacher professional learning reflects a global policy trajectory, one based on the premise that improvements in teacher quality can be gained through the development and use of such an approach (see Chapter Nine, this volume, for more detailed discussion on standards and accountability).

The individual standards in the suite of professional standards, which include provisional and full registration, career-long professional learning, and leadership and management for both middle leaders and for head teachers, are now inextricably linked to a number of other policy instruments. Taking a historical perspective, it is interesting to observe the gradual introduction of each standard over a period of time (the first formal standard was the Standard for Initial Teacher Education, which emanated from a merger of the competences to be achieved during ITE as published in the *Guidelines for teacher training courses* – SOEID, 1993 – and national university quality assurance procedures). Most notably, the introduction in August 2014 of Professional Update, has seen the professional standards take on a new significance. Professional Update requires all registered teachers to have their line manager confirm to the GTCS every five years that they have continued to engage in the professional review and development process and to progress their own professional learning. Positioned by the GTCS as non-threatening and developmental, this particular policy instrument started life being labelled by the Scottish Government as 'reaccreditation', and despite having been on the GTCS's agenda for some time, was undoubtedly exacerbated by the post-Shipman context in the medical profession (see Baker, 2006), which has had an impact on all professional bodies. While there currently exists very little research on the process of this policy development (with the exception of Watson and Fox, 2015), it would not seem unreasonable to consider the extent to which the consensus politics and network governance in teacher education policy development in Scotland have shaped the eventual outcome of something originally designed much more as an externally imposed accountability measure than as a developmental support process.

Conclusion

Teacher education policy in Scotland can be seen to be both distinctive and responsive to bigger global imperatives. There are clear links to the 'Scottish myth', evident through appeals to collaborative, democratic processes and to the privileging of academic integrity. However, despite the strength of this enduring myth, Scotland has not been immune to influences from elsewhere, particularly from neighbouring England. While education is a devolved matter, the location of all ITE within the university sector, together with UK-wide governance of aspects of higher education – in particular, funding and quality assurance arrangements – means that Scottish teacher education policy will continue to be a delicate balance between local, national and international imperatives and historical and contemporary influences.

Notes

[1] The Early Years Framework sets out ways of working with young children, their families and communities, which focus on early intervention and prevention.

[2] The new curriculum framework for learners from ages 3 to 18, focusing on skills and attitudes as well as traditional 'content'.

[3] A multi-agency approach to supporting children and young people.

[4] There was no public consultation prior to this decision taken by the Cabinet Secretary; many anticipated that LTS might merge with the Scottish Qualifications Authority (SQA) or Skills Development Scotland. LTS was formed in July 2000 following the merger of the Scottish Consultative Council on the Curriculum (SCCC) and the Scottish Council for Educational Technology (SCET) and had experienced an earlier restructure in 2004 – a key time in the development of the new school curriculum. On the merger with HMIE, LTS experienced a 60% cut in its funding and many of its employees, who were secondees from local authorities, returned to their substantive posts. Up to 60 staff accepted voluntary severance (Menter and Hulme, 2012).

[5] See http://www.ref.ac.uk/.

SEVEN

Teacher education in Wales: towards an enduring legacy?

Gary Beauchamp and Martin Jephcote

Introduction

An analysis of teacher education in Wales demonstrates that the processes of policy making and, in turn, their implementation are complex and non-linear and that disputation between government and 'stakeholders' and also between sometimes competing stakeholders opens up space for mediation. Closing that space, that is, the ability of government to ensure that its policies are enacted in the ways in which it intended, or indeed for a stakeholder to assert its priorities, depends on the exercise of power and control over those who, in different ways, may work to mediate and recontextualise policy. For any particular policy initiative there is a 'field' of actors each with its own ability to exercise power and control and, the more contentious and in the public eye the policy, the larger the field and the more dispute there is likely to be. Also, the bigger the field, the bigger the struggle that government is likely to have to make, implement and enact its policy. At the heart of such struggles are ideological differences but set within a wider set of social and political interests. So, as Taylor et al (1997) suggest, 'we need to observe politics in action, tracing how economic and social forces, institutions, people, interests, events and chance interact. Issues of power and interests need to be investigated' (cited in Ball et al, 2012, p 3).

These matters are influenced by many factors but are framed by the physical size and make-up of the country and its population. Wales is a small country that has a strong cultural and linguistic tradition. At the most recent census in 2011, it had a population of 3.06 million, which is the largest it has ever been (www.ons.gov.uk/ons/rel/census/2011-census/population-and-household-estimates-for-wales/index.html). As a report conducted for the Equality and Human Rights Commission (2011) points out, Wales is also a relatively poor nation within the United Kingdom (UK). Pupils' qualifications are strongly related to family income, and the report notes that approximately a fifth of the Welsh population live in poverty, and that individuals' earnings in Wales are lower than the UK average. Of those people who are both disabled and have a work-limiting condition, 74% are not employed, a rate three times more than the UK average. Thus, policy making in Wales is shaped by this context, including the educational landscape characterised by a continuing commitment to community-based education and comprehensive schools and the introduction of a Foundation Phase for three- to seven-year-olds, a direct response to the need for early intervention in young people's lives.

The Welsh language is central to government policy and, in the policy document *Iaith Pawb: A national action plan for a bilingual Wales* (WAG, 2003, p 1), it is asserted that the 'Welsh language is an essential and enduring component in the history, culture and social fabric of our nation. We must respect that inheritance and work to ensure that it is not lost for future generations'. One result of this is the existence of schools that use the Welsh language as the medium of instruction (referred to as Welsh-medium schools in this chapter, but *Ysgolion Cymraeg* in Welsh), with obvious implications for teacher trainers who provide teachers for both Welsh- and English-medium schools. Table 7.1 shows the number of schools in Wales in January 2015:

Table 7.1: Number of schools in Wales, 2014

Type of school	Nursery	Primary	Middle	Secondary	Special educational needs	Independent	Total
English language	13	895	2	157	39	66	1,172
Welsh language	0	435	4	50	0	0	489
Total	13	1,330	6	207	39	66	1,661

Source: January 2015 school census

Overall, there were 38 fewer local authority-maintained schools in January 2015 than in January 2014, but the total number of pupils in local authority-maintained nursery, primary, middle, secondary and special schools was 465,704, a rise of 623 pupils since January 2014. There were four less independent schools (http://gov.wales/docs/statistics/2015/150723-school-census-results-2015-en.pdf). In January 2015, there were 24,510.8 full-time equivalent (FTE) qualified teachers in local authority-maintained schools, 311.7 fewer than at January 2014.[1] These teachers are all registered with the Education Workforce Council [EWC], which replaced the General Teaching Council for Wales [GTCW]) in April 2015 as 'the independent regulator in Wales for teachers in maintained schools, Further Education teachers and learning support staff in both school and FE settings' (http://www.ewc.wales/site/index.php/en/what-is-the-ewc). It maintains a register of education practitioners and a related Code of Practice. It also administers the award of Qualified Teacher Status (QTS), Induction and Early Professional Development (EPD) on behalf of the Welsh Government.

Initial teacher training (ITT)[2] is thus a relatively small field in Wales. Control over allocating and managing teacher training numbers, and inspecting the resultant provision, are the responsibility of the Higher Education Funding Council for Wales (HEFCW) and Estyn (Her Majesty's Chief Inspector of Education and Training in Wales) respectively, both formed in 1992. In Wales, higher education institutions are independent of government, but government funds are distributed to them by HEFCW. HEFCW is also responsible for the accreditation of ITT and, significantly, both 'determining Initial Teacher Training (ITT) intake targets annually for each provider in line with national – Welsh – intake targets set by the Welsh Government' and 'working with Estyn to ensure that the universities providing ITT in Wales continue to meet requirements for ITT and that their provision enables students to achieve Qualified Teacher Status (QTS)' (https://www.hefcw.ac.uk/policy_areas/itt/itt.aspx). The latest available figures for ITT intake for the primary and secondary sectors, reported by HEFCW in December 2014 for 2015/16 (www.hefcw.ac.uk/documents/publications/circulars/circulars_2014/W14%2041HE%20ITT%20intake%20targets%202015_16.pdf), are shown in Table 7.2.

In Wales, ITT is provided by three regional 'centres', with two of the three being separate universities (with students enrolled by each university rather than the 'centre') working in collaboration, as shown in Table 7.3. Unlike in other parts of the UK, none of the universities has a direct denominational influence.

Each centre runs an accredited training programme, as well as managing and delivering an allocated number of employment-based training routes under the Graduate Teacher Programme (GTP) on behalf of the Welsh Government. These centres are often shared between different university campuses, but work to common policies and procedures. This presents many challenges, not the least of which is that each centre is inspected by Estyn as one 'provider', rather than having separate inspection and reporting of the provision provided on individual campuses.

Table 7.2: Intake targets for initial teacher education training, 2015/16

Intake targets 2015/16	Undergraduate	Postgraduate	Total
Primary	300	450	750
Secondary	95	785	880
Total	395	1,235	1,630
Secondary PGCE subjects			
Priority subjects Mathematics; chemistry; physics; modern languages; Welsh; ICT (Computer science)		323	
Other subjects Design & technology; English; geography; biology; general/integrated science; music; religious education; history; PE; art; business studies; dance & drama; and outdoor activities		472	

Table 7.3 Three centres of initial teacher training in Wales

South East Wales Centre for Teacher Education & Training (SEWCTET)	South West Wales Centre of Teacher Education (SWWCTE)	North and Mid Wales Centre of Teacher Education (NMWCTE)
Cardiff Metropolitan University University of South Wales (*recently merged Newport University and Glamorgan University*)	University of Wales Trinity St David (*recently merged Swansea Metropolitan University and University of Wales Trinity St David*)	Aberystwyth University Bangor University

The devolved journey so far

Outside of education, other tensions exist, which affect the ability of Wales to take control of its own destiny. The single most important factor is that for most of its recent history, control in Wales (including education policy) was centralised in England. Despite 'institutional lip service to differences in Wales' from the Education Act 1944 (Daugherty and Jones, 2002, p 108), there was little difference between the education policy of England and Wales. The impact of this was that a specific Welsh educational dimension was 'synchromeshed ...

out of existence' (Jones, 1997, p 2). This was despite the establishment of a Welsh Office (based in Cardiff) in 1964, which had some power over education policy. In reality, however, its influence was limited and there was little real deviation from policy in England until devolution (Griffiths, 1999).

This lack of power, however, did not indicate a lack of interest in education. There is a long history of education being valued highly in Wales, such that 'it may be contended that both culture and curriculum (in its broadest sense of the experiences children gain whilst at school) have in the past been inextricably linked, at least in the public consciousness' (Beauchamp, 2003, p 128). As Jones (1997, p 2) puts it, in Wales 'the appetite and respect for education is second to none'. This appetite, however, was for a *Welsh* education, reflecting both the culture and, as a visible symbol, the Welsh language. Indeed, education has been described as the 'bedrock upon which the Welsh language movement has flourished' (Williams, 2013, p 1).

Given this appetite, it could be suggested that a desire to develop a unique Welsh agenda further and exercise more control over education, and indeed all government policy, would have resulted in support for the devolution of such powers. However, when the-then Labour government in England offered a referendum in 1979, 'a long and tortuous campaign ... allowed internal dissent amongst "yes" campaigners to fester' (McAllister, 1998, p 156) and devolution was rejected significantly by the Welsh population. Jones and Roderick (2003, p 198) suggest that this 'seemed to leave Wales politically bereft of direction or, more correctly, with even less moral authority to withstand direction from outside'.

In the interim period before another referendum, it is perhaps ironic that a strongly unionist English Conservative government would introduce policies that inadvertently enhanced support for devolution, and actually safeguarded the Welsh language, an integral part of Welsh culture and heritage. Edwards et al (2011, p 535) summarise policies as:

> the subsidized development of Welsh language television through the formation of the Welsh 'fourth' television channel; the establishment of a statutory Welsh Language Board (WLB) in 1988, with a remit to protect and develop the Welsh language; the 1988 Education Reform Act, which led gradually to the Welsh language becoming a compulsory part of the school curriculum and, finally, the passing of a Welsh Language Act in 1993, which placed an onus on the public sector to treat Welsh and English equally.

In 1997, a second referendum was called as part of the manifesto of the newly elected New Labour UK government. The result was a narrow majority of 50.3% who supported devolution, with a majority of only 6,721 votes. This led, in 1999, to the devolution of limited powers (including education) to the new Welsh Assembly Government, now called the Welsh Government.

In Wales, and generally in education across the UK and much of the Western world, there is a narrative of increasingly centralised control underpinned by a neoliberal reform agenda seeking efficiency and improvement (attainment) gains. Furlong (2013b) points out that this has become a major area of government policy in many countries, driven by globalisation and neoliberalism. He suggests, however, that such ideas are not static, and that interpretations vary between countries over time, and reminds us of the significance of national politics in the development of teacher education policy. Such a situation potentially leads to 'national monologues' where 'England, Wales and Scotland are speaking to themselves, but not to each other' (Laugharne and Baird, 2009, p 238).

In contrast to fluctuating political pressures in England, Drakeford (2007, p 4) claims that 'Wales is the only part of the United Kingdom to have a genuinely long term commitment to left of centre redistributive politics, stretching for more than 150 years from 19th century Liberalism through 20th century Labourism to the present day'. Although, in recent years, political changes in England have produced many and rapid changes to educational policy (Beauchamp et al, 2015; Chapter Four, this volume), the same cannot be said for Wales. Here, a more stable political direction has been evident and, even though the 'vice-like grip of the Labour Party upon Welsh national life' has been weakened since devolution (Jones, 2014, p 185), the influence of the Labour Party has prevailed, although now more nuanced by negotiations with other parties to maintain this. These sometimes complicated negotiations are summarised by K. Reid (2011, p 440):

> Between 1999 and 2007, the Labour Party was responsible for the government of Wales (NAW 2000, 2006a). Between 2005 and 2007, the Labour Party managed as a minority Administration. After the Election of 2007 ... a Coalition was formed in Wales between the Labour Party and Plaid Cymru. Plaid Cymru is an ethno-regional party and not a nationalist party in the political sense like the British Nationalist Party (BNP). In some ways it is more akin to the

Scottish Nationalist [sic] Party (SNP) except that the Welsh language and its culture are at the epicentre of Plaid's values.

This situation was further complicated when no party gained an outright majority in the Welsh elections of 2001. The Labour Party ended with exactly half the seats in the Welsh Assembly (30), but decided to form a Labour-led administration, rather than form coalitions with either Plaid Cymru or the Welsh Liberal Democrats.

This relatively stable and Left-leaning political influence is important in understanding developments in a devolved Wales and the desire to make it different from a cultural, linguistic and educational perspective. The Welsh (Labour) First Minister, Rhodri Morgan, even announced in 2002 that he wanted 'clear red water' between his own administration and the 'New Labour' government in England (Rees, 2007). The resultant policies thus derive from 'a long period of intellectual soul searching about Welsh identity' and also signal an acceptance that 'the legacy of industrialization has produced a class structure very different from either England or Scotland ... [so] Wales has particular needs that require distinctive policy solutions' (Daugherty and Davies, 2011, p 5). In exploring these distinctive solutions, the implications for teacher education can be framed within an examination of the impact and legacy of three of the four ministers[3] responsible for education since devolution: Jane Davidson, Leighton Andrews and Huw Lewis.

Jane Davidson (1999–2007) – 'made in Wales, for Wales'

As the first Minister for Education, Lifelong Learning and Skills in 1999, Jane Davidson was part of a government trying to make the most of new powers to reflect political and national traditions. As discussed above, education had a proud tradition in Wales and, as such, was a high priority for the new government. It also offered the potential to provide highly visible policies that were radical and distinct from those in other countries, particularly England.

The tone was set in *The learning country* (National Assembly for Wales, 2001, p 2), where Jane Davidson wrote in the foreword that '[w]e share strategic goals with our colleagues in England – but we often need to take a different route to achieve them. We shall take our own policy direction where necessary, to get the best for Wales'. This distinctive educational policy agenda was influenced at various times by countries such as Canada, Finland and Scotland (K. Reid, 2011), but the rhetoric was of policy 'made in Wales' and 'for Wales'. It should be noted at the outset, however, that such changes inevitably had potential consequences for the content of ITT programmes and teacher training numbers.

Perhaps the most radical departure from existing policy was signalled by Davidson with the introduction of the Foundation Phase, 'a flagship policy of early years education (for 3 to 7-year old children) in Wales' (Maynard et al, 2013, p ii). Siraj-Blatchford et al (2007, pp 45-47) describe the policy as a 'sustained curriculum initiative' that 'advocates children learning through first-hand, experiential activities and play, and places a child's personal and social development and well-being at the heart of the curriculum'.

The extent of the changes introduced by the Foundation Phase (as opposed to the Foundation Stage in England) provided both opportunities and also challenges for many education stakeholders. For ITT programmes it presented challenges not only in adapting content, but also in reflecting a much stronger emphasis on the role of play in learning. While always a feature of early years teaching pedagogy, the premise of the Foundation Phase that children '[l]earn through first-hand experiential activities with the serious business of "play" providing the vehicle' (DCELLS, 2008, p 4) provided a fresh challenge to both serving teachers and those training new generations of teachers.

An additional major challenge for ITT came in 2006 when Davidson announced a major national review of provision. Led by Professor John Furlong, from Oxford University, the 'Furlong Review' concluded:

> Wales needs to ensure that it has the right numbers of high quality teachers to fill its current and future needs. It then needs to ensure that those new teachers have the right skills, knowledge and understanding to realise the full potential of Wales' increasingly distinctive educational agenda. (Furlong et al, 2006a, p 1)

The review made a total of 36 recommendations designed to improve ITT in Wales, but perhaps the most significant were the following:

- recommendation 5: 'as far as possible' avoid 'producing teachers unlikely to work in Wales' (p 3), leading to a reduction in ITT places with a suggested reduction of 50% in primary numbers and 25% in secondary numbers;
- recommendation 8: over a five-year period to move 'to an entirely postgraduate entry route for teaching and that the BA (Education) degree in Wales should be phased out' (p 7); recommendation 14: a reduction from seven to 'three main Schools of Education

> ... the North and Central Wales School of Education; the South East Wales School of Education; the South West Wales School of Education' (p 8).

Although the proposed move to an entirely postgraduate entry route for ITT did not fully materialise, the other two recommendations were implemented, leading to the current three 'centres' of teacher training outlined above. The Funding Council provided extra money to ease staffing and course issues, and some higher education institutions developed new courses (particularly educational studies) as a means to retain staff but others made staff redundant (Parkinson, 2011).

As a stakeholder group, ITT providers were increasingly positioned as responsive (rather than proactive) and, reflecting on the review after publication, some of the authors acknowledged that it was very much part of a 'messy, uncertain and essentially political world' (Furlong et al, 2007, p 129).

Also mentioned in the Furlong Review, and returned to in the later Tabberer Review (Tabberer, 2013), was the position of research in those higher education schools of education involved in ITT leading to qualified teacher status. Although encouraging the new schools to develop research, the Furlong Review also concluded that (at the time of the report):

> Within Wales, none of the HEI [higher education institution] providers is currently in receipt of core funding for research through the Research Assessment Exercise (RAE). This marks Wales out as very different from all of the other three countries in the UK where a significant number of providers have both strong ITT and research. Despite some good 'pockets' of research in Wales, research capacity in education is currently very weak. One consequence of this weakness is that those within education departments are not as able as those across the rest of the UK to contribute to the intellectual leadership of the field – either in relation to teacher education or in relation to schooling more generally. Given the very significant change agenda currently underway within the education service in Wales, this, we would contend, is a serious matter of concern. (Furlong et al, 2006a, pp 31-2)

Unfortunately, concerns about educational research in Wales remain to the current day and there has been a decline in the research capacity of universities. Despite funding for four extension projects in Wales by the Economic and Social Research Council's (ESRC) Teaching and Learning Research Programme (TLRP) aimed at providing opportunities for capacity building by collaboration between researchers in Wales, by 2007 Rees and Power (2007, p 93) reported that '[e]ducational research performance (at least as measured by the RAE) in these Welsh institutions is not very strong', with the inevitable result that the allocation of research funding has dropped.

This problem was recognised by the research community itself and resulted in the Welsh Educational Research Network (WERN) being funded by the ESRC between 2007 and 2009. This project attempted to facilitate 'collaborative research activity between educational researchers in different institutions, providing opportunities for joint activity and social learning between partners with varied levels of expertise and experience' (Davies and Salisbury, 2007, p 79). WERN offered competitive bursaries to groups of academics featuring a mixture of experienced and early career researchers, but crucially from different universities (including academic mentors from outside Wales) with the aim of developing research capacity. At the end of the project, despite inevitable tensions over workload and institutional collaboration, in his external evaluation Gardner (2008, p 5) reported that 'a degree of transformation was achieved by WERN'. Unfortunately, the end of the funding for the WERN project, combined with an ongoing process of reconfiguration of higher education institutions, meant that this transformation was short-lived.

Gilroy and McNamara (2009, p 332) report that in the 2008 RAE in Wales, 'six institutions returned a total of 41 staff which represented a further down-turn, even after excluding the previously 5*-rated department at Cardiff which was on this occasion returned to an alternative UoA [Unit of Assessment]'. In addition, 'half the institutions demonstrated no world-leading, and virtually no internationally excellent work'. This bleak assessment was echoed by Daugherty and Davies (2011, p 9) who asserted that 'education research in Wales is clearly not healthy, and compares unfavourably with the other three countries of the UK'. These concerns seem justified, in the short term at least, as in the most recent Research Excellence Framework (REF) exercise in 2014, only Cardiff University submitted an entry for education.

Leighton Andrews (2009–13) – 'challenge and change'

The appointment of a new, and more adversarial, Minister for Children, Education and Lifelong Learning in 2009 signalled a period of challenge for most sectors within education in Wales. Leighton Andrews, in his recently published account of his time in office, claimed to have 'a firm view of the challenges'. When first meeting the Director General of his department, Andrews' own retrospective view was that he 'set the tone' and:

> made it clear that I felt there was a real lack of urgency in the department. It was dysfunctional and not operating in a strategic fashion. I felt that there were too many empires within it, and insufficient focus on One Wales and Ministerial priorities. I thought some of the papers I had seen going to Cabinet Committees were weak.... I was determined that the department would improve its implementation.... As I said in interviews and articles in my first few weeks, 'Wales is a small country. I'm sure we can be simpler and smarter in the way we make things happen in education. ... Over recent years, the department has had to be focused on dragging the system into reality....'[4] (Andrews, 2014, pp 22-24, 51)

Andrews (2014, p 75) has also recently asserted that school governing bodies 'acted more like parent-teacher associations and cheerleaders for their schools, almost whatever they did, than serious governing bodies'; the GTCW was, he thought, 'highly conservative' (p 155); 'national leadership through HEFCW, also needed galvanising' (p 287); a Higher Education Wales meeting is described as 'directionless' (p 295); and he questioned the ability of the two largest teaching unions to 'demonstrate unequivocally that they were on the side of raising standards' (p 163). Even though these are retrospective views, the same potentially confrontational rhetoric was evident throughout his dealings with the whole education sector during his time in office.

One striking example was the ministerial reaction to Wales' poor performance in the 2009 Programme for International Student Assessment (PISA) (where Wales' scores were significantly lower than those in other parts of the UK), which at the time Andrews labelled a 'wake-up call to a complacent system' (Andrews, 2011, p 4).[5] Another example was provided by his attempts at a higher education reconfiguration agenda where the minister threatened, if necessary, the forced dissolution of universities. The end result was the merger of several universities providing teacher training, but not all.[6] His approach inevitably divided opinion, but his tenure as a minister certainly increased the pace of change and raised the profile of education in the media, both in Wales and beyond.

Of particular relevance to teacher education was Leighton Andrews' announcement in November 2011 of his intention that all newly qualified teachers would have the opportunity to follow a Masters in Educational Practice programme as part of their induction and early professional development. He contested that it was not itself an ITT initiative, but a response to perceived shortcomings in ITT and of the quality of the induction experience. In launching it he stated:

> Teacher training is not enough. Teachers need to continue to deepen and broaden their skills and knowledge once in post. It is imperative we embed a culture of lifelong learning, reflection and inquiry into the teaching profession.... Introducing a master's at this point in a teacher's career will help to address the inconsistency in the quality of induction and EPD [early professional development] that teachers previously received across the country. It will also provide a positive step towards reducing in-school and between-school variation in teacher quality and learner outcomes. (www.walesonline.co.uk/news/local-news/ministers-view---leighton-andrews-2024801)

Although the Masters in Educational Practice programme has recruited cohorts of students since its launch, its future, certainly in its current form, is uncertain and its impact limited by the fact that not all those eligible have chosen to take the qualification.

In 2012, Andrews turned his focus back to ITT and announced a review of ITT as part of a wider plan to raise standards. This was led by Ralph Tabberer, a former teacher and chief executive of the Teacher Training Agency for England (which became the Training and Development Agency in 2005).

Huw Lewis (2013 to the present) – the great reformer?

The Tabberer Review was published in July 2013 and received by Huw Lewis, who had a background in the Labour Party and was a former chemistry teacher, and took up post as Minister for Education in June 2013 following Leighton Andrews' resignation. This role was taken up just ahead of what was expected and then proved to be disastrous PISA results for Wales and concerns from local authorities that they might see some diminution of their powers.

The Tabberer Review made 15 recommendations and concluded that:

> [P]rogress to improve ITT since the 2006 review has been slow.... The new Centres have been slow to implement the stronger and more coherent management approach that they need.... Improvements will require stronger engagement between the regulatory bodies ... [and there is a need] for better management and more effective collaboration as the foundations for improving ITT in Wales. (Tabberer, 2013, pp 2-3)

Worryingly for ITT providers, the review concluded that 'providers should also understand that, if the current weaknesses persist and if they fall short, individually or collectively, the Department for Education and Skills and HEFCW have the powers to reallocate a sizeable proportion of trainee numbers to willing and capable providers' (Tabberer, 2013, p 3).

Responding to a specific recommendation of the Tabberer Review, in March 2014, John Furlong was appointed Wales' expert ITT adviser with a brief to work with the ITT sector to raise the standard, quality and consistency of teaching training and assessment in ITT across Wales.

In relation to educational research in Wales, and specifically the need to improve capacity among initial teacher educators, Tabberer (2013, p 25) recommended that 'ITT providers take urgent steps to strengthen research engagement among tutors and trainees so that teaching and teacher training are strongly influenced by practical, scientific inquiry methods'. He concluded that 'the current position, whereby research has a low status in a professional training environment, is untenable' (2013, pp 24-25). In attempting to address this, Tabberer pointed to the potential role of the Welsh Institute for Social and Economic Research, Data and Methods (WISERD) and to WISERD Education, an existing one million pound investment based at Cardiff University funded by HEFCW, to undertake research to sustain and enhance the quality of learning and the standards of teaching and teacher education in Wales. Its activities are, however, ongoing and it is currently too early to assess their potential impact.

Making sense: where are we now and where might we be going?

Furlong's report in his role as ITT adviser was published in February 2015. It builds on the Tabberer Review and coincided with, and was informed by, a review of the curriculum in Wales undertaken by Donaldson (Donaldson, 2015). Furlong outlines the need for change in the current system of ITT and puts forward a range of possible options the Welsh Government may consider in order to 'raise the quality of provision' (Furlong, 2015, p 1). These options, including revising the standards for newly qualified teachers and introducing competitive tendering for provision, introduce another layer of uncertainty for ITT providers until the Welsh Government responds to the report.

Despite outlining serious concerns about current provision, however, Furlong (2015, p 38) concludes optimistically that '[o]nce it is clear which of the ... options the Welsh Government wishes to adopt, then I am sure that the sector will seize the opportunities they provide, working together to give Wales the quality of teacher education that it needs for the future'.

Reviewing this sequence of initiatives since devolution, including Furlong's latest review, we can see that ITT providers have had to act in a responsive mode to a plethora of initiatives directed at schools, many with implications for ITT and continuing professional development provision. It is not only the amount of change that creates potential problems, however, but also the speed with which they are carried out, where they are leading and the level of stakeholder engagement. As the Organisation for Economic Co-operation and Development recently concluded (OECD, 2014, p 7), despite many strengths in the education system in Wales, 'the pace of reform has been high and lacks a long-term vision, an adequate school improvement infrastructure and a clear implementation strategy all stakeholders share'.

Education in Wales is currently at a crucial juncture. In 1921, Walford Davies (1921, p 2) noted that the 'manageable size and education system' of Wales made it possible to achieve things that were difficult for larger nations. This 'manageable size' remains both a source of strength and a source of weakness. The strength is that there is the potential to introduce national change quickly. At the time of writing this is typified by the acceptance by the Minister for Education of all of the recommendations of the far-reaching and radical review of curriculum and assessment in Wales (*Successful Futures*) led by Donaldson (2015). These recommendations, which cover all learners from ages 3–16, include removing key stages (to be replaced with progression steps) and the introduction of six areas of learning and experience (expressive arts; health and wellbeing; humanities; languages, literacy and communication; maths and numeracy; and science and technology) with three cross-curriculum responsibilities – literacy, numeracy and digital competence. In accepting the recommendations set out in *Successful Futures* in full, the minister himself described the change as 'one of the most ambitious and radical programmes of educational reform in our history', which is 'not about adjustments; they require us to rebuild our curriculum from the foundations up. These changes, by their very nature, are fundamental and profound' (http://www.yoursenedd.com/debates/2015-06-30-5-statement-the-welsh-government-response-to-the-donaldson-review).

Taken alongside the ongoing review of ITT, and the centralised control of government, there is potential for large-scale and radical change in a short period of time. For universities, with their relatively small scale and number, and apparently little influence over government policy, this may lead to formidable challenges and upheaval. The same can be said for the position of research in teacher education in Wales as, although '[t]eacher education policy assumes particular strategic importance in devolved governments … the nature of teachers' future engagement with research is uncertain' (Beauchamp et al, 2015, p 164).

Wales has a long and proud tradition of education. It is a small nation moving towards its own distinctive education system. At the time of writing, it is approaching a fulcrum where it tips away from its past and into an unknown, but distinctive, future with implications for both learners and providers, including those in ITT. This looks to be driven from the centre, that is, from central government, and in cases based on individual ministerial preferences and priorities. It appears that the space for other stakeholders to exercise their influence may have been marginalised. The current minister, although relatively new to office, and less confrontational than his predecessor, may yet turn into the 'great reformer' who oversees the largest and most far-reaching changes ever to education in general, and ITT in particular, in Wales.

Notes

[1] It is worth noting here, however, that prior to a major review of teacher training numbers as part of the review chaired by John Furlong (the 'Furlong Review') in 2006, which will be discussed in more detail below, these numbers were higher. The Furlong Review resulted in an overall 50% cut in primary teacher training numbers and a 25% cut in secondary numbers.

[2] The term ITT will be used throughout this chapter but the three centres prefer the terms teacher education (NMWCTE and SWWCTE) and initial teacher education and training (SEWCTET).

[3] Jane Hutt (2007–09) is omitted as no distinct or relevant policies were enacted as the result of her tenure.

[4] Interestingly, he also notes that '[t]he first item to be tackled would be policy on school closures', as this was the issue that would eventually lead to his resignation as he campaigned against the closure of a school in his constituency against his own departmental policy.

[5] Although he has recently stated that 'I made a mistake in that speech. I said we should aim for the top twenty of school systems measured in the PISA scores in 2015. The target was too ambitious, and it was naïve' (Andrews, 2014, p 109).

[6] This resulted in one the of the 'centres' outlined above becoming one university, making it easier to align systems, while others remained as separate universities (with students enrolled in each), making it more challenging to align systems.

EIGHT

Teacher education in the Republic of Ireland: a challenging and changing landscape

Teresa O'Doherty

Introduction

Teacher education in the Republic of Ireland is currently experiencing 'aggressive, ambitious programme and structural reform' (Smith, 2012, p 74). Initial teacher education (ITE) programmes, which are predominantly provided by universities/colleges, are the subject of profound reform in relation to their content, design, duration, process and quality (Coolahan, 2013); in addition, the number of state-funded providers is being rationalised and new structural identities/clusters are being formed. Within a system where the structures for teacher education have deep historical roots, this movement towards the reconceptualisation of teacher education across the continuum has been characterised by a period of incremental development and continuity, followed now by rapid reform and revision.

This chapter examines the last period of reform of Irish teacher education from 1965 to 1975, and then traces the development of teacher education policy from 1991 to 2006, which created both the springboard and capacity for the current phase of change. In a period of economic crisis and retrenchment, where sweeping changes are being made to the process of teacher education and uncertainty abounds as to the retention of colleges/institutions that have persisted and evolved over many decades, Irish teacher education is experiencing unprecedented 'turbulence'. Within this process there are both opportunities and challenges for teacher education.

1965–75 – the last period of reform in teacher education

Following independence in 1922, the newly formed state inherited and largely accepted the established structures in all areas of activity; Irish education experienced a high level of continuity with the past and as a consequence the structure and provision of primary teacher education between 1924 and 1974 was much as it had been since 1884, when state funding for denominational teacher education was sanctioned and teacher training programmes were extended to two years. During the first four decades following independence while the state financed teacher education, regulated the curriculum and set the examinations, the churches provided teacher education in single-sex residential institutions (four Roman Catholic colleges and one Church of Ireland co-educational college). Established in 1912, teacher education provision for secondary teachers, the Higher Diploma in Education, was a one-year, part-time postgraduate programme, provided by few staff within poorly resourced education departments. Reflecting the low status of education within the universities, the chairs of education remained vacant for varying periods and the infrastructure of university teacher education provision was underdeveloped (Coolahan, 2004a). Although the Registration Council for post-primary teachers was established in 1918, registration was not a prerequisite for appointment to a teaching position and given the dominant position of religious staff in schools, for many decades up to 50% of secondary teachers were unregistered.

Ireland's attendance at the 1961 Organisation for Economic Co-operation and Development (OECD) Washington Conference was a turning point in the course of Irish education (O'Sullivan, 2005, p 135 ff); aware of the need to engage in urgent economic reconstruction and of the emerging global discourse where education and human capital production were inextricably linked, the decision was made to open all aspects of education in Ireland to international review under the auspices of the OECD. The resulting report, *Investment in education* (Government of Ireland, 1965), served to shift domestic policy from one of cultural nationalism to that of human capital production, where the purpose and content of education was reformed to meet the needs of the economy. It illustrated the social and geographic inequalities of opportunity that existed in Ireland where one third of all children left full-time education on completion of primary-level education and only 59% of all 15-year-old children were in school; following the introduction of the free post-primary education and school transport scheme in 1967, this figure increased significantly and by 1971 three quarters of all 15-year-olds were attending school (Loxley et al, 2014, 180). In the decade that followed the publication of the *Investment in education* report, universal provision of second-level education was attained and the primary-level curriculum was radically reformed to reflect a child-centred philosophy. Teacher education was also reviewed and the report of the Commission on Higher Education (Government of Ireland, 1967, p 238) recommended that 'education should cease to exist on the periphery of university studies and should be established, and be seen to be established, in the mainstream of university work'. Furthermore, it stated that the 'isolation of teacher-training colleges and training courses from the rest of the higher education system should end' (1967, p 238).

Consequently, the programmes for primary teachers were restructured and extended, and the colleges assumed greater independence from the Department of Education. Staff numbers increased, libraries were enhanced and colleges became co-educational, with the requirement for student residence ceasing. The terminology of 'training colleges' gave way to 'colleges of education', which were autonomous denominational institutions affiliated with validating universities, but remaining on separate campuses. The introduction of the three-year Bachelor of Education (BEd) degree programme in 1974 was a significant landmark in the creation of teaching as a graduate profession (Coolahan, 2007, p 3). Education became the central discipline within programmes and was presented under three headings:

- foundation disciplines (philosophy, sociology, psychology, history of education);
- content of specific curricular areas, including the specific methodology of teaching these subjects/areas;
- methodology of teaching, which included lesson planning, evaluation, classroom management, and resource development and management.

Education was seen as both theoretical and practical and 'teaching practice (placement/practicum)' was a core part of programmes. In addition, approximately 40% of the programme was allocated to the study of liberal arts subjects, which were perceived to provide the academic respectability for the new degree within the university sector, on which recognition and validation depended (Burke, 2009, p 43). While the BEd was subject to the normal quality assurance processes associated with affiliated universities, the Department of Education and Skills (DES) retained control over the entry requirements and level of enrolment on courses, the duration of programmes, and the Inspectorate examined annually 10% of final-year students on teaching practice. Colleges continued to attract high-calibre students, and although the concurrent programme was the major route into primary teaching, a postgraduate programme was introduced intermittently in response to a shortage of primary teachers.

The Higher Diploma, which catered for the traditional 'academic' subjects for post-primary teachers, was restructured as a full-time one-year programme and universities appointed new professors and more full-time staff. Teaching and learning resources were improved and library facilities were enhanced to support increased research (Coolahan, 2004b). Reflecting the diversification of the types of second-level schools, a binary approach to second-level teacher education developed (Gleeson, 2004). Thomond College of Education in Limerick was founded in 1970 to provide concurrent teacher education programmes for specialist post-primary teachers of physical education, materials technology (woodwork and engineering) and science education. Specialist colleges for home economics teachers at Sion Hill in Dublin and St Angela's College in Sligo became associated with universities, while the National College of Art and Design (Dublin), which offered art education programmes, became more autonomous. Universities and colleges also began to offer a range of in-service postgraduate programmes and research associations were developed; the Reading Association of Ireland (in 1975) and the Educational Studies Association of Ireland (in 1976) were established and became central to the promotion of research among the teaching community.

Coolahan (2013, p 15) concludes that 'the decade 1965–75 was a momentous one for the teaching career and for initial teacher education in particular' when teaching became a graduate profession, existing teacher education providers modernised their programmes and established relationships with accrediting universities, and new colleges of teacher education were founded. Subsequent decades allowed for the embedding of new processes and curricula, and the creation of a much stronger and more vibrant teacher education presence within the academy. Teacher educators became accustomed to managing their academic affairs within the parameters of university norms, with little external regulation. Graduates of their programmes had automatic recognition as teachers by the DES (in the case of primary-level teachers) and the Teacher Registration Body (in the case of second-level teachers). The 'legendary autonomy' of teachers (OECD, 1991) translated into legendary autonomy for teacher educators (Conway and Murphy, 2013, p 28). In general, higher education developed in the context of 'light touch policy' where the number of institutions increased, as did the number and range of programmes (Harkin and Hazelkorn, 2015).

1991–2006 – a period of building momentum and capacity for change

The period 1991-2006, characterised by the review and analysis of Irish education at all levels, was bookended by OECD reviews carried out in 1991 and 2005. The *Review of national policies for education education: Ireland* (OECD, 1991) affirmed the professional and academic structure of existing teacher education provision, noting that 'initial teacher education is already of a good and appropriate standard' (Coolahan, 2007, p 6, citing OECD, 1991). The review supported investment in the continuum of teacher education, advocating the '3 Is' approach – good-quality Initial teacher education, followed by a structured form of Induction and greatly expanded In-service teacher education. It concluded that the principal challenges facing the teaching profession in Ireland were 'how to address in a comprehensive way the needs and aspirations of talented and well-educated young teachers ... as they progress through their careers' (OECD, 1991, p 98). This review provided the stimulus for the Green (policy) Paper *Education for a changing world* (Government of Ireland, 1992), which initiated wide-ranging debate throughout the country, generating a thousand written submissions. To analyse these submissions the National Education Convention (NEC) was convened, a process that represented a 'celebrated example of the partnership approach to education policy-making' (Gleeson, 2004, p 50). This two-week convention facilitated structured multi-lateral dialogue and the resulting report became the foundation document for the White Paper, *Charting our education future* (Government of Ireland, 1995). The White Paper acknowledged that 'initial teacher education cannot be regarded as the final preparation for a life-time of teaching' (p 128) and called for the establishment of a Teaching Council that would 'give the teaching profession a degree of control over and responsibility for its own profession' (p 146). The White Paper directly influenced curricular reform for all stages of the education system and was the catalyst for a range of educational legislation, including:

- the Universities Act 1997;
- the Education Act 1998;
- the Education (Welfare) Act 2000;
- the Equal Status Acts 2000–04;
- the National Qualifications Authority Act 2001;
- the Teaching Council Act 2001;
- the Education for Persons with Special Education Needs Act 2004.

This legislation provided the legal framework for education that hitherto had been absent, and clearly set out the policy direction for teacher education.

The economic climate of Ireland changed dramatically during the late 1990s and early 2000s; typified as the 'Celtic Tiger', Gross Domestic Product (GDP) growth accelerated sharply in the second half of the 1990s, averaging 9.75% per annum, while the average growth in GDP during the period 2000–07 was 5.7% (Government of Ireland, Department of Finance, 2011). Given the clarity of the agenda for change, the commitment of policy makers, the level of engagement with the extensive consultative process throughout the 1990s and the thriving economy, expectations for reform in teacher education were high:

> One might expect that, with the help of a buoyant economic context, the stage was now set for early direct action to implement these key dimensions of government policy on teacher education. However, this was not the case and the impressive momentum which had built up on teacher education lost its urgency, and, what might be termed, a period of policy drift set in. (Coolahan, 2007, p 16)

Although the state had become more 'activist in its approach' during the 1990s, it had not become 'interventionist', a legacy of the powerful role of the churches and the resulting restraint on state autonomy in education during the previous half-century (O'Sullivan, 2005, p 175). In a review of the DES in 2000, Cromien (2000, p 4) criticised the Department's lack of clarity in policy formation, which he claimed 'has led to a certain passivity in the Department in relation to new developments'. While there were substantive and landmark reforms in education emanating from the NEC in areas such as inclusion, multiculturalism and information technology, teacher education was to remain an area of particular government passivity; action was deferred in favour of the commissioning of two separate reviews: *Preparing teachers for the 21st century: Report of the working group on primary preservice teacher education* (Kellaghan, 2002) and the *Advisory group on post-primary teacher education* (Byrne, 2002). Mindful of the rapid rate of change in Irish society and the increasing complexity of teaching within the technological age, both reports called for 'a root and branch reform based on the reconceptualisation of teacher education' (Kellaghan, 2004, p 20) and were viewed by teacher educators as 'the vehicle to leverage for change ... but nothing happened' (Nic Craith, 2014). DES participation in *Teachers matter* (OECD, 2005) heralded the establishment of the Teaching Council, which was officially launched in 2005 and attained statutory recognition in 2006, more than 10 years after its establishment had been agreed. Referring specifically to the considered pace of policy development, it was later observed that 'whatever faults may be imputed to the system, precipitate action is not one of them' (Coolahan, 2007, p 22).

An 'unexpected' development of the period (Coolahan, 2007, p 22) was the introduction of an alternative entry route to teaching in August 2003 when the DES recognised a part-time blended learning programme for primary teacher education provided by a private agency – Hibernia College. The introduction of this programme, validated outside the traditional university structures, created a market in teacher education where a for-profit organisation could recruit and qualify unlimited numbers of teachers, within an essentially unregulated profession. Galvin (2009, p 279) identifies this development as an example of a new policy model, representing the business/information technology sector solution to a 'pressing and potentially expensive education sector "problem" – the need to ramp up the production of credentialed primary teachers without incurring substantial costs in doing so'. This commercial initiative, established initially to provide a course to address the needs of unqualified teachers already employed in schools, has grown to become the largest single provider of teacher education for primary-level teachers and has been responsible for one third of all new entrants to the profession over the last five years (Smith, 2012, p 86; Teaching Council, Consultative Forum on Teacher Supply, 15 April 2015).

The Teaching Council – creating the swell for a new wave of reform

The establishment of the Teaching Council in 2006 raised the profile of teacher education policy and created the swell for a new wave of educational reform. Designed to 'promote teaching as a profession', the Teaching Council's remit is to develop and maintain standards in relation to all aspects of the professionalisation of teaching, including reviewing and accrediting programmes of ITE, establishing procedures for induction into the profession and developing a framework for the continuing professional development of teachers (Lawlor, 2011). Representation on the 37-member council is dominated by teachers, with only four teacher education nominees, reflecting 'the perceived marginality of teacher education' (Gleeson, 2004, p 52). The Teaching Council Act 2001 provided 'an overall cohesive agency to co-ordinate multi-faceted action' (Coolahan, 2007, p 36) and the early phase (2006–11) of the work of the Teaching Council was characterised by extensive consultation and the commissioning of a substantial review of international research and practice (Conway et al, 2009). In the absence of documentation that articulated the values and standards of teaching in Ireland, the council generated and circulated the *Draft codes of professional conduct for teachers* in 2007 and initiated an extensive programme of meetings with partners including nine public regional consultation fora (Teaching Council, 2007a; Mulcahy and McSharry, 2012). Premised on an understanding of teaching as an extended and complex profession and informed by research, the *Codes of Professional Conduct for Teachers* (Teaching Council, 2007b, 2012), reflective of the specific culture of teaching in Ireland, are based on the core values of respect, care, integrity and trust. Influenced by the work of the Teaching Council in Scotland (Lawlor, 2009, p 11; 2011), the Teaching Council's policies echo the reform motifs articulated by Donaldson (Smith, 2012, p 76) and reveal an ambition for teaching that is rooted in the teaching profession's 'distinguished record of service in Ireland' (Teaching Council, 2012, p 3).

Acknowledging the discourse on the continuum of teacher education, the council has prioritised assuring the quality of ITE programmes. Identified as a 'new era for teacher education and the engagement of the teaching profession' (Coolahan, 2013, p 9), the council's evaluation of programmes and the resulting prescription of content have paralleled a period of both unprecedented attention in teacher education internationally (Cochran-Smith, 2012) and a 'rising tide' of accountability, compliance with regulation and adherence to professional norms (Conway and Murphy, 2013, p 12), with a focus on outcomes and quantification. Recognising the 'Procrustean exercise of super stretching and pulling' (Deegan, 2012, p 193) of ITE programmes to accommodate curriculum innovations, and aware of the Teaching Council's emerging role as the key agent for revision, teacher educators engaged in a collaborative manner with the accreditation of programmes. While reports emanating from these pilot accreditations repeatedly recommended the reconfiguration and extension of teacher education programmes (Teaching Council, 2011d), the authority to implement such change resided with the DES (Teaching Council, 2011c, p 6), and initially little advancement was made. The convergence of a number of factors creating the 'perfect storm' provided the context for radical reform (Conway, 2013, p 53).

Ireland experienced 'extreme financial difficulties within a global recession' (Clarke and Killeavy, 2012, p 134), which resulted in an economic bailout funded by the European Central Bank, the European Commission and the International Monetary Fund; while coping with the severe austerity measures imposed under the conditions of the bailout, disappointing Programme for International Student Assessment (PISA) results (OECD, 2009) 'shocked' the Irish people. The-then newly appointed Minister for Education, Ruairí Quinn (2012), criticised previous administrations for their 'lack of political will and vision to champion change' and, supported by senior officials within the DES, determined to tackle perceived 'long-standing issues and challenges in Irish education' (Hislop, 2011, p 18). The confluence of these factors opened a policy window for the transformation of teacher education' (Smith, 2012, p 77) and transitioned teacher education from policy limbo, where it had existed for many decades, to being a policy problem within an aggressive 'reform agenda' (Quinn, 2012).

Reflecting an almost linear relationship between policy, teacher quality and students' achievement on benchmark tests (Cochran-Smith, 2012), the government's strategy, Literacy and Numeracy for Learning and for Life, contained a detailed action plan to 'improve the quality and relevance of initial teacher education' (Department of Education and Skills, 2011, p 32). It contained the 'dramatic' announcement (Coolahan, 2013, p 20) that the duration and configuration of all ITE programmes were to be revised – the BEd programme (primary teacher education) was to become a four-year programme for all entrants in 2012–13, and all postgraduate ITE programmes (primary and post-primary) were to be extended to two years for entrants in 2014–15. In a push towards increasing the relevance of the BEd programme, the humanities/liberal arts component was removed in favour of optional courses that would focus on developing professional knowledge and pedagogical skills. Subsequent Teaching Council documents – *Initial teacher education: Criteria and guidelines for programme providers* (Teaching Council, 2011a) and the *Strategy for the review and professional accreditation of existing programmes* (Teaching Council, 2011b) – identified prerequisites for accreditation, thereby centralising control of the content and nature of ITE. The council identified mandatory areas for inclusion in programmes, balancing the foundations of education (philosophy, sociology, psychology and the history of education) with professional studies and pedagogy, all of which were to be underpinned with a strong inquiry and research dimension. Clinical placement was to comprise 25% of the programme, and the integration of theory and practice throughout programmes was promoted. While current university–school relationships are informal and teachers act voluntarily as mentors or guides for students teachers (Long et al, 2012), the council's articulated ambition is to formalise and structure these relationships. The reconceptualisation, design, validation and accreditation of BEd programmes within one academic year, particularly at a time of unrelenting austerity reflected in significant year-on-year budget cuts and reductions in staffing, was extremely challenging. Cognisant that change in Irish teacher education is a rare occurrence, teacher educators embraced the long-awaited opportunity to radically reform programmes.

Given the ultimate speed of the decision making and the absence of consultation, policy makers gave little consideration to the level at which the higher education sector would validate the extended postgraduate/consecutive programmes; reflecting the Bologna principles that 120 postgraduate ECTS [European Credit Transfer System] satisfy the requirements for a Masters qualification, university registrars agreed that postgraduate teacher education programmes would be validated at Masters level. While this decision brings Ireland a significant distance towards achieving an all-Masters teaching profession, as exists in Finland, this unanticipated outcome reveals the continuance of an ad-hoc approach to teacher education policy. The absence of a cost-benefit analysis and strategic planning on the part of policy makers has resulted in no additional investment in teacher education to implement this significant policy development; rather, resources allocated to initial teacher education have diminished during this period.

Structural coherence agenda

As the Irish economic crisis deepened in 2011–12, higher education structures became the focus of government reform; the Higher Education Authority (HEA) published its strategy for the consolidation of higher education institutions and enhanced collaboration and coherence between institutions, indicating that its immediate priority was to 'enhance the quality and cost-effectiveness of provision through shared collaborative provision' (HEA, 2012, p 9). Within a number of weeks, a separate review of ITE was initiated, where the HEA was asked 'to identify possible new structures for teacher education ... to envision innovative strategies so that Ireland can provide a teacher education regime that is comparable with the world's best' (Hyland, 2012, p 3). Initial teacher education was being provided by 19 state-funded institutions; both the fragmentation of provision and the oversupply of teachers were identified as concerns to the system. The international panel, comprising Professors Pamela Munn and John Furlong, and chaired by Professor Pasi Sahlberg, made significant recommendations on the consolidation of teacher education provision. Despite the continued existence of an alternative teacher provider operating outside the higher education sector (Hibernia), locating teacher education as a research-based activity within higher education for all other providers was uncontested. However, advocating the establishment of centres where early childhood, primary and post-primary teacher education were co-located, thereby creating a critical mass that enables 'staff and students to conduct research at a high level' (Sahlberg et al, 2012, p 19), the panel recommended the rationalisation of provision whereby two providers be discontinued and that the remaining 17 providers be consolidated into six clusters (Sahlberg et al, 2012, p 20).

The first institutional movement was a voluntary merger led by the institutions themselves, and predated the Sahlberg et al (2012) report, when Froebel College (primary, Catholic college) agreed to merge with the-then NUI Maynooth (now called Maynooth University). Froebel initiated the transition and registered its students with NUI Maynooth in September 2011 and began the process of terminating its relationship with its accrediting body, Trinity College, and relocating its student and staff cohort onto the university campus in September 2013. The college now comprises one department within a school of education and works in parallel with two other departments of post-primary and adult education. Staff and students are now full members of the Maynooth University community.

Following the recommendations of Sahlberg et al (2012), four Dublin institutions have agreed to amalgamate, creating the Dublin City University (DCU) Incorporation, whereby St Patrick's College Drumcondra (SPD, primary, Catholic college), the Church of Ireland College of Education (CICE, primary, Anglican college), Mater Dei Institute (MDI, post-primary, Catholic college) and DCU (post-primary, civic university) will merge to form a single Institute of Education within the university. Assisted by external experts and consultants who have been advising on the process of merger over a two-year period (Bennetot Pruvot et al, 2015, p 42), staff and students of the various institutions will begin to relocate to the redeveloped St Patrick's College Campus in Drumcondra in September 2015. This 'incorporation project' recognises the significant cultural differences between the institutions, of which three are autonomous teacher education colleges that are much older than the university into which they are merging. These colleges have strong religious affiliations (two Catholic and one Anglican) and provide faith formation for their students, while DCU is a secular institution. The intention is to provide combined neutral core education within the larger secular institution (Bennetot Pruvot et al, 2015, p 52) while the distinctive identity and values of teacher education of the incorporating colleges will be maintained through the establishment of two centres for denominational education within the new institute of education. The incorporation process recognises the challenges involved with the loss of autonomy and the potential impact on identity, ethos and organisational culture, while also underlining the personal and professional opportunities the incorporation will bring.

Mary Immaculate College (primary, Catholic college), the University of Limerick and the Limerick Institute of Technology (both civic/secular institutions), identified by the Sahlberg report as a potential 'centre of excellence for teacher education', have collaborated to establish the National Institute for Studies in Education (NISE); while retaining institutional autonomy, this trans-sectoral and regional cluster involving a university, institute of technology and a denominational college of education, is committed to working in closer alignment to promote teacher education across the continuum. Building on a bottom-up and positive collaboration project, developed through the Shannon Consortium Partnership, which was spurred by the HEA's Strategic Innovation Funding policy of 2005–10, NISE plans to engage in curriculum mapping and sharing of modules/programmes, and while creating greater academic coherence and availing of potential financial efficiencies, there is no expectation that closer alignment will result in merger/amalgamation.

In Cork, while teacher education programmes in art and design are now being jointly offered by Crawford College (Cork Institute of Technology) and University College Cork, the traditional independence of the institutions is not contested. On the west coast, St Angela's College (post-primary home economics, Catholic college) is being merged with NUI Galway. While St Angela's College courses have been accredited by NUI Galway since 1978, and in 2006 the two colleges agreed a strategic partnership to provide university-level education in the north west, the merger is an example of direct involvement of the HEA imposing a merger process – St Angela's merger with NUI Galway has created significant difficulties for the staff in the smaller institution where mutual recognition of their employment status has not been agreed, resulting in a number of one-day strikes by lecturers. The two providers identified for closure by Sahlberg were permitted to recruit students in 2014, and so their continuance has been extended to 2018 at least.

While significant developments have been undertaken to consolidate provision of ITE across the state, revision of institutional arrangements is inextricably interwoven with issues of ethos, identity and autonomy, and require extended periods to negotiate and establish. Although Sahlberg et al did not comment on the denominational provision of teacher education, nonetheless the integration/merger of providers will challenge institutions to maintain their particular ethos within civic universities, with potentially as few as one autonomous denominational college remaining on the landscape. In a context where almost 90% of all primary schools are under Roman Catholic patronage (Coolahan et al, 2012), and the DES is promoting a policy of reduced church governance of primary and post-primary schools within an increasingly pluralist and secular society, the revision of the structures of teacher education has initiated a wider review of the values underpinning teacher education and has challenged providers to articulate their position and contribution to contemporary Ireland.

Challenges and opportunities

The recent changes in the content, duration and thrust of ITE provide opportunities to strengthen teacher education – the prioritising of research and teacher inquiry in extended programmes, and the movement to a Masters qualification, will invigorate and enhance the professionalism of teaching. Developments over the last decade have resulted in the repositioning of teacher education within public discourse and have served to reaffirm the position of state-funded teacher education within the academy. The commitment to a balanced programme of study, encompassing educational disciplines, pedagogies and practicum, has endorsed deeply held views on what constitutes appropriate initial teacher education. The extended exposure to classroom practice within ITE and the movement towards greater partnership with teachers open up opportunities for enhanced engagement for all, as does the Teaching Council's commitment to teaching as a complex activity underpinned by research and reflection, which requires renewal and learning across the teaching career. Within this context the Teaching Council has taken significant steps to highlight the role of the teacher as researcher. In addition to commissioning research, awarding research bursaries to teachers, hosting a number of national and international conferences and providing registered teachers with access to a vast array of electronic research resources, the council has established an annual 'Research Alive!' event where teachers are invited to showcase their research. The active promotion of the teacher as researcher is evident in the policy and practice of the council, and serves to signpost the council's commitment to a renewed approach to teacher professionalism across the continuum.

The absorption of teacher education provision within the university sector may unlock the potential of teacher educators, but it cannot be assumed that cross-fertilisation and transfer of knowledge will automatically occur where independent departments are co-located on one campus. While the opportunity exists to break down the chasm between primary and post-primary teacher education, the relocation of ITE from dedicated colleges to universities, with the associated increase in academic respectability, may be a mere 'devil's bargain' (Burke, 2000) for Irish education. The traditionally limited commitment of universities to teacher education and its low status on university campuses is a cause of concern. In addition, the extent to which the articulation of a shared identity and values in newly formed entities will be a spur to form fresh new cultures or be a root of dissent that inhibits development, has yet to be demonstrated.

The progression of accreditation by the Teaching Council may be both an opportunity and a challenge; while conceived as a means of protecting standards, the implementation of a process that stipulates that all programmes comply with specified guidelines may result in homogenised teacher education programmes (Burke, 2009). The council's approach to accountability and its willingness to engage in meaningful consultation with teachers and ITE providers will be pivotal to the future of ITE. Given the high esteem in which teachers are held and the rich historical legacy associated with teaching in Ireland, movement towards a reductionist approach to accountability could undermine the status of teaching and the goodwill of those engaged in accreditation processes.

Implementing ambitious and demanding reform of teacher education during a period of sustained austerity is a grave concern for all teacher educationists; the capacity of providers to deliver on their commitment to reconceptualised, research-intensive programmes is dependent on significant investment. The extent to which investment in ITE materialises in the coming years will influence the depth and impact of reform.

The greatest challenge may emanate from the current problem of teacher oversupply. Currently teacher education in Ireland attracts highly qualified candidates and becoming a teacher is a very popular career choice that carries strong social prestige (Sahlberg, 2012, pp 5, 19); in addition, retention and success rates among students in colleges of education are the highest in the higher education sector (Clarke and Killeavy, 2013, p 117). While the number of student teachers recruited to college-based programmes remains controlled by the DES, there is no control on the number of candidates being recruited by the private operator, which is now the largest single provider of teacher education. It is also notable that a substantial number of primary-level teachers undertake their teacher education programmes in the UK. Figure 8.1 illustrates the number of newly qualified teachers (NQTs) on the Teaching Council Register, 2009–14, and the rank order by size of the higher education providers.

Figure 8.1: Newly qualified teachers and higher education institution rank

			Number of NQTs on register (2009-14)	HEI Rank
Primary	Hibernia College	Ireland	3,334	1
	Mary Immaculate College of Education	Ireland	3,207	2
	St. Patrick's College of Education	Ireland	3,197	3
	Marino Institute of Education	Ireland	1,047	4
	Froebel College of Education	Ireland	576	5
	Church of Ireland	Ireland	198	6
	St. Mary's Coll Strawberry Hill	England	147	7
	University of East London	England	139	8
	University of Glasgow	Scotland	112	9
	Brunel University	England	105	10
Post Primary	University of Limerick	Ireland	2,378	1
	National University of Ireland Galway	Ireland	1,700	2
	University College Cork (NUI)	Ireland	1,538	3
	University College Dublin (NUI)	Ireland	1,436	4
	National University of Ireland Maynooth	Ireland	1,411	5
	Trinity College Dublin	Ireland	856	6
	Dublin City University	Ireland	787	7
	Hibernia College	Ireland	589	8
	Mater Dei Institute of Education	Ireland	376	9
	St. Angela's College	Ireland	298	10

Source: Teaching Council, data presented at a Consultative Forum on Teacher Supply, 15 April 2015

Recognising the threat to quality, the Sahlberg et al (2012, p 20) report stated: 'The issue of supply is also closely linked to that of quality. Where there is an oversupply of teachers, with the consequent reduction in opportunities for employment, it may not be possible to continue to attract high calibre entrants into teaching.' Graduate employment statistics reveal a sharp reduction in the proportion of BEd graduates securing permanent full-time teaching posts, declining from 17% in 2009 to 4% in 2013, while the proportion securing substitute or part-time teaching declined to 64% in 2013 from 79% in 2012 (HEA, 2014, p 91). The attractiveness of teaching in Irish society is under severe threat, and to retain the high quality of its entrants to the profession, the oversupply of teachers must be addressed.

Conclusion

Teacher education policy in the Republic of Ireland has remained relatively stable for the last five decades; this has ensured that some of the values and processes lost in other jurisdictions have been retained. Informed and influenced by European Union policy and OECD documents and reports, a substantial policy platform had developed over previous decades, when Minister Ruairí Quinn announced the extension of the duration of teacher preparation programmes in 2011. Spurred by the poor performance of Irish students in the PISA and recognising the core role of teacher education in the economic reconstruction of the nation, reform of teacher education became a priority on the political agenda. While the compression of events during this period may mirror those experienced during the last wave of reform (1965–75), it could be argued that the intensity and velocity of reform have been unprecedented. The appointment of an ambitious and reform-oriented minister became the catalyst in transitioning teacher education into the political arena at a time when international policy was focusing on competence, accountability and benchmarked, quantifiable outcomes. The commitment of the minister (who stepped down from his post in July 2014) to transform the quality and infrastructure of teacher education has not been matched by HEA/DES investment and the capacity of institutions to implement appropriately such radical reforms is a concern. Teacher education is at a critical juncture; while the historical evidence illustrates that the growing swell and tide is favourable for education change, nonetheless the extent to which a genuine and positive transition in teacher education can be achieved, and sustained, depends on the continued political and financial commitment of policy makers.

Part Three:
Critical issues in teacher education policy: home international analyses

NINE

Standards and accountability in teacher education

Aileen Kennedy

Introduction

An increased international focus on teacher quality has brought with it an increased focus on the use of standards as a means of encapsulating expressions of what it means to be a good (or satisfactory) teacher. Sahlberg (2011b, p 177) suggests that 'a widely accepted – and generally unquestioned – belief among policymakers and education reformers is that setting clear and sufficiently high performance standards for schools, teachers, and students will necessarily improve the quality of desired outcomes'. This 'generally unquestioned belief' has been translated into policy measures that are arguably not informed sufficiently by a rigorous evidence base, and the link between the publication of standards-based policies and their impact on the practice of teachers and ultimately the educational achievement of pupils, has not been subjected to sufficient empirical scrutiny.

This chapter considers how the drive for accountability in terms of teacher quality is enacted through the production of professional standards for teachers in the four nations of the UK and neighbouring Republic of Ireland. We have seen in the foregoing chapters how standards and accountability are major concerns in all five of these countries. Through discourse analysis of the standards documents, the chapter presents an analysis of the espoused aims, the content and the structure of the various conceptualisations of standards, illustrating in each a range of explicit and implicit purposes. It considers how the concept of 'accountability' is made visible through the existence of standards-based approaches, identifying both commonalities and divergent themes across and between nations. What it does not do is analyse how such policy documents are enacted, and it is acknowledged that this is of course important and these processes have been described to some extent in the chapters in Part Two of this book. However, the standards documents themselves present the official version of the discourse, as authorised by those charged with overseeing teacher governance, be they governments themselves or professional bodies. And, indeed, the location of the ultimate governance over such issues is in itself worthy of analysis, as this chapter reveals.

There follows an overview of the policy context and discussion of key areas of debate in the literature. The chapter then presents an analysis of each of the five sets of standards before concluding with a discussion that brings the analysis together and draws on a range of theoretical perspectives in offering some possible readings of the commonalities and divergences revealed in the analysis.

Contemporary issues in policy and literature

The development and use of professional standards for teachers is now firmly situated as a key policy lever by which countries might improve student outcomes and, ultimately, their economic standing (Scheerens, 2010). Indeed, in 2005 the Organisation for Economic Co-operation and Development (OECD) asserted that '[t]here is widespread recognition that countries need to have clear and concise statements of what teachers are expected to know and be able to do' (OECD, 2005, p 9) and that countries should have 'profession-wide standards and a shared understanding of what counts as accomplished teaching' (p 10). This 'common-sense' approach of developing professional standards to guide teachers' practice, on the assumption that this will improve pupil outcomes, seems to have been broadly accepted as a logical way forward by policy makers globally. However, even in 1999, Darling-Hammond was warning that professional standards for teachers should not be considered as a panacea, and that the impact of other factors such as curricula, resources and dysfunctional institutional structures could not be counteracted by the introduction of professional standards. This warning serves as a leveller, and although the central focus of this chapter is on standards and their relationship to accountability, it is important to bear in mind that this is but one aspect of an education system through which accountability might be demonstrated.

Over the past 10 years in particular, as political interest in the development of professional standards for teachers has increased, so too has academic interest. Most of this academic literature has tended to focus on country/state-specific developments, with much of it taking an explicit political focus, exploring the meaning of standards in context and the extent to which they enable control over, or by, the profession (eg, Stevens, 2010, Evans, 2011 and Goepel, 2012 in

England; Hagan, 2013 in Northern Ireland; Han, 2012 in China; Mayer et al, 2005 in Australia). In addition to the bulk of literature that looks at general aspects of specific standards, there also exists a small body of literature that explores specific aspects of standards more generally, such as Ryan and Bourke's (2013) study, which explores the extent to which reflexivity is apparent in professional standards, and Clarke and Moore's (2013) exploration of the 'ethics of singularity' promoted by professional standards, which serve to shape, and arguably standardise, teacher identity. What this body of literature illustrates is the enactment of 'vernacular globalisation' (Appadurai, 1996; Chapter Three, this volume) – that is, the local adaptation of global trends, in line with local cultural, historical and social practices. Although the national contexts represented in the literature vary, a number of key themes arise across discussions, including:

- the definition and purpose(s) of standards;
- standards as a means of accountability;
- perspectives on professionalism evident in professional standards.

Defining 'standards' and their purpose(s)

Despite the almost universal acceptance that standards are an appropriate way forward for the teaching profession, there is a surprising lack of unanimity in relation to how the term is understood. Indeed, Stanley and Stronach (2013, p 293) suggest that rather than thinking about how to define standards, we should be thinking about them 'much more as what probability theorists would call a "sample space", that is, a range of semantic possibilities'. The literature reveals a number of different conceptions of what standards are and what they are for, including a means of 'standardising' quality of practice (usually at a baseline level), suggesting a state to be achieved rather than a commitment to continuing development and improvement. Sachs (2003a), while not promoting standards as an entirely good thing, outlines three broad claims from the literature that underpin some of the arguments for their use – standards serve as: a 'common-sense' outline of what teachers should know and be able to do; a facet of accountability and quality assurance; and a means of promoting quality improvement. While the last of these suggests an aspirational purpose, standards are often taken to denote a common, or standard, level of practice. Where standards are taken to denote 'standardisation' – as is implicit in such iterations that purport to provide a baseline for competence/licensing – the implication is that they provide some written and agreed quality threshold that can be uniformly applied to all teachers. However, Clarke and Moore (2013, p 489) suggest that when such versions of standards set out requirements for what teachers should know and be able to do, they are:

> rendered so vague by the fundamental impossibility of taking account of the idiosyncratic and the contingent in teaching and learning as to result in their being reduced to mere statements of the obvious – rendering judgments regarding the extent to which they have been achieved overly subjective despite their requirement to 'demonstrate' and 'provide evidence'.

However, while there exists a powerful critique of the notion of standards-based conceptions of teaching, there are some alternative views as to their purposes. Storey (2007, p 257) describes the academic attack on 'performativity', of which standards are seen as a central feature, as suggesting an 'attempted imposition of an alien architecture of managerialism in place of traditional professional values'. She goes on to suggest that such performativity tools are less 'alien' to new entrants to the profession, particularly to mature career-changers, than they might be to more established teachers, as these new entrants have experienced, and indeed accepted, such practices as 'normal'. While this position challenges the dominant critique, it is perhaps non-deficit rather than a ringing positive endorsement. From a more positive perspective, Ingvarson (1998) has been a longstanding advocate of professional standards as a means of supporting professional and career development, and Darling-Hammond (1999) presents a strong argument in favour of using standards as part of a profession-led developmental approach to teaching.

It is apparent that definitions and claims about purpose are neither simple nor straightforward. It is feasible that one set of standards could be seen to fulfil more than one purpose, and indeed, that different stakeholders may privilege different purposes depending on their particular perspective.

Standards are usually promoted as a means of enhancing teacher quality and, as such, are an obvious means of demonstrating accountability. While usually associated with top-down, externally imposed accountability, it should be acknowledged that accountability can also be evidenced by teachers themselves using standards as one means of exemplifying good practice. It is important, therefore, that we do not automatically assume accountability to be a pejorative term, and that we consider the capacity for standards to be used by and for teachers in accounting in a positive and empowered way for their own practice. Nonetheless, there exists trenchant criticism of the tendency for standards to describe teaching in a reductive way that fails to recognise the complex, contingent and human nature of practice. Stevens (2010, p 189), for example, refers to the 'simplistic "obedience" model of professionalism' that is implied by some such reductive standards documents. While Goodwin (2010, p 30) points out that 'calls for scientific evidence, best practices, and standardized strategies bypass the reality that learning to teach does not rest on techno-rational skills or proceed in a linear, predictable fashion'.

Regardless of one's perspective on the purpose and usefulness of professional standards, it seems clear that they are, at least for the time being, a central part of most countries' teacher education and development policies. However, despite being supported by transnational bodies such as the European Commission (2013), there is a paucity of evidence to support any direct links between the existence of professional standards and improved pupil outcomes. There are studies such as Walker et al's (2010) investigation of the impact of 'new professionalism' on teachers' work, which concludes that many teachers, especially headteachers, believe that standards improve teaching and learning, but these perception studies do not provide unequivocal evidence of a clear link between teacher standards and pupil outcomes. Perhaps, then, the continued and growing existence of standards is evidence of something else: a means of defining and shaping professional culture, or 'teacher professionalism'.

Discourses of professionalism

Regardless of their stated purposes, professional standards present an 'official' representation of teachers and teaching in particular national contexts. The analysis of these standards can therefore reveal much about how teacher professionalism is constructed, and about how it is intended to be enacted. The foregoing discussion reveals a tension between the use of standards to support professional growth and bottom-up accountability, and their use as a top-down, hierarchical and managerial means of ensuring compliance and performativity. These perspectives can be understood to be conceptualisations of 'professionalism', and exploration of theoretical constructs of professionalism can prove illuminating in seeking to analyse sets of professional standards.

The contrasting uses of standards as outlined above can be seen to characterise two distinctive contemporary discourses on professionalism. Sachs (2001) draws a contrast between the discourse of 'managerial' professionalism, which values efficiency, compliance and technical-rational responses, and the discourse of 'democratic' professionalism, which values social justice and equity, and seeks to 'demystify professional work' (p 252) through collaborative and transparent practice with students, parents and communities. In the former discourse, teachers are what Gale and Densmore (2003, p 86) refer to as 'state functionaries', while the latter discourse positions teachers as activist, autonomous and able to exercise agency (see also a similar but four-fold categorisation of teacher professionalism offered in Chapter Two, this volume).

Whitty (2008) draws on these ideas in proposing four 'modes' of professionalism, which he uses to illustrate developments in professionalism within the English context. Despite the nation-specific context of their derivation, these modes provide a useful analytical framework for the analysis of professional standards documents more generally. The four modes comprise:

- *traditional professionalism*, which positions teachers as trusted members of society who exercise autonomy by virtue of their knowledge and expertise;
- *managerial professionalism*, in which the state takes 'a much more assertive role in specifying what teachers are expected to achieve, rather than leaving it to professional judgement alone' (p 38);
- *collaborative professionalism*, which focuses on inter-professional collaboration rather than collaboration across and within teaching;
- *democratic professionalism*, which, while acknowledging the need to form strategic alliances across and beyond professional boundaries, has at its core the notion that teachers are agents of change, able to work proactively on behalf of the pupils they teach to promote social justice and equity.

It is not suggested that any one policy document might necessarily reflect wholly one of these modes, although this is of course possible. Rather, these modes are seen as useful in identifying and 'naming' the sometimes conflicting discourses present in individual policies.

Analytical approach

This chapter presents an analysis of the professional standards documents for the five countries under consideration here: the four jurisdictions within the UK – namely England, Northern Ireland, Scotland and Wales – and the Republic of Ireland. In so doing it adopts a critical discourse analysis (CDA) approach; it takes an explicitly politically engaged perspective on the ways in which the standards documents have been discursively constructed. MacLure (2003, p 8) puts a strong case forward for this kind of research, describing it as '(re)mobilizing discursive literacy in educational research'. It is important to stress that CDA is much more an approach than a specific methodology. Indeed, Fairclough et al (2011, p 358) view it as 'a form of intervention in social practice and social relationships', acknowledging that 'CDA sees itself not as a dispassionate and objective social science, but as engaged and committed'. While there exists a range of discourse analysis approaches, what defines CDA is the critical theory element of it, which 'focuses on the ways discourse structures enact, confirm, legitimate, reproduce, or challenge relations of *power* and *dominance* in society' (van Dijk, 2001a, p 353, emphasis in original). Or put simply, 'CDA is a – critical – perspective on doing scholarship: it is, so to speak, discourse analysis "with an attitude"' (van Dijk, 2001b, p 96).

CDA is, however, criticised in some arenas for its explicit political engagement (Widdowson, 1995), and is met with challenges in relation to its rigour. While 'political engagement' is not in itself necessarily negative, and indeed might be expected in a book that deals with policy matters, it is important, nonetheless, that in refuting these criticisms, critical discourse analysts approach the task in hand with a clearly devised, transparent and systematic structure for the analysis of the discourse(s) in question.

The CDA approach in this analysis is informed by Scott's (2000, pp 18-20) nine continua for policy analysis (see below) and Whitty's modes of professionalism.

Scott's continua for policy analysis

- prescriptive/non-prescriptive;
- wide focus/narrow focus;
- open/concealed;
- authoritative/non-authoritative;
- generic/directed;
- single-authored/multiple authored;

- visual or diagrammatical/written text;
- referenced to other texts/free of references to other texts;
- coherent/fragmented

(Scott, 2000, pp 18-20)

These constructs have been applied to the specific 'problem' under investigation: the discourse of accountability apparent in professional standards for teachers across these five countries. This overarching approach led to the identification of a more detailed and specific analytical framework, which poses four questions of the various standards documents, namely:

- *Genesis*: Whose standards? Where did the mandate come from?
- *Purpose*: Stated purpose? Guidance on operationalisation?
- *Structure*: How is the document structured and presented, including choice of language?
- *Status* of standards: Advisory, guidance, mandatory, legislative, aspirational ...?

Alongside these specific questions, attention is paid to what is not said as well as what it stated explicitly. The analysis for each standards document is then considered in relation to Whitty's four modes of professionalism, followed by a synthesis of key themes across all five sets of standards.

Analysis of the standards documents

England

The English *Teachers' standards* (DfE, 2013a) are owned and published explicitly by the government, and more specifically, are 'published by the Secretary of State for Education' (p 2). The current version has 'introduced some significant changes in terms of structure, content and application' (p 2) and the document is therefore 'designed to assist those who will be using the standards to understand those changes and to implement the standards effectively' (p 2). This opening paragraph conveys an explicitly managerial purpose, evident in the wording above, which instructs the user to 'implement' them, rather than to reflect on them, or to draw on them. Indeed, further down page 2 it is noted that 'Part 2 of the Teachers' Standards, which relates to professional and personal conduct, is used to assess cases of serious misconduct', thereby implying a deficit purpose. They are presented as the baseline standard for teach*ing* (not teach*ers*), whether that teaching be by fully qualified teachers, those working and training to be teachers on flexible routes such as Teach First or those from the further education sector with qualified teacher learning and skills (QTLS) status. The first subsection is entitled 'Introduction, legal standing and interpretation', foregrounding the legal status of the document, which is further expanded by mention of the use of standards in conduct cases, thereby highlighting the disciplinary function.

Perhaps unsurprisingly, given the managerial tone and deficit positioning, there is no mention of the profession itself being involved in the development or publication of the document. It might therefore be suggested that these standards are not designed to be in any way developmental. The focus on baseline thresholds for competence and conduct is reinforced by the declaration that the standards apply to 'the vast majority of teachers regardless of their career stage' (p 3).

The overall appearance of the document serves to further convey the message that this is a business-like, official document: the title is simple and descriptive with no apparent need to appeal to notions of professionalism or such like; the only non-text is the official government logo; and the language used is brisk and business-like, with numbered paragraphs containing instructive and prescriptive text. The language used conveys a performative perspective, employing terms such as 'appraisal', 'assessed' and 'performance', with a notable absence of language that might be considered to communicate a more developmental or aspirational discourse. The introductory sentence stem for each of the specific standards is 'a teacher must...'.

Overall, the document conveys a behaviourist/performance-based perspective on teaching and does not consider issues of values, beliefs and attitudes, other than in the rather disconcerting reference to teachers 'not undermining fundamental British values' (p 10). The document conveys quite clearly what Whitty (2008) would categorise as a 'managerial' perspective on professionalism, specifying in detail 'how to teach', and using this specification as a performative tool.

Northern Ireland

The Northern Irish document is entitled *Teaching: The reflective profession* (GTCNI, 2007), and interestingly does not contain the word 'standard' or 'standards' anywhere in either the title or in the body of the text. It was published in 2007 by the General Teaching Council for Northern Ireland (GTCNI) and is explicit about the development process, which it says involves discussion, debate and agreement with 'the broader education service, and most importantly, with classroom practitioners themselves' (p 5). Not only does this demonstrate a collaborative process, but it also privileges the position of the classroom teacher over the employer or the state. This provides a stark contrast to the managerial focus outlined in the English document discussed above, which rather than being produced by the professional body, was produced and published by government.

The stated purpose of the Northern Irish document is manifold, including serving as a stimulus for both individual and collaborative reflection and informing teacher education programmes. The stated purposes are open, positive and flexible. Fundamental to the document is the explication of the underpinning philosophy of teaching, rendering the status of the document as guiding and informative rather than legislative or directive.

This is a relatively long document of 50 pages, although the statements of competence do not begin until page 16. The first part of the document is devoted to presenting an argued position on professionalism, which makes explicit its alignment to a particular perspective, that of the 'activist teacher'. This position statement is informed by relevant, albeit dated, research texts. In arguing its position it seeks to meet potential criticism head-on, for example on page 8 the document states that:

> Some might suggest that the Charter and Code reflect an idealism that sits ill at ease with the realities of school life. However, such a view fails to recognise that the profession, if it is to claim true professional status, must value idealism as an underpinning characteristic of the professional persona.

Professional values and ethical and moral purposes are therefore very much to the fore, with technical descriptive language much less prominent. Interestingly, the second page introduces the subtitle 'incorporating the Northern Ireland teacher competences'. The term 'competence' is often considered to convey a technicist approach to teaching, breaking a complex and context-dependent practice down into observable behaviours in a reductive way. However, the Northern Irish document defines its use of the term explicitly, asserting that 'in endorsing this approach, [the General Teaching Council for Northern Ireland] has been conscious that the teacher competences must be considered holistically and not treated as a series of discrete entities, divested of values or a sense of mission and professional identity' (p 5).

In summary, Northern Ireland's 'standards' document expresses explicit alignment with a democratic perspective on professionalism, promoting the notion of teachers as reflective and activist practitioners, and acknowledging the importance of both individual and collaborative action.

Republic of Ireland

The Republic of Ireland's *Code of professional conduct for teachers* (second edition) was published by the Teaching Council in 2012 in accordance with the requirements of the Teaching Council Act 2001, and following consultation with a wide range of teachers, other stakeholders and the general public (Teaching Council, 2012). It outlines three specific, but linked, purposes:

- to act as 'a guiding compass for teachers' (p 3);
- to be used by 'the education community and the wider public to inform their understanding and expectations of the teaching profession in Ireland' (p 3);
- to provide legal standing as part of the disciplinary process.

These three purposes suggest broad alignment with a traditional discourse on professionalism where upholding public trust is central. However, the document then goes on to spell out the context in which 'The Code' is to be considered, highlighting the Teaching Council's Policy on the Continuum of Teacher Education, and envisioning teachers as reflective and supportive of students and new teachers. This discourse moves towards a more democratic perspective, one that also acknowledges the wider societal context in which teachers work.

In terms of overall structure, two pages are devoted to outlining the purpose and context and then one page is devoted to explicating the ethical values underpinning the standards. There then follow three pages of competence statements – 33 in total grouped into six categories. These categories take an interesting diversion from the more common, threefold categorisation that centres broadly around: values; knowledge and understanding; and skills and abilities. The six categories in the Irish document are:

- professional values and relationships;
- professional integrity;
- professional conduct;
- professional practice;

- professional development;
- professional collegiality and collaboration.

The relatively minor proportion devoted to 'practice' in comparison with other standards documents perhaps reflects the Irish document's status as a 'code of professional conduct', rather than primarily as a specification of teacher competences or behaviours associated with initial licensing/registration.

The status of the document is interesting: it simultaneously holds legislative status through its relationship to the Teaching Council Act 2001 and concomitant use in the disciplinary process, as well as proving a strong ethical steer in relation to teacher professionalism as 'a guiding compass as teachers seek to steer an ethical and respectful course through their career in teaching and to uphold the honour and dignity of the profession' (p 3). So while the document as a whole is entitled *Code of professional conduct...*, the text of the document does also refer to 'standards', acknowledging explicitly the range of potential purposes of such documents. The language appeals much more obviously to notions of teacher professionalism than it does to notions of externally imposed accountability. In so doing, it reflects a traditional perspective on professionalism that promotes the professional ethics and status of the occupational group and requires a unifying code of professional conduct to which members sign up.

Scotland

Scotland has a 'suite' of professional standards, published by the General Teaching Council for Scotland (GTCS), the latest iteration of which was published in December 2012 following revision mandated through the Donaldson review of teacher education (Donaldson, 2011). The suite encompasses three separate documents:

- *The standards for registration: Mandatory requirements for registration with the General Teaching Council for Scotland* (GTCS, 2012a);
- *The standard for career-long professional learning: Supporting the development of teacher professional learning* (GTCS, 2012b);
- *The standards for leadership and management: Supporting leadership and management development* (GTCS, 2012c).

While published by the GTCS, there is no discussion of the process of development or of the individuals or stakeholder bodies involved in the writing process. In terms of situating this iteration in its historical context, the documents make reference to the previous versions, in particular to the former Standard for Chartered Teacher (not revised in this iteration as the Chartered Teacher Programme has been discontinued) and to the previous Standard for Headship. It also lays claim to the new Standard for Career-Long Professional Learning (SCLPL) being based on 'sound national and international research' (GTCS, 2012b, p 2), although no research is cited.

Despite being billed as a 'suite' of standards, the documents claim different purposes. The Standards for Registration (SfRs) profess to outline 'standards of capability ... in which ... the wider community can have confidence' (GTCS, 2012a, p 2), revealing an explicit regard for external accountability, yet purposely giving no guidance as to how judgements are to be made. The SCLPL provides a framework for teachers to use when planning their professional learning, and should not be seen as a standard to be 'achieved', but does make explicit links to other quality processes. The Standards for Leadership (SfLs) list a number of purposes, including:

- aiding individual reflection;
- informing the design and quality assurance of leadership programmes;
- as an aid to recruitment and selection;
- as a means to promote dialogue.

Like the SCLPL, the SfLs also make links to their use as a part of other quality processes.

Just as the stated purposes vary, unsurprisingly, so too do the status of the respective standards. The SfRs, for both initial and full registration, are clearly linked to licensing and therefore are mandatory for all teachers, providing the 'benchmark of teacher competence for all teachers' (GTCS, 2012a, p 2). The SCLPL, in contrast, is optional, for teachers who choose to reflect on it, and purports to be aspirational. The SfLs sit somewhere in the middle, providing guidance to 'support self-evaluation and professional learning' in role-specific contexts.

In terms of structure, all three sets of documents start with an 'onion' diagram illustrating the suite of standards and their relationships to each other, and then contain the same statement about 'professional values and personal commitment'. There is also a common discourse permeating all three documents, which privileges values, sustainability and leadership as three key pillars. The remainder of each document is devoted to outlining elements of professional knowledge and understanding, and skills and abilities, listing 'professional actions' for each element.

Because of the multiple underpinning purposes, the differences in structure and status, it is perhaps unsurprising that the standards reflect different discourses on professionalism, despite being badged as a suite that might suggest a greater element of unanimity. Yet the SfRs, with their emphasis on registration/licencing, reveal a managerial perspective on professionalism, while the SCLPL, appealing to a managerial perspective in terms of its relationship with other quality assurance purposes, also supports a traditional perspective in that it supports the project of professionalisation through its voluntary nature and aspirational aims. The SfLs support a managerial perspective in terms of their links to other quality assurance processes, yet at the same time also reveal a collaborative perspective on professionalism through their emphasis on leaders working collaboratively with other professions and agencies.

So this 'suite' is perhaps a suite in name only as it portrays a varied set of purposes and expectations. It perhaps knows what it *doesn't* want to be: 'it is not intended that the Professional Actions should be used as a checklist' (GTCS, 2012a, p 2), yet lacks coherence in terms of what it *does* want to be, demonstrating a raft of possible purposes.

Wales

The *Revised professional standards for education practitioners in Wales* document was published by the Welsh Government in September 2011. There is no statement about the genesis of the document other than a reference to the standards that were being replaced by this revised document. The document does make clear, however, that the standards apply to all education practitioners, but contains no directive language about operationalisation, simply that 'these standards should be used by education practitioners in Wales at the appropriate stage of their careers' (p i). This provides an interesting contrast to the English standards, which dictate that they should be deployed by headteachers, conveying an overt and hierarchical performative purpose. The Welsh document allows for profession-wide engagement and use of the standards, perhaps allowing for accountability to be more evenly distributed.

The document contains 16 pages in total, starting with a succinct statement of audience, overview and action required. It then goes on to list 'standards' for each occupational group covered:

- higher level teaching assistants: three categories, 36 statements;
- practising teachers: three categories, 55 statements;
- leaders: six categories, 66 statements.

While stopping short of legislative status, the document, being published by the Welsh Government as a circular, renders its status as (strongly) advisory. There is no explicit mention of mandatory status, but strong guidance that it should apply to each of the above occupational groups. The style of expression is perfunctory; there is no performative focus, but neither is there any explicit mention of professionalism or aspirational agenda, and no attempt to articulate an underpinning philosophy of teaching/teachers.

The document makes a clear statement about its overall purpose being 'to raise standards of teaching and to improve learner outcomes throughout Wales' (Welsh Government, 2011, p 1). The absence of any overt evidence base for this illustrates the point made earlier that policy makers appear to see standards as a 'common-sense' solution to improving teacher quality and therefore enhancing learner outcomes. In terms of operationalisation, the document promotes the standards framework as a means to 'enable practitioners to identify their performance management objectives' (p 1), suggesting a performative, managerial perspective. However, this managerial, performative discourse is not sustained strongly throughout the document.

In terms of alignment with a particular perspective on professionalism, the deliberate use of the phrase 'education practitioners' rather than 'teachers' perhaps hints at a collaborative (although not inter-professional) perspective, although again, there is no explicit, sustainable alignment with this discourse either. Overall, the document suggests a reactive response to global policy messages about the 'best' way of enhancing student outcomes, without any clear evidence of an underpinning philosophy or purpose.

Discussion

The standards documents analysed here are all published either by the government (England and Wales) or by the relevant Teaching Council (Northern Ireland, Republic of Ireland and Scotland), revealing at the outset differences in the shape of professional governance within the various jurisdictions. The English Teaching Council was abolished in 2012, so was no longer in existence when the current version of the standards was published, leaving Wales as the only jurisdiction in which a Teaching Council exists but in which government published the standards. This leads to some interesting observations about the extent to which political and professional governance dominate, although even where Teaching Councils have ownership of the professional standards, that does not necessarily mean that they are not also required to take cognisance of government policy direction and advice. This is evident through the range of mandates that have precipitated the production or revision of the various standards documents, and the range of bodies that have been consulted in the process. For example, while the GTCS now enjoys full independent status, its revision of the suite of professional standards was mandated through a government-initiated review of teacher education.

The structure and style of the documents varies greatly, from the official and perfunctory style of the English and Welsh standards to the more narrative, argued and contingent style of the Northern Irish document. The size of documents ranges from eight pages in Wales to 50 in Northern Ireland, again suggesting significant differences in intention and use. The style of language varies accordingly, as does the extent to which each document makes reference to other texts: the Welsh document contains no references; the English, Republic of Ireland and Scottish documents refer to other relevant professional and/or legislative documents; while the Northern Irish document adopts a more academic style in referencing a few academic texts.

As might be expected when the genesis, structure and style vary so much, the various standards documents also reveal a wide range of stated purposes, both across and within national boundaries. While the English document is more focused in its stated purpose – it is clearly concerned with performative/disciplinary issues – the Northern Irish and Republic of Ireland documents are expressly manifold in their stated purposes. The Welsh document is somewhat generic in its purpose of raising standards for all learners, while the Scottish suite reveals clear, but differing purposes for each of its three documents.

It is in statements about the respective status of the documents, however, that underpinning discourses on professionalism are perhaps most readily revealed. The legislative, disciplinary status of the English standards is evident not only through explicit statements about status, but also in the more general managerial discourse of performativity and externally imposed accountability. The Republic of Ireland document also reveals a managerial discourse relating to its legislative status via the disciplinary function, but at the same time, privileges the ethical nature of the document in its role as a 'code of conduct', appealing much more overtly to a traditional discourse of professionalism. The Scottish suite of documents reveals the variation in status being accorded to different standards, ranging from the mandatory status of the SfRs, to the theoretically optional status of the aspirational SCLPL. This suite of standards also therefore reveals both managerial and traditional discourses on professionalism, and in the SfLs, hints in a small way at a collaborative discourse through mention of headteachers working with other professions. Interestingly, despite being published by government, the Welsh standards' status as a 'circular' falls short of full legislative status, holding a strong advisory standing, suggesting perhaps a weak managerial discourse. The Northern Irish standards sit much more clearly within a democratic discourse, their status being to provide an informative, guiding contribution to ongoing discussion and debate; they are much more obviously an ethical code of conduct than they are a performative list of behaviours or actions.

Clearly, individual standards, or suites of standards, can appeal to more than one discourse, but interestingly, using Whitty's (2008) four modes of professionalism, there is very little evidence of a collaborative discourse that sets teachers' work within a wider inter-professional context. This is interesting in terms of wider accountability in that it suggests that professional accountability has primacy over accountability, which might come from the demands of the wider public policy agenda. It also suggests that the ultimate unit of accountability is the individual teacher rather than groups of teachers, or institutions, or wider networks of professionals extending beyond teachers. This pathologisation of teachers neglects to take account of other influences on the quality of an education system. As Sterman (2000, p 28) argues: 'The attribution of behavior to individuals and special circumstances rather than the system structure diverts our attention from the high leverage points where redesigning the system of government policy can have significant, sustained, beneficial effects on performance.' This line of reasoning might help to explain why standards exist in some form or another across all five of these countries, yet their genesis, structure, form, purpose and status vary considerably. If we look to attribution theory by way of explanation, then we can consider the existence of professional standards as exemplification of what Guimond et al (1989) term 'person-blame' as opposed to 'system-blame'. That is, policy makers seek to advance accountability for quality education through a focus on the responsibility of the individual teacher, rather than accountability of the system. This particular perspective allows us to see the various iterations of professional standards as perhaps having more in common than might otherwise be seen.

The move to develop professional standards at national levels is, of course, not unique to these five countries and, as outlined earlier in this chapter, there is consistent policy advice being given from transnational institutions that supports this policy trajectory. It would be easy simply to attribute this growing policy phenomenon to globalisation, and to attribute the differences in enactment of the global policy trajectory to 'vernacular globalisation' or 'glocalisation'. Schwinn (2012), however, critiques this view as simplistic, suggesting that there is a need for a more nuanced single conceptualisation that encompasses both the global and local aspects, or what he terms 'globality and locality' (2012, p 526). Part of the complexity of this analysis, particularly when adopting a comparative perspective, is encapsulated in Louis and van Velzen's (2012, p 2) question: 'Is the meaning of common linguistic elements translated into practice in the same way across countries? In other words, is the apparent emergence of global trends real or illusory?' This is particularly apposite in the context of professional standards documents, which may or may not, as is the case in Northern Ireland, use the term 'standards', yet can be considered alongside documents that do use it, and may also use the term alongside the notion of 'code of conduct'. These terms all have subtle cultural and historical differences, which make any comparative analysis somewhat problematic.

In conclusion

While the bulk of the analysis in this chapter has focused on illuminating the detail of the individual national standards, the foregoing discussion questions the extent to which such a comparative analysis is a useful means by which to explore issues of similarity and difference in national responses to seemingly global influences. However, in returning to the central aim of the chapter – to explore standards as a means of promoting or enacting accountability – the analysis does reveal some interesting issues. First, it is perhaps ironic that while all four nations of the UK are promoting the concept of 'evidence-informed teaching' (BERA and RSA, 2014b), the continued use of professional standards appears to be accepted without evidence of their contribution to enhancing pupil outcomes. Perhaps if there was more and better empirical evidence available, individual nations could make more informed decisions about the primary purpose of standards, the most appropriate structure and the likely impact on the quality of teaching. Second, the pathologisation of teachers, and the resulting responsibility being placed on individual teachers' shoulders, might usefully be rebalanced through greater consideration of accountability across the system as a whole, and the evidence-informed development of locally appropriate quality enhancement and accountability approaches.

TEN

The place of research in teacher education

Gillian Peiser

Introduction

This chapter explores (a) how different types of research are fundamental in informing programme content (research *in* teacher education) and (b) how teacher education research is also useful in influencing programme design and structure (research *on* teacher education) (Cochran-Smith and Demers, 2008). The discussion of research *in* teacher education will present a rationale for research-rich teacher preparation and development and then review three different types of research: pedagogical content knowledge, professional enquiry, and innovative modes of integrating theory and practice. The analysis of research *on* teacher education will pay particular attention to the insights gleaned into how teachers learn, and illustrate how this knowledge has informed the content of teacher preparation courses. In addition to exploring the benefits and value of research in and on teacher education, the chapter will examine some of the associated challenges:

- the tensions between competence-based teacher standards and a wider professional understanding;
- the contested nature of 'valid' educational research;
- issues related to teacher educators' research capacity;
- the difficulties in developing an evidence base in teacher education.

The focus of this book is on teacher education across the UK and the Republic of Ireland. This chapter focuses primarily on the four nations within the UK, although many of the points made have clear relevance to the Republic of Ireland (and see also Chapter Eight, this volume, where the place of research in Irish teacher education is discussed) and indeed internationally. It begins with a brief overview of the policy context for teacher education research in each of the four jurisdictions of the UK. Those issues will then be readdressed in the discussion section with respect to the key points made in the chapter.

Policy context

The analysis by Beauchamp et al (2013) sees the contribution of research to teacher education as having broad institutional acceptance in Scotland, Wales and Northern Ireland, but as currently contested in England. England's position as an 'outlier', however, may be seen as a relatively recent development (Beauchamp et al, 2013), following the election of the coalition government in 2010.

Prior to that election, Hulme et al (2009) noted that all the teacher standards across the jurisdictions of the UK made reference to the fact that 'accomplished' teachers would need to draw on research to inform or improve professional practice. The then New Labour government advocated that teaching should become a Masters profession (DCSF, 2008) and starting in 2002, various state-funded 'applied' Masters degrees for in-service teachers were introduced:

- in England, the Masters in Teaching and Learning (Training Development Agency for Schools, 2009);
- in Scotland, the Chartered Teacher (CT) Scheme (SEED, 2002);
- in Wales, the Masters in Educational Practice (MEP) (GTCW and Welsh Government, 2012) (see Chapters Four, Six and Seven respectively for more detailed accounts of these).

At a European level, the status of research had been bolstered by the Bologna agreement in 1999, which required all postgraduate qualifications in the European Union to be at Masters level. On postgraduate routes into teaching then, even in England, it often became an expectation that student teachers not only engage with educational research, but also conduct some empirical research on practice.

At the time of writing this chapter, the Scottish and Northern Irish teacher standards continue to make explicit references to the significance of research-informed practice. Although, in Wales, there is no reference to research in its standards, its importance is highlighted in the non-statutory guidance documents that outline expectations for teacher education providers. The financial backing of the Welsh government for the Masters in Educational Practice for newly qualified teachers was also indicative of political support for research-informed practice. When the coalition government came to power in 2010, funding for the Masters in Teaching and Learning in England was withdrawn and the new English teachers' standards, introduced in 2012, make no explicit mention of the importance of research. These policy developments illustrate how government policy may promote or impede research-informed teacher education and how views about what should constitute teacher knowledge may be seen as inherently political.

Research *in* teacher education

Why research-rich teacher education?

In response to the 'diverging policy and provision for teacher education and heightened attention to the use of evidence and research', the British Educational Research Association (BERA) together with the Royal Society of Arts (RSA) commissioned an inquiry into the role of research in teacher education (BERA and RSA, 2014a), in order to provide an evidence base for its importance. The BERA and RSA report advocates teachers' 'research engagement', namely 'the involvement of teachers and school and college leaders in the doing of research' (BERA and RSA, 2014b, p 40) and 'research literacy', that is, that teachers should be 'familiar with a range of research methods, with the latest research findings and with the implications of this research for day-to-day practice, and for education policy and practice more broadly' (BERA and RSA, 2014b, p 40).

Within the inquiry, one of the papers by Winch et al (2013) argues that research-rich content in teacher education is fundamental so that beginning and in-service teachers are able to draw on a wide body of collective knowledge, pooled from a variety of different perspectives. In their critique of teaching narrowly conceived as a 'craft', as in some prescriptions from the government in England (Gove, 2010), Winch et al (2013, p 5) highlight the need to discriminate between common sense and good sense. They contend that the former is a 'conservative and potentially unreliable basis for professional judgement' and that 'good sense' decisions about teaching should be underpinned by reference points found in research.

As the final report of the inquiry (BERA and RSA, 2014b) argues, research-informed teacher education reaches further than promoting theoretical understanding in its own right. It also advocates evidence-based instruction that makes a practical contribution to the lives of young people. Furthermore, 'research literacy' not only empowers teachers to become autonomous evaluators and improvers of their work, but can also enhance professional identity.

MacBeath (2011) has argued, along similar lines, that programmes which prioritise experiential learning in the workplace without reference to research not only undermine the body of wisdom on teaching that has grown, but also fragment future knowledge, as new insights are more difficult to aggregate when learning is organised at the local level. Although experiential learning within the workplace is very important in helping teachers to develop their understanding of 'what works' in practice, learning from context alone can be limited as it ignores alternative (and potentially superior) approaches or solutions outside the immediate environment (Eraut, 2014).

The importance of research-based knowledge and research literacy to inform educational practice is clearly recognised in Finland and Singapore (Tatto, 2013) – two countries that score highly in international attainment comparative analysis tests. In Finland, there is a very close relationship between schools where students learn to teach and the universities (Kansanen, 2014). Indeed, teacher education is based on the idea of teacher-as-researcher of their own professional practice. In Singapore, research informs the design, structure and content of its teacher education programme and there is a strong emphasis on academic and pedagogical knowledge based on national and international research (Tatto, 2013).

However, as Tatto (2013) also indicates, it is difficult to make a causal link between high attainment of pupils and a research base for teacher education and, thus, the connection can only be inferred. Nonetheless, international and meta-studies would suggest that even if connections cannot be directly proven, they are often widely assumed in the literature on teacher education. For example, the Organisation for Economic Co-operation and Development (OECD) has claimed that in order to address the needs of lower achievers and in so doing, raise educational attainment, teachers will require a wide pedagogical repertoire that meets the individual needs of students, coupled with expertise in supporting students' meta-cognitive processes (OECD, 2012). As Mincu (2013, p 4) identifies, it is very difficult to see how teachers can acquire such a repertoire without research-based teacher education.

Diversification of research in teacher education

Over the years, research-informed teacher education has developed in different directions. In the Anglophone world, there has been a shift away from the study of the sub-disciplines of the study of education (eg, sociology, psychology and the history of education) to more pragmatic and applied forms of knowledge that seek to make a practical contribution (Furlong, 2013a). A particular focus for research-informed content in teacher education has been on pedagogical content knowledge (PCK) (Shulman, 1986), that is, the knowledge base of teaching that rests at the intersection of subject content and pedagogy, and the powerful influence of its application on student learning (eg, see Chiesa and Robertson's [2000] study on 'precision methods' in mathematics and Graham and Macaro's [2008] research on explicit strategies for teaching listening in foreign languages). Teacher education informed by research into PCK is of great significance given that Seidel and Shavelson's (2007) meta-study on the impact of different factors on student knowledge building uncovered that domain-specific learning, that is, how students develop and learn in specific subject areas, has the greatest effect size on student progress.

While a great deal of attention continues to be paid to research on PCK and effective teaching and learning strategies to inform 'evidence-based' practice, there has been some diversification away from a 'process-product approach', that is, the 'processes' that were considered reliable in achieving desired goals or 'products' (Hagger and McIntyre, 2000, pp 485-6). Teacher educationalists have problematised the concept that certain processes inevitably lead to desired goals due to the complexities of diverse educational settings and the particularity of beliefs and practices of individual teachers (Stuart and Tatto, 2000). In light of this knowledge, research in teacher education has had to become relevant to the context in which student teachers find themselves and take account of teachers' beliefs and values.

Practitioner enquiry and teacher research

Rather than focusing entirely on theory or research generated by others, practitioner enquiry is concerned with developing research skills in order to inform and develop practice and promotes active learning in context (Hardy and Rönnerman, 2011), where teaching is conceptualised as a 'problem to be solved' (Dickson, 2011, p 269). The purpose of practitioner enquiry is to generate knowledge *for* practice *from* practice, where the professional context acts as the site for enquiry (Cochran-Smith and Lytle, 2009). In this way, ownership and production of research shifts from the 'ivory tower of academe' to teachers or student teachers within their own contexts, who seek new insights into the processes of teaching and learning, effectively bridging the theory–practice divide (Burton et al, 2014). That is not to say that those who conduct practitioner enquiry do not engage with more substantive research from external sources or a larger knowledge base. Indeed, rigorous practitioner, or action research, is a cyclical process that systematically investigates the application of aspects from a wider knowledge base in a particular context. Cochran-Smith and Lytle (2009, p 94) present it as a hybrid of conceptual research and empirical research, enabling teachers to make decisions based on evidence.

Practitioner enquiry not only helps teachers to engage in and with research that is contextually applicable; it potentially has more far-reaching benefits. As Ross and Bruce (2012) established, teachers who conducted action research reported improved confidence in their professional abilities. Similarly, Dickson (2011) and Truxaw et al (2011) found that practitioner enquiry helped student teachers to develop their professional identity and perceptions of self-efficacy. Although teacher confidence cannot be directly equated with impact on student learning, in her systematic review of the impact of work-based professional learning, Cordingley (2013, p 1) established that enquiry-orientated learning and a focus on refining teaching and learning 'working towards aspirations for specific pupils side by side with theory' were key characteristics of effective continuing professional development (CPD). Similarly, Mincu (2013, p 10) claims that teachers who engage in onsite collaborative enquiry processes 'make a vital contribution to ensuring effective teaching and learning processes are in place and in building capacity for whole school improvement'. These studies demonstrate how teacher research may serve different purposes, ranging from the professional development of the individual to school improvement.

While action research is a typical form of practitioner enquiry, teacher research can may take on a multiplicity of forms. As Baumfield et al (2013) note, teacher research commonly involves a process of investigating questions that arise directly from classroom experience and can therefore fall in a middle ground between reflection and action research. Indeed, it is debatable whether reflective practice is a form of research in itself. For example, Richardson (1994) claims that Schön's (1983) notion of 'reflection-in-action' and its potential to improve practice has often been referred to as teacher research, whereas Burton et al (2014, p 150) argue that 'so-called evidence' generated from reflective practice is 'often anecdotal and derived from *ad hoc* experiences'. Nevertheless, reflective practice is frequently drawn on in teacher education as a gateway to research. Taking its origins in the work of Dewey (1933), and particularly influenced by the work of

Schön (1983, 1987), various typologies of reflective practice have been created for the teaching profession (eg, Calderhead and Gates, 2003; Moon, 2004; Pollard and Collins, 2005). These approaches prompt teachers to consider the goals and values that guide their work, how their own biographies may influence practice (Brookfield, 2002) and the critical exploration of the perspectives of different stakeholders in the workplace. On several teacher education courses (for both pre- and in-service teachers), the examination of alternative perspectives through reflective practice is used to scaffold critical engagement with research and theory. For example, the Masters in Teaching degree developed by the London Institute of Education continually involves students 'in a [conversational] discourse about their own learning and that of their peers [which then made] reference to relevant conceptual and theoretical frameworks' (Daly et al, 2004, p 104).

Innovative ways for integrating theory and practice

Some teacher educators (eg, Griffiths and Tann, 1992; Korthagen and Kessels, 1999) have reconceptualised the importance of theory with a 'big T', arguing that beginning teachers are likely to find this too abstract and difficult to make sense of and, indeed, that taking this conservative view of theory may even contribute to the further polarising of theory and practice. Korthagen and Kessels (1999) propose that attention should first be paid to theory with a 'small T', namely the exploration of students' personal and subjective reflections on teaching practice. It is only after personal theories are worked through that these should be linked with theoretical notions from a wider and more abstract knowledge base. In this way, learning to teach is based on a constructivist notion that it is a subject to be created rather than a 'ready-made' subject (Korthagen et al, 2006).

While reflective practice in different guises has gained widespread popularity as a 'research springboard', the Oxford Internship Scheme (McIntyre, 1990a), first developed in the 1980s, rejects 'more elaborated notions of experiential learning that emphasise "reflective practice", in which it is experience alone that constitutes the focus for reflection' (Burn and Mutton, 2013, p 2). Instead, the Oxford programme is designed to enable the integration of experiential learning and research-based knowledge, where school and university knowledge are interrogated in the light of each other, based on a model of 'research-informed clinical practice' (Burn and Mutton, 2013) and promoting 'practical theorising' (McIntyre, 1995). On this programme, beginning teachers are trained and supported to adopt research-informed practice rather than imitating experienced teachers or proceeding through trial and error. The purpose of this process is to enable the important 'interplay between the different kinds of knowledge that are generated and validated within the different contexts of school and university' (Burn and Mutton, 2013, p 1). The Oxford Internship Scheme presents teaching 'as a process of hypothesis-testing, requiring interpretation and judgement in action, rather than routinised application of learned repertoires' (Burn and Mutton, 2013, p 4). Similar 'research-informed clinical practice' schemes have been promoted and developed in Scotland, the United States, Australia, the Netherlands and Finland. For example, the University of Glasgow developed a clinical practice scheme that involved the cooperative working of university tutors and school mentors in a cluster of volunteer schools with sustained presence of university staff (Conroy et al, 2013). Together, university tutors, school mentors and student teachers were engaged in collaborative enquiry into authentic pedagogical problems. A full discussion of other schemes involving these and similar examples of research-informed clinical practice can be found in a review by Burn and Mutton (2013).

Issues and challenges for research in teacher education

As it has become apparent, the research element within and across teacher education programmes can take on a variety of forms. Within the confines of this chapter, we have drawn attention to an applied form of research (PCK), an evaluative form of research (practitioner enquiry) and innovative ways of integrating theory and practice, although there are several others. Within the university context, diversification of research types has led to deliberation about the most suitable content for teacher education programmes. There is debate among academics about whether to foreground the focus on more substantive forms of research, such as how children learn or subject knowledge, or to concentrate on PCK, practitioner research skills or the scholarship of reflective practice (Stuart and Tatto, 2000). There are also questions about the most appropriate times in a teacher's development for these foci and how they should be integrated with experiential learning (Stuart and Tatto, 2000). As Furlong (2013) notes, the field of education has had difficulties in establishing itself as a 'discipline' due to the diversity of areas with which it is concerned. While such variety can be considered as healthy as it enables programmes to 'evolve, change, and develop out of the local context and in response to the perceived needs of the time and place' (Stuart and Tatto, 2000, p 511), in some quarters this can lead to uncertainties about which type of research to foreground, especially if theoretical approaches are questioned by policy makers and the time afforded to research-informed elements is restricted.

Indeed, higher education institutions across the UK face considerable tensions between supporting their students to meet teachers' standards or competences, a prerequisite for qualified teacher status, which are demonstrated in practice, and developing a professional understanding linked to wider perspectives (see Chapter Nine, this volume). These difficulties are further compounded when, as in England, only a third of postgraduate course time is spent in the university. As Beauchamp et al (2013) note though, even on such courses, most university initial teacher education provision has continued to combine perspectives from educational research with meeting the imperatives of making programmes practical and relevant, making use of practitioner enquiry or action research modes of learning.

However, even when research in teacher education is used to provide helpful explanations or a theoretical underpinning for defined standards (Hagger and McIntyre, 2000) and universities organise research-informed teaching in this way, there is potential to focus on educational research that marries with the current political agenda and, by consequence, to dismiss alternative perspectives. In fact, what counts as 'valid' educational research in and for teacher education is part of a larger and highly contested issue.

For example, since 2010 the Department for Education in England (DfE) has been lending high levels of support to quasi-experimental research through its investment in randomised controlled trials (RCTs). The purpose of the RCT is to establish which teaching strategies are most likely to deliver the best results for 'closing the gap' between the educational attainment of young people from contrasting socioeconomic backgrounds (DfE, 2013b). The DfE, however, is less enthusiastic about other types of research that may contribute to educational understanding, as is evident in the former Secretary of State for Education, Michael Gove's, critique of the 'ideologically driven theory' (Gove, 2013) promoted by schools of education in universities.

Across all universities in the UK, the Research Excellence Framework (REF) also influences what counts as 'good' research. The REF assesses the quality of research to inform allocation of research funding in UK higher education institutions 'in terms of originality, significance and rigour' (REF, 2014) and to provide research benchmarking information. In funding terms, the emphasis is on research that is internationally excellent. Small-scale, practitioner-orientated research, which may well have limited international excellence or impact, is simply unable to compete with more 'scientific' types of research within this framework and is thus less likely to receive acclaim and recognition. So while practitioner-orientated enquiry is promoted within teacher education programmes for the sake of professional development, teacher educator professionalism and improvements in teacher education, it is less likely to be recognised as 'high quality' by a wider audience within the university sector.

The ramifications of the REF can also impact negatively on research capacity building in university schools of education (Christie et al, 2012). The fact that there are winners and losers of research funding has been recognised to affect the ways in which teacher educators engage in scholarship (Jones et al, 2011). Where funds are absent, this may hinder or even sever links between teaching and research, denying opportunities for teacher educators to undertake research as an essential part of their professional development (Murray et al, 2009).

As the final report of the BERA and RSA inquiry (BERA and RSA, 2014b) underlines, research-informed teaching may be less prevalent if the teacher educators and mentors teaching on initial teacher education programmes lack research experience. Teacher educators in the UK tend to be former school teachers, who by consequence of their career routes, have often not acquired research expertise before arrival to university posts (Harrison and McKeon, 2008). The constant pressure to develop programmes that are highly practically orientated means that many universities are more interested in recruiting staff with 'professional rather than academic capital' (Furlong, 2013a, p 143) and that some universities are less likely to develop or invest in the academic profiles of their staff when neither government directives nor inspection frameworks pay tribute to research (Furlong, 2013a). According to Menter et al (2010b), only one third of staff working as academics in departments or faculties of education in the UK were returned research active in the Research Assessment Exercise in 2008 (the predecessor to the REF). There may therefore be a gulf between educational research and those who 'mobilise' or teach this knowledge, as highlighted by Nelson and O'Beirne (2014, p 36), when they call for more and better brokerage between the producers and users of research through a centrally coordinated 'knowledge mobilisation infrastructure'.

The next section of this chapter illustrates how the type of research promoted *in* teacher education has been strongly influenced by research *on* teacher education, in particular in the area of how teachers learn and develop knowledge. We will see that research *on* teacher education also faces challenges, particularly in providing answers to policy questions about which modes of preparation are likely to 'create' the most effective teachers.

Research *on* teacher education

Research *on* teacher education is of interest to both policy makers and teacher educators. Policy makers are concerned with finding evidence for justifying a particular model of teacher preparation at the macro level and therefore seek out research that is able to establish cause–effect relationships between pre-service training and teacher effectiveness (measured in terms of pupil attainment). However, research of this nature is very difficult to conduct and, as yet, is still to provide clear-cut findings about such relationships.

One of the major reasons for this lies with issues of methodology. Most research on teacher education in the UK has adopted interpretive or practitioner enquiry genres (Menter et al, 2010b) and is thus similar to the type of research conducted *in* teacher education. Commenting from a United States perspective, Borko et al (2007, p 8) also note the predominance of these approaches and explain their popularity by saying that they 'lend themselves to study the teaching and/or learning processes, a topic of deep interest to most teacher educators; in addition, studies within these genres often can be conducted by individual scholars and without external funding'. While this type of research has been helpfully applied at the micro level of teacher education to inform curriculum development, the challenge of aggregation has resulted in the absence of a coherent knowledge base that can be used to inform larger policy decisions (Tatto, 2013; Borko et al, 2007; Murray et al, 2009; Menter et al, 2010b).

Research on teacher education has tended to focus on understanding how teachers develop and acquire knowledge, and has explored the diversity of experiences in learning to teach. This body of knowledge has contributed to programme design and has been very influential on the types of research discussed earlier in the chapter.

How teachers learn and develop knowledge and the impact on programme design

Since the 1970s, there has been extensive research revealing the centrality of teachers' lives, beliefs and values in their practice and development. We know from this work (eg, Ball and Goodson, 2002; Goodson, 1991; Hagger and McIntyre, 2000; MacLure, 2001) that teachers' professional choices and actions frequently reflect the negotiation of their identities and values within structural parameters and that these are likely to vary in strength at different stages of their careers, depending on the strength of these factors. In light of this knowledge, teacher education has looked to support student teachers in their exploration of professional identities and sense of mission, providing them with opportunities not only to ask themselves what they and others consider to be important, but also to reflect on whether their actions mirror their beliefs (Korthagen, 2004). Teacher education programmes also seek to engage beginning teachers in developing a vision for teaching, or set of images, of 'the possible' (Feiman-Nemser, 2001, cited in Hammerness et al, 2005, p 386). While some beginning teachers need help in actualising an already identified teacher identity, others require support in undergoing a 'transformation of self in the endeavour to become, or change into, a teacher' (Hobson and Malderez, 2005, p 132).

The proliferation of reflective practice-orientated programmes, supported by conceptual models and 'reflective tools' such as critical incident analysis (see Tripp, 1994) and narrative enquiry for the purpose of professional development (Conle, 2000), can also be viewed as a response to research on how teacher biography may shape teacher behaviour. These approaches not only enable support tailored to individuals but also provide frameworks for navigating the emotionally charged experiences that we know are commonly encountered by beginning teachers (Hobson and Malderez, 2005; Hobson et al, 2006).

Parallel to the findings on the centrality of teachers as individuals, enquiry into teachers' professional learning has established the powerful impact of the social and cultural contexts in which knowledge is acquired and used (Feiman-Nemser, 2008; Timperley, 2008). As learning to become a teacher has been increasingly recognised as an active and constructive process in a 'community of practice' (Lave and Wenger, 1991), teacher education courses have supplemented their focus on knowledge *for* practice with attention to the development of knowledge *in* practice and *of* practice (Cochran-Smith and Lytle, 1999). Programmes have paid attention to the need for learning tasks *within* the practicum to be carefully graduated and the importance of allocated time for collaboration and dialogue with colleagues, mentors and expert teachers. When conditions allow for the latter, beginning teachers are able not only to reflect on their own practice, but also to access expert teachers' articulation of their decision making, 'making their tacit craft knowledge explicit' (Burn and Mutton, 2013, p 2).

In order to take full advantage of learning within a community of practice, teacher education has stressed the importance of creation of knowledge *of* practice (Cochran-Smith and Lytle, 1999), which is generated when classrooms and schools are treated as sites for enquiry and practice is evaluated and interpreted in light of larger social, cultural and political issues and the theory and research of others. In creating this practice–theory loop, theoretical study in teacher education maintains its relevance as it is explicitly linked to teachers' work (Hobson et al, 2006; Korthagen et al, 2006).

In addition to the study of teacher individuality and the impact of social and contextual factors on how teachers learn, scholars have also examined the nature of teacher expertise. The development of expertise has frequently been conceptualised in light of stage theories, whereby teachers progress over a period of time (of usually five to seven years) from being concerned with themselves, and learning the basic elements of the task, to gradually becoming more aware of issues related to students and student learning and developing the ability to respond appropriately in a variety of different situations (Berliner, 1994). Studies have established that more expert teachers also engage more frequently in meta-cognition (see Hammerness et al, 2002, cited in Hammerness et al, 2005). In view of this, programmes scaffold learning so that novice teachers can progress through the stages more rapidly and develop strong levels of meta-cognitive competence earlier than might otherwise be expected (Hammerness et al, 2005).

Research on teacher education has thus provided much knowledge that has helped to inform programme design. It has highlighted how teacher education must recognise that teachers themselves are the 'central actors' in their own development (Hagger and McIntyre, 2000), the necessity of creating courses that best support professional learning within a community of practice, and the need to scaffold learning in such a way that enables teachers to progress to the expert stage as early as possible.

Challenges in establishing an evidence base for teacher education

While the body of research discussed earlier has revealed much about how teachers learn and has helped to inform programme design at a micro level, it has, as indicated previously, been less successful in ascertaining the relative effectiveness and outcomes of different models of teacher education (Tatto, 2013). As Menter et al (2010b) established in their study of teacher education research in the UK, there is a distinct absence of research on teacher education that adopts experimental methods of enquiry that supports the evidence-based education movement. Although there have been some exceptions to this general picture – for example a study conducted by Tatto et al (2012), which established that top-performing countries relied on university-based teacher education with a strong emphasis on subject content, pedagogical content knowledge and carefully constructed links between theory and practice – a well-developed research infrastructure for studying the impact of particular practices in teacher preparation has yet to be established.

Cochran-Smith (2005a) explains that many of the problems here are related to the fact that there are difficulties in building a chain of evidence that links:

- teacher education and student learning;
- student learning and their practices in the classroom;
- practices of the teacher and how much their students learn.

However, Cochran-Smith (2002a, p 285) also argues in an earlier publication that questions about how to best prepare teachers can never be answered on the basis of research evidence alone, as such questions 'also have to do with ideas, values, and beliefs about teaching and learning ... and the purposes of education in a democratic society'. In spite of this philosophical argument and the difficulties in establishing a chain of evidence, Borko et al (2007) argue that the investigation of these relationships should now constitute the research agenda. They call for larger and more complex studies, which draw on multiple methods and take advantage of new technologies for processing and analysing larger datasets.

Grossman and McDonald (2008) point out, however, that many problems lie within the newness of the field, claiming that in comparison with research on teaching, which is now an 'adult' discipline, research on teacher education is still in its 'adolescence'. They stress the need to establish common conceptual frameworks with a common language and a universally recognised vocabulary in order to enable greater precision for describing and analysing teaching. Their views on language are concordant with those of Korthagen et al (2006), who suggest that the development of a shared professional language among teacher educators and researchers is a prerequisite for developing a knowledge base on which to build teacher education practices in different settings and countries.

Indeed, Korthagen et al (2006) conducted a meta-study in three different countries in order to establish common principles that underpin effective teacher education. Their work investigated the factors that best enable programmes to be responsive to the expectations, needs and practices of teacher educators and student teachers. From their findings, they established seven principles for student teacher learning and programme change in teacher education. They surmised that learning about teaching:

- involves continuously conflicting and competing demands;
- requires a view of knowledge as a subject to be created rather than as a created subject;
- requires a shift in focus from the curriculum to the learner;
- is enhanced through (student) teacher research;
- requires an emphasis on those learning to teach working closely with their peers;
- requires meaningful relationships between schools, universities and student teachers;
- is enhanced when the teaching and learning approaches advocated in the programme are modelled by the teacher educators in their own practice.

While such principles offer a helpful conceptual framework for future research, the teacher education community still has some way to go in developing a multi-methods and multidisciplinary research infrastructure with theoretical tools that are able to address the critical questions asked by policy makers.

Discussion

Research *in* teacher education, then, is able to greatly enhance course content in providing a wide professional knowledge base, assisting beginning and experienced teachers in making critically informed judgements and contributing to the development of broad pedagogical repertoires. The development of 'research literacy' (BERA and RSA, 2014b) enables teachers to enquire into and improve their own practice and can help to develop professional identity. The significant contribution of research-rich content and research literacy in teacher education is clearly recognised in the top-performing countries in educational attainment in the world (Tatto, 2013).

In spite of these compelling arguments, there are practical challenges in making research a high-status aspect of teacher education. The principal constraints in the UK are imposed when policy prioritises instrumental knowledge over a wider professional understanding. In Scotland and Northern Ireland, where there is a more collaborative and cooperative approach between universities and policy makers to teacher education, there are relatively strong commitments to research-rich teacher initial teacher education. In England, however, the absence of reference to research in the teachers' standards, and a policy drive to shift teacher preparation away from university-led programmes to more school-based programmes, render the status of research less stable. While, from a positive perspective, there is policy support for research within teaching schools' alliances, whereby research and development (R&D) constitutes one of the 'big six' responsibilities of teaching schools (NCTL, 2014a), and evidence-based practice based on the results from RCTs is promoted (DfE, 2013b), there are reasons to be concerned about the fragmentation of research knowledge in teacher education and the sidelining of the wide-ranging types of research that contribute to teacher understanding.

Although there is a commitment to research-rich pre-service teacher education in Scotland and Northern Ireland, the BERA and RSA (2014b) inquiry highlighted issues related to research-orientated CPD. The inquiry revealed that, in Scotland, teachers' experiences of CPD, and their engagement with research within this, are disjointed. Similarly, while there are clear references to reflective practice and research engagement expressed in the General Teaching Council for Northern Ireland's Code of Values and Professional Practice and Teacher Competence Framework, these have not yet been widely developed beyond initial teacher education (BERA and RSA, 2014b). Thus, there is work to be done in Scotland and Northern Ireland in making research engagement and literacy characteristics of teachers' lifelong learning.

Policy embodied in changing curriculum frameworks and 'quality assurance' measures also poses challenges to the prominence of research within teacher education in the UK. As Furlong (2013a) has highlighted, constantly changing national curricula for schools, revisions of teachers' standards and accountability measures that interfere with the detail of teacher education, create uncertainty within the teacher education community about what professional knowledge is and what research elements contribute to this. Accountability measures in England, where the outcomes of rigorous inspection procedures of ITE (which pay little concern to research activity) impact on the allocation of resources, may render research-rich teacher education and research building capacity as a lesser priority for some schools of education. All four nations of the UK, however, are affected by the necessity to deliver high-quality taught programmes, which has an impact on the way in which tutors are deployed. A report by the OECD (2014, p 73) uncovered that, in Wales, most staff 'were consumed with teaching responsibilities, leaving them with no flexibility to accommodate research'. The 2015 report on initial teacher education in Wales by Furlong (2015) focused very directly on the dearth of educational research in the institutions with responsibility for pre-service teacher education. Even in universities that invest in research excellence to raise prestige and reputation and to improve funding levels through the REF, there can be a 'dual economy of teaching and research and a corresponding dual labour market' (Menter et al, 2010b, p 122). Leitch (2009) note that in Northern Ireland, where there is 'a climate of openness between policy-maker and researcher communities' (p 355), the RAE created a gulf between research-active and 'not research-active' staff (p 358). Similarly, the Department of Education and Skills (2012) in the Republic of Ireland notes a lack of critical mass for research purposes and, in fact, recommends the merging of providers in order to enhance research-building capacity.

Conclusion

This chapter has demonstrated how both research *in* and *on* teacher education has much to offer those in the business of teacher preparation but that both types face a variety of challenges. Research-rich teacher education, in its variety of forms, ultimately supports teachers in making judicious decisions based on wide professional knowledge that are likely to contribute to improved outcomes for young people. The diversification of research has resulted in a compromise between theory and practice, with a commitment to both theoretical aspects of knowledge and to the desire to make a practical contribution to the field. Although the status of research in teacher education in the UK is strongly influenced by regional politics, unresolved questions about the precise nature of teacher knowledge among the academic community, and barriers in the way of research capacity building, make research-rich teacher education more vulnerable in the face of political scepticism about its value.

While the teacher education community has studied how teachers learn and develop (research *on* teacher education), and this has been helpful in informing programme design, there is an urgent need to research different modes of teacher education at the macro level, so that the sensible rationale for research-informed education can be further interrogated in light of empirical evidence.

This issue is particularly pertinent in a policy context where there is an emerging plethora of different preparation routes. Drawing on a domestic and international evidence base, the BERA and RSA inquiry has started the ball rolling here. However, if the so-called 'adolescent field' of teacher education is to grow up quickly and find its adult voice, investment is required in large-scale, longitudinal studies so that teacher preparation policy is informed by reliable datasets rather than politics and ideology.

But research of this nature requires substantial financial backing of a funding body that will need convincing of the research rationale, aims and strategy for this work – no mean feat in a period of economic austerity. In critical times, however, where teacher education has become a political football, these challenges need confronting head-on.

ELEVEN

Teacher education and higher education

Jean Murray

Introduction

In 1984, Alexander et al (1984, p xv) famously conceptualised pre-service or initial teacher education (ITE) as 'suspended between the worlds of school and higher education (HE)': 'One provides its raison d'etre and the occupational imperatives to which it is bound to respond, and the other the framework within which such responses must be located, and which has its own cultural and academic imperatives.'

Taylor (1983) conceptualised teacher education as 'Janus-faced', another dualistic conceptualisation, offering an even starker sense of difference and opposition between the two 'faces' of ITE – one looking towards the school and the other looking, in opposition, to the university.

Underlying this dualism around the two sites of learning in ITE is, of course, another dualism of theory/practice as separate and distinctive, primarily generated in and 'belonging to' only one location: theory as the knowledge domain of the university and practice as the domain of schools. As these authors from the 1980s pointed out, these constructions of dualism in the field of ITE were not new; they had characterised teacher education in England since its first establishment in the HE sector over a century previously (Dent, 1977); and in 1984, these dualisms clearly still had considerable validity and power as ways of conceptualising ITE and the contestations it then involved.

At the time of writing, in some ways both of these dualisms continue to be influential elements in the 'public discourses' of ITE (Popekwitz, 1987). They still, all too often, bring with them a sense of the two locations and the two types of knowledge traditionally associated with them as separate and distinctive domains, even though both schools and universities are, of course, involved in the common enterprise of educating high-quality teachers. This chapter argues that in some key ways these dualisms have been unhelpful continuities in ITE since 1984, and that they are also increasingly inaccurate and inappropriate for conceptualising the field. This is not least because they overlook significant changes in the knowledge domains of ITE and the often more integrated ways in which knowledge is generated in and across each location.

Yet it is also clear that, to some extent, these constructions of HE and school as separate and distinctive *locations* still reflect the common sense of ITE as it is currently structured in the majority of the United Kingdom (UK) and the Republic of Ireland (RoI). The experience of learning in the school workplace is still an essential element of all ITE courses. But most students and teacher educators involved in ITE across these five nations are still based primarily in higher education institutions (HEIs) of some kind and still work on programmes taught and validated within HE; most ITE students, especially in Scotland, the RoI and Northern Ireland, still spend the majority of their time in HE settings; and most of the teacher educators preparing them to be teachers are still employed within universities. For these groups, this location predominantly in HE means that they must have particular awareness of the imperatives of that sector, in addition to knowledge of the professional priorities and practices of the school sector.

But this is not solely an issue of HE as a *location* for ITE; it is more about the enduring legacies of the power and influence of HE and its domains of knowledge. Even in England where, as Chapter Four indicates, there are emerging school-led ITE cultures in which 'the university' is not directly involved and may be tacitly or explicitly positioned as 'other', the discourses and practices of HE still have some influence, not least through the 'apprenticeship of observation' (Lortie, 1975, p 61), which school-based teacher educators will have experienced during their own ITE. Those involved in teacher education, then, are therefore all influenced by at least some of the cultural, social and epistemological imperatives of the HE sector, at the same time as they attend to the multiple demands of the school sector for ITE.

This chapter focuses in the main on the HE sector as the location for part of ITE; it also analyses the 'theory' of ITE or its research base as part of the knowledge traditionally claimed by the sector. In this sense, the chapter may seem to work with the dualisms outlined above, but it also attempts to deconstruct them and to argue that overlaying and alongside their often misleading senses of continuity, there are now distinct changes to the traditional knowledge domains of ITE and to the sense of two separate and distinctive types of knowledge within them. These changes make it increasingly difficult and inappropriate to talk in dualistic terms.

In looking across all five nations, this analysis also shows the commonalities and continuities of 30 years ago breaking up as teacher education becomes increasingly diversified, certainly by national policy and provision, but also by type of university and by profile of education within it – and at the level of individual agents in the field – also by habitus and affinities (Bourdieu, 1987). This fragmentation has resulted in increasingly divisive and intensive manifestations of the discourses, practices and modes of knowledge in teacher education, which now play out differently in the structures and cultures of HE and in the lives of those who study and work in teacher education in the five nations.

A recent, seminal book by Furlong (2013a) entitled *Education: An anatomy of the discipline* presents an analysis of the historical and contemporary instantiations of education as a discipline within the universities of the UK. The book includes detailed commentary on teacher education since Furlong (2013a, p 4) argues that 'as a discipline, education has always been dominated by its involvement with teacher education ... the field as a whole has been profoundly shaped by its engagement with professional preparation'. Rather than repeating many of the important arguments made in that book, this chapter draws on it and other sources to discuss the impact that changes in the specific relationships between teacher education and HE have had on institutions and individuals between 1984 and 2014.

The chapter structure is as follows: the first section offers a conceptual framework for understanding the differing ways in which teacher education is located in HEIs – predominantly, but not exclusively, in the university sector – across the five nations under discussion in this book. Broad themes identified and discussed here include:

- the differentiated status of teacher education as a field within the HE sector;
- the changing institutional contexts;
- 'turns' to the practical and to the university;
- the impact of research intensivity, including the research audits in the UK;
- the nature of research in and on ITE (picking up on themes in Chapter Ten).

The chapter then gives brief examples of how the fragmentation of the field has affected teacher educators, arguing that their work has become increasingly heterogeneous, under-valued in some universities, but 're-valued' in some of the more managerialist and entrepreneurial parts of the HE sector.

Conceptualising teacher education within the higher education sector

As Chapters Four to Eight show, all HEIs in the UK and RoI have experienced extensive changes since 1984 during times of profound social change and economic cycles of 'boom and bust'. These social and economic reconfigurations have often triggered reform of the HE sector. In the RoI, for example, the economic rollercoaster brought a time of unprecedented economic prosperity in the 1990s and early 2000s – the era of 'the Celtic Tiger' – but has been followed by severe austerity measures after the global economic crisis of 2007/08, during which HE structures for teacher education have been subject to radical reform.

During the past 30 years, drives for higher levels of student participation in HE, alongside global and national pressures for excellence, have led to an expanded and seemingly more diverse university sector (Barnett, 2000, 2003; Morley, 2003). These factors in combination with neoliberal performativity regimes have resulted in larger and more diversified institutions, increased marketisation, far-reaching structural and cultural changes and more intensive managerialist practices, including extensive audits, and new, corporate governance structures. Changing employment practices in HE have also brought a 'casualisation' of some of the academic workforce and the introduction of 'teaching-only' contracts in which being an active researcher is no longer seen as an essential part of academic work.

The HE sector in the UK and RoI is highly differentiated in an essentially hierarchical system, with universities occupying relative positions of dominance, subordination or equality in relation to one another. These positions relate not only to the current forms of the institutions, but also to their histories through the processes of institutional sedimentation (Kirk, 1986) over time. While in many ways the HE system has certainly become more diversified (Furlong, 2013a), global quests for excellence have provided further reinforcement for many of the traditional signifiers around institutional status – often in the same spaces as the diversification agenda. For example, the research 'excellence' and 'productivity' of each institution are often key parts of the methodologies used to draw up international and national league tables. This has led many universities to place increasing significance on research activity and quality (Stromquist, 2002), particularly in countries such as the UK, Australia and New Zealand where research audits occur regularly. It is therefore possible to argue that, alongside diversification, an emphasis on entrepreneurialism and more corporate visions of the sector, the power of the elite, and a traditional and research-led model of the university persists, alongside an often enhanced status around 'elite' fields of activity and traditional disciplines, particularly those in science, technology, engineering and mathematics areas.

Internally, HEIs are, of course, far from homogeneous entities, not least because of the ways in which the disciplines and fields within them reflect differing epistemologies, discourses and practices, both historical and contemporary. Teacher education across the UK and RoI has particular histories of gendered power relations (Maguire, 1994), with the majority of provision growing not within the traditional university sector with all its elite academic associations, but within the social and intellectual 'poverty' of the normal schools or teacher training colleges of the late 19th and early 20th centuries (see Chapter One; also Dent, 1977; Heward, 1993; Coolahan, 2004a). Consequences of these 'lowly' origins include perceptions of the field's reduced status and marginality within the university sector and its struggles for legitimacy (Hencke, 1978; Aldrich, 2002; McCulloch, 2011).

In some research-intensive and 'old' universities, education in general – and teacher education in particular – is still not highly esteemed in relation to other traditional disciplines (Coolahan, 2004a); indeed, in some elite institutions, teacher education may still be positioned as 'a backwater of the mainstream of universities' (Hencke, 1978, p 10). But, in contrast, in many HE colleges and newer universities, teacher education is often highly valued as an important part of the core business (and financial health) of education departments, or even of the institution as whole (Universities UK, 2014). As Furlong (2013a) comments on the situation in the UK and Hyland (2012) on that in the RoI, for many universities, ITE provision may be seen as a 'cash-cow', subsidising other activities and institutional structures.

Other types of vocational courses for public sector work, including social work and nursing, are now located in HE where they also face explicit government regulation and multiple, sometimes conflicting, imperatives from the university and their professional fields. Nevertheless, as Furlong et al (2000, p 3) identify in discussing reforms between 1984 and 2000, 'perhaps because of the historically tenuous hold that teacher education has had within teacher education (Gardner, 1996), the scope and depth of the reforms were particularly strong in our own field'.

At the time of writing, the regulations and reforms faced by HE-based teacher education across the five nations, but particularly in England, are often more radical and ideological in their forms and intents than those faced by other professional fields (Browne, 2013).

Teacher education is conceptualised in this chapter as a professional field, set within the general discipline of education, instantiated within academic organisational units that are variously termed faculties, departments or schools of education (the latter term is used for the remainder of this chapter). These schools are specific territories within HEIs; they are the physical, structural and ideological spaces where the discourses, practices and knowledge modes of the discipline of education in general, and of the field of teacher education in particular, are instantiated; they are the sites of struggle where accommodations are made and resistances forged between the missions and imperatives of the wider university and the specific practices of teacher education. Becher and Trowler (2002, p 5) argue that there are complex inter-relationships between the *territories* of a discipline (or field) and its organisational structures and modes of knowledge and the distinctive and clearly identifiable patterns of behaviours that create disciplinary subcultures and disciplinary-specific identities for academics (the *tribes*). Following this argument, changes in the territories of ITE are likely to bring changes to the patterns of behaviour and identity found in the tribe of teacher educators working within them.

The institutions currently offering ITE programmes in the five nations range from long-established, research-intensive universities, well placed in international league tables, to teaching-intensive universities and colleges. The latter group may have good national and professional reputations but are often still striving to establish their place in the 'marketplace' of the modern university sector. As described in Chapters Four to Eight, ITE in Northern Ireland is offered by two universities and two higher education colleges; in Scotland, ITE is located in eight universities, most of them 'old' or 'pre-1992'. The only routes into teaching in both these nations are through studying at a university or university college. In Ireland, following the Sahlberg Review (Sahlberg et al, 2012), 19 state-funded HE institutions providing ITE are to be reduced to 17 and consolidated into six regional clusters; here an independent company, Hibernia College, also provides online ITE as an alternative – and controversial – route into teaching. In Wales, following the first Furlong Review (Furlong et al, 2006a), six universities currently collaborate to form three regional 'centres' for ITE. In England, 70 universities currently offer ITE courses, the majority in the 'new' or 'post-1992' university sector, but there are also an increasing number of alternative routes outside HE or with tenuous relationships to it (these include school-centred initial teacher training [SCITT] centres, School Direct and Teach First). Wales also has a limited number of alternative routes.

Behind these summaries and the different patterns of current provision, however, lie many changes at various times in the last 30 years; it is these changes and the ways in which they have impacted on teacher education in HE that are the focus of the next section.

Patterns of institutional, social and cultural changes: 1984–2014

Institutional volatility and academic drift

In 1984, as Alexander et al (1984) describe, teacher education institutions in the UK were to be found on either side of the 'binary line' that divided the traditional universities from the polytechnics, institutes and colleges under public sector governance. In the RoI, some teacher education was also located in universities as well as in colleges of education. While there were a number of programmes, usually at postgraduate level for secondary school teachers in the traditional universities, the majority of ITE students across all five nations in 1984 studied to become teachers in teacher training colleges or other public sector institutions.

Alexander et al (1984, p xviii) refer to 'the challenge of unprecedented institutional change' in ITE in the UK between 1963 and 1984, change that had had a considerable impact on both organisational arrangements and institutional cultures. Since 1984, teacher education has experienced further institutional turbulence, driven by shifts in national policy for HE, demographic shifts in pupil numbers and teacher demand levels, specific changes to teacher education – often government imposed – and the impact of national research audits.

Many of the HEIs providing teacher education programmes have been caught up in the processes of 'academic drift' (Pratt, 1997) or 'universitisation' (Menter et al, 2006). These processes have caused considerable structural changes to institutions, sometimes involving mergers or other types of enforced institutional collaborations. These changes have occurred at different times in each nation. In Scotland, after the rationalisation of the teacher education colleges in the 1970s and 1980s, mergers between the surviving colleges and universities were a distinctive feature of the 1990s. In Northern Ireland and the RoI, as Chapters Five and Eight describe, from the 1970s to the 1990s many teacher education institutions experienced fewer mergers and hence less overt disruption than this. But in both countries, recent policy recommendations have meant considerable changes, either already implemented or in prospect soon.

In England and Wales, changing demographics in the 1970s and early 1980s triggered a sudden reduction in ITE numbers, profound institutional turbulence and the consequent closure or merger of large numbers of teacher education colleges (Hencke, 1978). This left the majority of teacher education provision in England in the public sector as diversified HEIs or polytechnics (Alexander et al, 1984).1 The 'academic drift' of those institutions meant that many became the 'new' universities of the 1992 onwards, after the abolition of the 'binary line' between the public sector HEIs and the 'old' universities.

The impact of demographics and teacher demand on ITE institutions has also been an important factor in other nations. Recent examples in the UK include the reduction in student teacher numbers in Scotland in the first decade of the 21st century, which caused institutional turbulence and staff losses (Menter, 2011b), and in Wales, the combination of changes in teacher demand levels and the results of the Furlong Review of 2006, which brought a round of mergers or enforced collaborations for the schools of education.

Reorganisations resulting from internal institutional volatility have also been significant in each nation; these have taken some schools of education from being single-discipline, organisational units to becoming part of large, multidisciplinary faculties or colleges. As Menter (2011b, p 299) comments on the situation in Scotland in particular, mergers whether internal and external often bring 'the reduction of the visibility and prominence of teacher education as a distinctive element of public provision'. In a curious twist on this idea of reduced visibility, however, the 'teacher training college' as the location for ITE is remarkably persistent in the imagination of the public, press and government alike. In 2010, for example, at a time when all HE-based ITE in England was located in the university sector, Michael Gove, then Secretary of State for Education, promised to 'reform teacher training to shift trainee teachers out of college [sic] and into the classroom' (Gove, 2010, p 6). The UK press also frequently uses the term (see, for example, *Daily Mail*, 2012; *The Daily Telegraph*, 2013). It is intriguing to consider what the longevity of this anachronistic term says about public perceptions of the status of teacher education and its under-recognised – or less visible – place within the university sector.

Turning to the practical: university responses

All schools of education in the UK now compete in various ways for internal and external funding to ensure their continuing economic viability. In teacher education the main source of such funding is usually government-funded programmes for pre- and in-service education. As Chapter Four describes, in England, this has become an increasingly competitive and unstable 'marketplace'. The situation is much less 'market-led' in the three other UK nations, but in all of them such government funding underpins – to varying degrees – the financial health of many schools of education (BERA and UCET Working Group on Education Research, 2012). A similar situation exists in the RoI.

Threats to income derived from pre-service funding, then, have major implications for the economic viability of many schools and for the maintenance of their range of activities, including postgraduate degrees and educational research. In England, for example, as Chapter Four describes, it is feared that School Direct will threaten the financial stability of schools of education and their institutional abilities to plan strategically (McNamara and Murray, 2013). In current policy contexts, then, meeting all professional requirements for ITE, ensuring good student 'outcomes' and complying with all relevant regulation and quality assurance mechanisms are vital for universities across the five nations to maintain the income flows from ITE provision.

ITE is often used as a policy lever to address concerns about the quality of school education, as measured by international comparative surveys such as the Programme for International Student Assessment (PISA). In response to this imperative, the 'practicum turn' in teacher education (Mattson et al, 2011) has been a noted feature of recent teacher education policy internationally in the last decade. As Groundwater-Smith (2011, p ix) articulates, this 'practicum turn' has involved exploring 'professional practice knowledge and the ways in which our understandings impact upon the design and enactment of ... "the practicum curriculum"'.

Faced with the need to accommodate this 'turn', universities have engaged in various forms of knowledge generation on/into practice, as part of their changing teacher education provision; this has, however, played out differently across various countries and institutional settings. In some countries, it has involved the explicit rejection of the theory/practice dualism and of 'theory into practice' models through attempts to integrate knowledge generation *across* and *between* schools and HE, drawing on the relevant knowledge and expertise located within each of those sites. In Finland and some institutions in the UK and Australia, for example, strong and effective models of collaborative partnership in ITE have been developed to ensure that programmes are integrated across schools and universities using models of 'research-informed clinical practice' (Burn and Mutton, 2013). In such approaches, research has clear relevance to inform the workplace learning of student teachers while they are on practicum in schools.

In other settings in Australia and the United States, the 'practicum turn' has become a 'practice turn' (Reid, J., 2011), including the exploration of how practice-related skills for eventual use in the workplace might be explicitly taught in the university (Grossman et al, 2008; Reid, J., 2011). And in the RoI, Conway et al (2013) have focused on how what they term 'learningplace [sic] practices' can generate new knowledge and forms of integrated pedagogies across schools and universities for students on practicum. Key aspects of all these initiatives have been to make a 'practicum or practice turn' that focuses on student teacher learning in schools as 'practice', generating new forms of research-informed knowledge in the process.

In England, as Chapter Four discusses in more detail, placing increased focus on school partnerships and on the practicum has involved a 'turn to the practical' (Furlong and Lawn, 2010, p 6, quoting Hoyle, 1975) and a distinct change in the epistemologies of ITE. Here recent governments – of all political persuasions – have worked to change the control and locus of teacher education from HE to schools, around a predominantly practical, relevant and school-led curriculum framework. There is an unquestioning belief that gaining more experience in schools by extending the practicum[2] will automatically lead to better-quality learning for pre-service teachers. Despite the importance of research-informed knowledge in ITE, the revised teacher standards focus on 'teachers' behaviour, rather than on their attitudes and their intellectuality' (Evans, 2011, p 851) and contain very little explicit reference to teachers' engagement with (and in) research (see also Chapter Nine). These standards – and the designation of teaching as a simple 'craft' in policy pronouncements (Gove, 2010) – exemplify the impoverished constructions of teacher knowledge and the processes of learning to teach, which the 'turn to the practical' has brought to ITE policy and some practices in England. In these visions, there is often a devaluation of the overall place of universities in supporting teacher learning (McNamara and Murray, 2013) and of research-informed knowledge, still frequently mis-characterised as irrelevant 'theory'.

The 'turn to the practical' has also occurred across the other countries of the UK (Beauchamp et al, 2013), albeit in different and less extreme forms than in England. Scotland has certainly experienced something of a 'practical turn' (Menter, 2011b), which has also involved the introduction of standards across all phases of teacher education (see Chapter Nine). But the Scottish standards, unlike those in England, balance this 'turn' by specifically referring to research being used 'to challenge and inform professional practice' (GTCS, 2012a, p 18). They also ask teachers to 'engage in practitioner enquiry to inform pedagogy, learning and subject knowledge; lead and participate in collaborative practitioner enquiry' (GTCS, 2012b, p 10). Here again, there is evidence of more integrated forms of teacher knowledge developing during ITE.

These standards were followed by a call for enhanced school–university partnerships in the Donaldson Report (2011) (see Chapter Six). While that same review acknowledged the importance of the 'craft' components of teaching, it also stated that these must be 'based upon and informed by fresh insights into how best to meet the increasingly fast pace of change in the world which our children inhabit' (2011, p 5). In terms of the practicum, it went on to state:

> Simply advocating more time in the classroom as a means of preparing teachers for their role is therefore not the answer to creating better teachers.... The nature and quality of that practical experience must be carefully planned and evaluated and used to develop understanding of how learning can best be promoted in sometimes very complex and challenging circumstances. (Donaldson, 2011, pp 4-5)

In other parts of the report, the practicum was also clearly linked to research as a 'site for experimentation' in 'well researched innovation' by 'research aware teachers' (p 102) and providing 'the opportunity to use practice to explore theory and examine relevant research evidence' (p 90).

The generation of sets of standards has also been a feature of teacher education in Wales. Here, teacher education policy was closely linked to that in England until devolution in 1999, but since that date there has been considerable policy diversification (see Chapter Seven; Beauchamp et al, 2013) including in the teacher standards. In Northern Ireland, where ITE policy has long been distinctive, there are a set of teacher competences but the rationale for these describes the profession as activist and reflective and emphasises research (see

Chapter Five). In Ireland, the Teaching Council's emphasis on revised Codes of Professional Conduct for Teachers has similarly been seen as part of a shift towards the practical, in the perception of many (Conway and Murphy, 2013), moving ITE further from HEI autonomy to professional control and the domination of teacher education by professional norms and practices (see Chapter Eight). As discussed below, however, in Northern Ireland, the RoI and Scotland, these 'turns to the practical', have been counterbalanced by 'turns to the university' and the emergence of new and more integrated forms of teacher knowledge in ITE.

The university turn: teacher education moving further into HE?

At the same time – and often in the same HE spaces or 'territories' – as these 'turns to the practical' are occurring in differentiated ways across the five nations, there have also been consolidations in the position of ITE as it is located within the university sector. This is termed here 'the university turn', and it too has brought epistemological changes.

One common element in a 'university turn' across all five countries, as in most European Union states, was the Bologna Process. This culminated in the Bologna Accord of 1999, which formed a European HE Area with a common qualifications framework in which between 90 and 120 ECTS (European Credit Transfer and Accumulation System) were normally needed to satisfy the requirements for a Masters qualification. This meant that many one-year postgraduate ITE programmes in the UK were re-validated to give credits towards the attainment of a Masters-level qualification. Masters-level qualifications are important signifiers of the value of the research-based knowledge traditionally associated with HE. This level of qualification in ITE involves more time in the university and more sustained student teacher involvement in the development of research literacy, the use of existing research to inform practice and active engagement in personal research (BERA and RSA, 2014b); in short, the depth and breadth of student engagement in the research-rich environments of the HE sector increases. ITE provision at Masters level, then, signifies national commitments to strengthening the 'academic' and 'cognitive' elements of ITE (DEL, 2014, p 44).

The strongest examples of changes brought by the 'university turn' in ITE are to be found in the RoI, where the majority of ITE is to be relocated to the university sector (from colleges of education) and all teacher education programmes are in the process of being reconfigured and extended, with undergraduate primary teacher education becoming a four-year course and all postgraduate provision (both primary and secondary) extended to two years and validated at Masters level. Here there is clear influence from the Continental European policy of countries such as Finland and Portugal where all ITE is already at Masters level, and Norway and the Netherlands, which have made significant policy moves in this direction. The ITE curriculum in the RoI retains emphases on the distinctive knowledge base of teaching to be acquired in the university, including focus on the four traditional educational disciplines of sociology, psychology, history and philosophy, but it also includes practice-focused research and teacher inquiry within the new programmes.

In Scotland, teacher education policy has also taken a 'university turn', albeit of a different kind. With ITE consistently based in universities since the 1990s, the Donaldson Review gave further importance to the role of the HE sector in ITE as 'central to building the kind of twenty-first century profession which this Report believes to be necessary' (2011, p 104). But Donaldson (2011, p 88, emphasis added) recommended undergraduate ITE degrees that 'combine in-depth academic study in areas *beyond* education with professional studies and development [which] involve staff and departments beyond those in schools of education'.

The schools of education have therefore needed to engage far more with other disciplines, revising their programmes to become more diversified and, in some cases, to include some five-year ITE Masters qualifications.

Teacher education policy in Northern Ireland seems to be evolving in the same European-influenced direction as the RoI. Recent policy statements (DEL, 2014, p 38) have recommended the extension of the Post Graduate Certificate of Education (PGCE) to two years, resulting in a Masters degree in teaching. The same review stated that all teacher education needed 'to be strengthened academically and cognitively. Provision has not yet been sufficiently infused with the intellectual power which university involvement in teacher education makes possible. That intellectual power derives from the universities' research activities' (DEL, 2014, p 44).

In Wales, the recent Tabberer Review (2013, pp 24-25) recommended that the research element of ITE within universities be strengthened as current provision gave it too low a status. The Masters in Educational Practice (MEP), introduced for newly qualified and early career teachers, in response to perceived shortcomings in ITE and induction provision, was a three-year part-time programme (see Chapter Seven). It had a strong emphasis on professional enquiry and was focused around a series of government-determined learning areas, closely related to practice and national priorities for schooling, and supported by university-led online learning materials and in-school mentoring. This initiative shows considerable potential to form new and integrated forms of teacher knowledge, but whether or not it can be seen as part of a 'university turn' for continuing professional development (CPD) in Wales is still open to question, not least because the future of the programme is uncertain and its impact limited by lower than anticipated participation rates.

Although much official English policy does advocate the importance of research in teacher education and schooling, many of these statements omit or de-emphasise the contribution of the university (Beauchamp et al, 2014) and funnel a considerable proportion of research funding to the teaching schools networks. England has certainly not made the kinds of clear and consistent 'university turns' for Masters-level study– with all that those 'turns' signify about teacher knowledge and the processes of learning to teach – found in the other four nations. Although elements of the PGCE have now been validated at Masters level, repeated calls over time for the course to become a two-year full Masters qualification have gone unanswered. Now, as Chapter Four shows, a recent review of teacher education (DfE, 2015 – the Carter Review) has suggested that student teachers should be much better informed about the option of gaining a teaching qualification (QTS) only through assessment against the Standards and without studying for a PGCE or indeed any other professional qualification offered by HEIs. The findings of this review reflect the contested place of HE in ITE and the dominant constructions of knowledge for teaching as practical and focused around the immediate demands of contemporary practice in schools. Despite this, most university providers of ITE – and some school-led providers – in England have maintained a strong commitment to combining perspectives from educational research with meeting the official imperatives of providing the required relevant and practical programmes.

Mention should also be made here of the CPD provision at Masters level offered in England before 2011 and a pilot initiative to set up a practice-focused Masters in Teaching and Learning (MTL) for newly qualified teachers, which was derailed by the outcome of the 2010 General Election. This scheme, implemented by both universities and schools, had the potential to offer research-informed perspectives on practice. Despite the results of the British Educational Research Association and Royal Society of Arts review (BERA and RSA, 2014b) reiterating the importance and effectiveness of research in teacher education and many policy pronouncements supporting this idea in theory (see, for example, DfE, 2015), there are few signs of M-level provision through either ITE or CPD being offered in the foreseeable future in England.

Growing research intensivity, research audits and their effects

Historically, across the UK – and RoI – there have been close relationships between educational research and teacher education provision, particularly ITE (Furlong, 2013a). Schools in old, research-intensive universities are more likely to have diversified income streams because of their research status (BERA and UCET Working Group on Education Research, 2012; Furlong, 2013a), with additional funding coming, for example, from national and international students on Masters or doctoral programmes and more core research funding. These schools have different positions in teacher education, since less dependence on government funding for pre- and in-service programmes means more autonomy and more choice around future actions (Furlong, 2013a). Additionally, as specified above, many universities now place increasing significance on research 'excellence' and 'productivity' as parts of the methodology used to draw up league tables (Stromquist, 2002). This is a particular factor in countries where research audits occur regularly.

Part of the 'university turn' in teacher education and a very significant factor in prompting social and cultural changes in the schools of education in the UK has then been the effects of the quinquennial, national research audits on research and knowledge related to ITE. These audits have become what Gilroy and McNamara (2009, p 322) describe as 'a key feature of university life in the last twenty years'. The various audits, once known as Research Assessment Exercises (RAEs) but now as the Research Excellence Framework (REF), conducted since 1986, have brought epistemological changes in education as a discipline, as well as varying consequences for teacher education research and for schools of education (Gilroy and McNamara, 2009; Oancea, 2010; Furlong, 2013a).

Historically, there was little sustained research activity, beyond practitioner action research and curriculum development, in the public sector institutions from which the schools of education in new universities developed (Fish, 1995). But when they became part of universities – whether in 1992 in England and Wales or through the 1990s in Scotland – the newly (re)formed schools of education had to pay immediate attention to the economic and cultural imperatives of the university sector, making distinct changes in their communal cultures and priorities. This included the need to increase levels of research productivity in order to participate in the RAE of 1992, the first in which they could be included. For the new universities, there was a degree of optimism about the financing of their future research capacity building (HEFCE, 1997).

In the subsequent RAE (1996), the schools of education in the new universities demonstrated an increase of more than 40% in submissions, to the extent that the 'fledgling research cultures' they had created (Bassey and Constable, 1997, p 3) outnumbered the submissions from schools of education in the old university sector. The results and the funding formula of the 2001 RAE, however, meant that between 2001 and 2008 only one school of education in a new university in England received any core research funding at all. As new universities already had lower institutional baselines for research engagement, this left many institutions with large ITE programmes without funding to develop their research and had particular consequences for teacher education and its knowledge bases.

The 2008 RAE was a more selective and strategic exercise in which fewer education staff were submitted in comparison with previous audits; this was in part as a consequence of revised criteria for research excellence and a changed funding formula privileging 'internationally excellent' research. This increasing pressure meant that many of the practitioner research studies, traditionally undertaken by teacher educators, were excluded from the exercise. The RAE Panel for Education stated that, while some other areas of education research showed increased strength in terms of quality and quantity of submissions, teacher education research was 'less strongly represented than previously' (HEFCE, 2009, p 2).

This RAE also left schools of education in each nation in different positions in terms of education research. In Wales, the position was very poor as none of the schools of education engaged in teacher education received research funding, while in Northern Ireland only two out of four teacher education providers did. The position in Scotland was much stronger as all the schools of education in the 'old' university sector achieved highly (Menter, 2011b). In England, where only 25% of the eligible schools of education offering ITE entered the RAE at all, the results were predictably dominated by old universities, but with 'pockets' of research excellence found in some new universities with large teacher education programmes.

After these mixed results, research capacity-building projects were funded in Wales (the Welsh Education Research Network – WERN) and in the North West of England, the Teacher Education Research Network (TERN). Across Northern Ireland and the RoI, the research element within the Standing Conference on Teacher Education, North and South (SCoTENS) network performed similar networking and capacity-building functions for teacher education research. All of these projects were influenced by a major Scottish initiative, the Applied Educational Research Scheme (AERS), which ran between 2004 and 2008. Funding for research capacity building on these models has not been sustained, however (Murray et al, 2012). All these capacity-building programmes happened alongside the Teaching and Learning Research Programme (TLRP), the Economic and Social Research Council's largest ever investment in education research, which was initiated in 2000 and ended in 2011/12 and at least 70 projects, across all education sectors.

For the REF of 2014, most universities became increasingly focused on international research and even more strategic around the researchers submitted. When the results were published, for education they show a mixed picture, with a good proportion of research at the highest level (4★) but also a significant amount at the lowest (1★) level (Pollard, 2014). This, and the continued dominance of the old universities at the top of the league tables and the position of education as the least inclusive area in terms of the percentage of staff (27%) submitted (THE, 2015, p 36) led Andrew Pollard (2014, p 1), the chair of the education panel for the REF, to state: 'I anticipate these outcomes will trigger wide-ranging discussion of research purposes and activity in education, particularly when seen in the context of the rapid changes which are also taking place in teacher education.'

Overall, the repeated research audits since 1992 have, then, had differential impacts on schools of education and on the academics within them (Gilroy and McNamara, 2009), with the exact nature of that impact depending on a range of structural and cultural factors. These include the national system, the trajectory of the HEI, the configuration of the school of education and the types of work undertaken within it and the various affinities and aspirations of individual academics working there. Certainly, the audits have increased tensions around involvement in teaching, research and academic management and the differential degrees of esteem attached to those activities in schools of education providing ITE programmes (BERA and UCET Working Group on Education Research, 2012).

The RoI does not conduct national audits of research activity, but here too there is growing emphasis on internationally recognised research. There are, for example, institutional pressures on staff to publish selectively with a view to achieving impact factors and citations; these are part of performance management and workload structures within universities and reflect clear awareness of the audits in the UK. It can be argued, then, that growing research intensity in the RoI has had broadly similar effects on teacher education and its underpinning research as those found in the UK.

Given the very mixed fortunes of research in, on and for teacher education since 1984, these effects of growing research intensivity have been to reinforce the status quo in terms of institutional hierarchies in the subject (Gilroy and McNamara, 2009). 'What counts' as good educational research – and hence what is recognised as valued and legitimised knowledge in the HE sector and within schools of education – has been reconfigured over time by research auditing. Further effects have been to devalue practitioner and pedagogical research and to inhibit many teacher educators' participation in research (Sikes, 2006; Murray et al, 2012). It can be argued that, cumulatively, these factors have undermined the development of the 'young' field of teacher education research (Menter et al, 2010b), limited the development of research-informed ITE and contributed to ongoing questioning of the value and impact of educational research and the unique contribution that universities can claim to make in teacher education.

Yet a counterargument would be that what are sometimes termed 'REF-able' or 'REF-worthy' research outputs are now an increasingly narrow selection of all research and scholarly activities in education. There are also questions around what types of research literacy and/ or active research engagement teacher educators might need in order to provide research-informed ITE (BERA and RSA, 2014b). It is, then, becoming clear that non-inclusion in the REF – or in other measurements of research performativity – can no longer be automatically equated with *lack* of research engagement in, on or for teacher education, at either individual or institutional levels.

Reflecting this, Pollard (2014, p 2) commented:

> The [research] activity required to compete successfully [in the REF] in social scientific terms is, in my opinion, becoming increasingly distinct from the activity required to flourish in the rapidly changing fields of teacher education. The pressure which this puts on staff working in Education is sometimes extremely acute.

Effects on teacher educators' work and identities

This section of the chapter explores briefly how the wider patterns of institutional, social-cultural and epistemological changes outlined above have affected the diverse professional identities and work of HE-based teacher educators.

Some indication of the diversity here is given by a small sample of studies. For example, Menter's (2011b) analysis of university schools of education in Scotland, approximately 10 years after the mergers of universities and colleges were completed, indicates the existence of four 'sub-tribes' within the teacher educator workforce. Stratified by the recent history of institutional change and personal career histories, the four groups are defined as:

- former college staff;
- longstanding university staff;
- staff appointed to the university since mergers between college and university;
- staff on temporary contracts.

Each of these groups has brought different experiences and attitudes into the university, with differences emerging in the study around how each group engages in research, and the degree and type of their commitment to students and personal constructions of what counts as 'good practice' in teacher education.

A study by Murray (2014) of 36 teacher educators in two case study universities in England showed three modes of professionalism constructed, each deploying diverse repertoires of resources to claim credibility in both schools and HE. Here some of the differentiations around professionalism were clearly related to time spent in the university; teacher educators new to HE, for example, constructed their 'recent and relevant' experiences of schooling as giving them powerful knowledge. Other differentiating factors, however, included varied constructions of teaching, different modes of practice as a teacher educator and degrees of care and support offered to student teachers. The most significant variables also included personal engagement in research and the deployment of status gained from this as valuable professional capital in the university.

Struggles around teaching and research engagement also become powerful signifiers of credibility and value in other studies of teacher educators' work and identities (Murray et al, 2012; Brown et al, 2014). In the work of Ellis et al (2012) with staff in schools of education in

England and Scotland, some categories of teacher educators' work, including forging partnerships with schools and what is termed 'relationship maintenance' – a category of work in which teacher educators act as diplomats to smooth relationships between school, student and university structures – took up large amounts of time.

Recent studies of teacher educators in England, facing the rapid changes initiated by School Direct (Brennan et al, 2014; Brown et al, 2014), show new roles and forms of professional knowledge emerging in response to the growing 'market' in ITE. Some senior teacher educators, for example, were engaged in what were effectively marketing and sales roles on behalf of their universities in the work of Brennan et al (2014). Teacher educators' identities and knowledge were diversifying further; their work was becoming increasingly heterogeneous – undervalued in some universities, but re-formed and re-valued in some of the more managerialist and entrepreneurial parts of the HE sector.

These findings have significant implications for HE-based teacher educators, including:

- the fragmentation of an already diverse occupational group;
- the emergence of new roles and work patterns;
- changes to professional knowledge bases and identities;
- diverging opportunities around further career development.

Conclusions

This chapter has focused in the main on the HE contexts for ITE over the nations of the UK and the RoI. It has analysed two of the dominant dualisms of ITE in the 1980s – university/school and theory/practice, acknowledging that these dualisms might still be found in the 'public discourses' of ITE (Popkewitz, 1987) and that to some extent they reflect ongoing common sense about the locations of ITE, as it is currently structured in the majority of the UK and RoI. But it has also presented arguments to deconstruct these dualisms since, in many important ways, they are seen here as unhelpful continuities in ITE. They are also increasingly inaccurate and inappropriate for conceptualising the field, not least because they overlook significant changes in the forms and domains of knowledge.

Looking across all five nations, this analysis also shows teacher education in HE becoming increasingly diversified over the last 30 years, certainly by national provision but also by type of university and by profile of schools of education within each country. Changes to practices, discourses and forms and domains of knowledge have been identified and analysed. Instantiated within the many and various schools of education in the five nations, these differing – and oft-times competing – constructions of teacher education exist alongside one another, sometimes resulting in increasingly divisive and intensive manifestations of practice, which play out very differently in the structures and cultures of HE. As the territories of teacher education (Becher and Trowler, 2002) diversify and fragment, they become increasingly heterogeneous. Given this diversification and the complex relationships between these territories of the field and the academics operating within them (Becher and Trowler, 2002), it is not surprising to find the fragmentation of the diverse occupational group of teacher educators, the emergence of new roles and work patterns and changes to professional knowledge bases and identities.

Notes

[1] While ITE in the university sector at this time was largely protected from the effects of the rapid expansions and contractions experienced by the colleges (Plunkett, 1984), it did experience cuts (Taylor, 1984); some universities also experienced mergers with colleges (Shaw, 1984) and lived through subsequent cultural shifts.

[2] Student teachers on a PGCE course in England now spend more than 66% of their time on practicum. In contrast, the Teaching Council in the RoI requires that only 40% of the course time should be spent in schools on postgraduate programmes.

TWELVE

Partnership in teacher education

Trevor Mutton

Introduction

Partnership in teacher education encompasses differing notions of collaborative working in a range of different contexts but most frequently designates the relationship between providers of initial teacher education (ITE) and the schools with which they work most closely, although similar partnerships might be in place involving schools and universities working together in relation to the continuing professional development (CPD) of teachers. Partnership working has been at the heart of teacher education, both in the United Kingdom (UK) and in many international contexts, for the last three decades but the way in which individual partnerships function can vary greatly, with the actual concept of 'partnership' itself being open to interpretation and the source of underlying tensions. These tensions, however, may not always be openly acknowledged. Teacher education has been identified by Cochran-Smith (2005b, p 3) and many others since as a 'policy problem', with partnership working, particularly in the UK, having been promoted by both policy makers and those responsible for programmes of initial teacher education as an integral part of what can be done to address this perceived problem. There is, however, less explicit acknowledgement of the potentially problematic nature of the concept of partnership itself. As early as 1984, Alexander was identifying some of the key issues and arguing that the dialogue of 'professional partnership' had been 'difficult to promote' not least because of differences in the models of professional learning favoured by schools and universities respectively. He concluded that 'the comfortable language of 'partnership' conceals more intractable issues' (1984, p 142).

It is the way that teacher education policy and practice has tried, over the years, to accommodate some of these 'intractable issues' that this chapter will seek to address by examining the way in which the notion of partnership has developed in light of the changing landscape of teacher education within the UK and Republic of Ireland (RoI).

This chapter begins by looking at the way in which teacher education policy has led to a particular rhetoric of partnership ('the comfortable language') and how this may be reflected in the practical arrangements for partnership working across the five jurisdictions under examination here. It then examines partnership as an 'epistemological and pedagogical concept' (Furlong et al, 2008), focusing both on the contexts in which beginning teachers acquire professional knowledge and skills and the problems of the potential disconnect between the various elements of the programme if partnership fails to work effectively. Finally, the chapter examines the practice of partnership working itself and the issues that may arise from such working.

Partnership as a policy issue

Teacher education programmes have always depended on universities working in partnership with schools but, in England and Wales, it was the policy developments from 1984 onwards that marked a period of significant change (for a more detailed chronology, see Furlong et al, 2000; Brisard et al, 2005). The publication of circulars 9/92 and 14/93 (DfE, 1992, 1993) introduced the requirement for universities to establish formal arrangements for partnerships, which would in turn 'exercise a joint responsibility for the planning and management of courses and the selection, training and assessment of students' (DfE, 1992, para 14). It was the differing interpretations of the way in which these activities might be managed (including the nature of the integration between the university-based and the school-based elements of the programme) that saw the emergence of a number of different models of partnership, while the rhetoric around partnership often allowed for uncritical acceptance of a range of diverse practices, values and perspectives (Dhillon, 2009). The Modes of Teacher Education (MOTE) project, carried out after the introduction of the reforms of the early 1990s, concluded that there were, in fact, three dominant models in operation following the introduction of the new requirements in England and Wales (Furlong et al, 1996, 2000). The MOTE researchers described the three models respectively as 'collaborative', 'complementary' (or 'separatist') and 'higher education institution (HEI)-led', the last of these making up the greatest proportion of the partnerships that were studied. Briefly, the collaborative models they identified were characterised by schools and the university working together in terms of the planning, delivery and evaluation of the teacher education programme so as to achieve integration and coherence; programmes operating complementary partnerships were characterised by schools and the university having separate but complementary responsibilities, but with little integration between the two; finally, HEI-led partnerships were those in which the university defined what it is that trainee teachers needed to learn (both in school and at the university) and in which schools were seen as providing the resource that enabled the identified learning opportunities to take place. What all three of these models have in common, however, is the notion of partnership as an 'epistemological and pedagogical concept' (Furlong et al, 2008), that is to say the acknowledgement that both schools and universities contribute to teachers' professional learning in distinctive ways and that while both are necessary, neither alone is sufficient (Hagger and McIntyre, 2006). Evidence from successful teacher education schemes across the world likewise highlights the necessity of such interdependence (Schleicher, 2012). Furlong (2013a) acknowledges that partnership work is challenging but argues for models of partnership in which each partner 'contributes from its own strengths, its own essential purposes, where neither is in the lead, but where each institution learns from the other' (2013, p 187). Sachs (2003b), likewise, emphasises that a collaborative partnership is not the result of university staff facilitating the professional development of teachers through partnership but rather one that is mutually beneficial to the professional development of both. The former is a 'one-way' activity characterised by an 'expert–client' relationship where 'academic/theoretical knowledge is privileged over practitioner know how'. Sachs (2003, p 66) argues instead for a model that represents 'a two-way model of reciprocity'.

While teacher education policy may differ significantly across all jurisdictions of the UK and RoI (see Chapters Four to Eight), the notion of partnership is nevertheless a central tenet of each. The following brief analysis of partnership within individual national contexts demonstrates, however, that the aspiration to achieve such a 'two-way model of reciprocity', often expressed in policy documentation as a drive towards more collaborative models of partnership working, is not always evident in practice.

England

During the last 30 years, partnership in England has become an increasingly important policy issue, strengthened by successive government circulars, but the 'comfortable language' that Alexander

(1984) refers to has continued to mask some of the underlying issues. A case in point was the development by the Teacher Training Agency (TTA) of the National Partnership Project (NPP) in England from 2001 to 2005 under the Labour government of the time, which had two clear aims – to increase both the quantity and the quality of school involvement in initial teacher training (ITT). A significant amount of funding was made available to develop projects at regional level, as well as to support the development of partnership promotion schools, which would receive funding to do outreach work with schools in their region. Furlong et al (2006b), who carried out a national evaluation of the scheme, suggested that although the programme did have some benefits in terms of securing more school places for trainee teachers and greater levels of collaboration, in some areas, between providers themselves and between providers and schools, this was nevertheless being carried out within a competitive market-led teacher education policy landscape. They also found that little of the underlying practice of partnership had changed since the MOTE study of the 1990s and argued that the project actually 'further undermined the pedagogical and epistemological dimensions of partnership' and encouraged instead the development of a 'technical rationalist approach to teacher education' (2006b, p 32). The cooperation between providers through involvement in the NPP that led, for example, to agreed common formats for documentation across ITT providers within a region, is not seen by Furlong et al as a positive outcome of the project but rather as a reductionist approach that denies the complexity of the process of professional learning.

Market-driven approaches to teacher education continued under the coalition government from 2010, with the introduction of School Direct, one of the main policy aims of which was to enhance the role of schools in ITT by building on the best practice that already existed and to encourage the development of more collaborative partnership working (particularly in relation to the recruitment of trainees and the planning and delivery of ITE programmes). The control mechanisms for ensuring that HEI providers did actually move more fully towards greater school involvement in partnerships were twofold. First, a new Osfted (Office for Standards in Education) inspection framework would 'recognise the features of outstanding university-school partnerships' (DfE, 2011, p 13, para 9); and second, the allocations of ITT places by central government would 'prioritise providers that have such arrangements in place so that only universities and other providers who demonstrate extensive school involvement and high quality training continue to have a role in ITT' (DfE, 2011, p 13, para 9).

While there has, to date, been little research focusing on the nature of partnership models following the above policy changes, a report in 2014 by Universities UK noted the increased level of engagement by HEIs with schools as a result of the introduction of School Direct and that the allocation of ITT places to schools working in partnership with a designated HEI had led to more collaborative working in relation to the design and delivery of training programmes (Universities UK, 2014).

Northern Ireland

In Northern Ireland, suggested procedures and responsibilities for partnership working were provided in a framework document, first produced in 1998 (NITEC and CEPD, 1998), which set out key responsibilities for different stakeholders in terms of supporting the learning of beginning teachers through their initial training and the early stages of their career but within a voluntary framework. One of its key aspects was to ensure a continuum for professional learning with designated support as appropriate (see Brisard et al, 2005, for a detailed account of the development of policy in relation to partnership working in Northern Ireland). The original Northern Ireland partnership framework identified lead partners for each phase of a beginning teacher's career (HEIs for initial teacher education, the education and library boards [ELBs] for induction and schools for early professional development). Moran et al (2009), however, drawing on a study of induction arrangements, highlight the need for a re-conceptualised model of partnership working in Northern Ireland. Such a model should, they argue, have three key characteristics, namely 'consistency, continuity and community' (2009, p 957) but they acknowledge the challenges of developing any revised model within a complex policy context. Earlier attempts to reform teacher education which began in 2003 and led to the subsequent Osler (2005) report, had likewise emphasised the need for continuity from initial training through induction and ongoing professional development but did not result in any significant change because of the complexity of policy implementation at the time. The ongoing identification of the need for enhanced partnership working remained, however, and is central to each of the four options for teacher education reform suggested by Sahlberg et al in their review for the Northern Ireland government (DEL, 2014), including the suggestion of establishing a 'Partnership Concordat' 'to oversee partnership between universities, schools, and employers....' (p 44, para 8.9). Their report, drawing on international evidence, also highlights the effectiveness of models of research-informed clinical practice and suggests that one such model might be for 'the initial teacher education institutions to work in close partnership with chosen schools to ensure that they become places for clinical teaching practice similar to the teaching hospitals that are part of faculties of medicine in many countries' (2014, p 11, para 3.18). It remains to be seen to what extent these suggested reforms become a feature of teacher education policy in Northern Ireland in future years.

Republic of Ireland

One key feature of the partnership arrangements between teacher education providers and schools in the RoI is that they have traditionally been largely voluntary and have relied on the goodwill of schools to be involved. For many years, initial teacher education arrangements resembled more the pre-1984 position in England (and elsewhere), with universities and the teacher training colleges taking on most of the responsibility for the planning, delivery and assessment of the programme and the schools being the sites for 'teaching practice'. The recognition of the need to provide more meaningful (and, in many cases, more extensive) school-based experiences for trainee teachers had been identified over a long period but the issue in making this a reality appeared to have been primarily one of resourcing (Cannon, 2004). The review of teacher education in the RoI carried out by Sahlberg et al in 2012 made clear recommendations for the development of partnerships between universities and schools, both in initial teacher education and to support ongoing professional development. Their conclusions are also reflected to a certain extent in the work carried out by the Teaching Council to produce guidelines for school placement (Teaching Council, 2013). This work, involving the Teaching Council and appropriate stakeholders, was instigated in order to support the previously published national criteria for programme providers, which had, in turn, called for 'new and innovative school placement models ... using a partnership approach, whereby HEIs and schools actively collaborate in the organisation of the school placement' (2013, p 3). As in other jurisdictions, the move towards more collaborative partnership working may still be reflected more in a policy steer than in day-to-day teacher education practices but the trend in the RoI, as elsewhere, is clearly towards the development of more collaborative partnership models.

Scotland

Likewise in Scotland, the last 30 years have seen the development of ITE partnership arrangements that have aimed to produce more 'complementarity' in terms of the roles played by HEIs, schools and local authorities but it needs to be understood that this is within a context in which universities are responsible for all ITE. In Scotland, there have been no equivalents of employment-based routes into teaching or initiatives such as School Direct. Following developments in the early 1990s such as the Moray House Project and the Mentor Teacher Initiative (see Brisard et al, 2005, for a detailed account of these initiatives) and the General Teaching Council for Scotland (GTCS) report of its Working Group on Partnership (GTCS, 1997), there seemed to be an openness to developing models of partnership in which more 'complementarity' could be achieved but also an acknowledgement of the resource implications of any related policy change. Significant changes in partnership working did not, however, materialise in significant ways in subsequent years, in spite of further reviews of teacher education in Scotland such as the 2005 Second Stage Review, which called for 'local authorities and universities to establish new, effective and proactive partnerships' (Scottish Executive, 2005, p 8). The need for a more 'proactive approach' was likewise highlighted by the Donaldson Report (2011), which contains numerous references to the need to establish stronger ITE partnerships and to move from notions of complementarity to more collaborative approaches. The report also examined in detail the nature of teachers' professional learning and called for more integration between the differing aspects of the ITE programme. One of the key recommendations of the report was: 'New and strengthened models of partnership among universities, local authorities, schools and individual teachers need to be developed. These partnerships should be based on jointly agreed principles and involve shared responsibility for key areas of teacher education' (Donaldson, 2011, p 91).

One further interesting suggestion in the report is the possible development of 'hub teaching schools', which would have a stronger focus than others on teacher education and would work collaboratively with other partners, both in ITE but also in CPD and ongoing professional learning.

Wales

In Wales, the partnership arrangements established following circulars 9/92 and 14/93 (DFE, 1992, 1993) have been subject to a number of studies, which have both identified the positive aspects of ITE partnership working and highlighted a number of constraints, including resourcing issues, consistency in the quality of mentoring in schools and the apparent imbalance between HEIs being required to work in partnership with schools while at the same time there is no such obligation on schools to work with HEIs (Bassett, 2003). The current requirements and the associated guidance (Welsh Government, 2013) make it clear that it is the responsibility of providers 'to ensure that schools are full partners in ITT in every way: not only do they contribute to the delivery of training; they also participate in planning training, and in selecting and assessing trainees (2013, p 45, para R3.1) Although the rhetoric of partnership is clearly evident in government publications such as the above, the actual nature of partnership working between HEIs and schools has been identified as being in need of further development.

Two major reviews in recent years have identified that establishing effective partnership working is one key factor in improving quality in ITE in Wales. The Furlong Review (Furlong et al, 2006a, p 74, para 5.18) was clear that '[r]egional partnerships of schools and HEIs, in which there is genuine equality and reciprocity, have the potential to become key agents of change'. Likewise, the more recent review carried out by Tabberer (2013, p 27, para 101) highlighted that '[i]n Wales, as in many other countries where ITT is devolved to providers serving different regions, the success of ITT is strongly affected by the quality of school partnerships'. Tabberer's recommendation that the Welsh Government should consider setting up a network of 'training schools' can be seen as encouraging those schools that are most committed to teacher education to develop their current role as part of the process of 'improving school-based practices' (2013, p 22).

Summary

Across the five jurisdictions, partnership is clearly central to both current and proposed models of teacher education and, where there have been calls for reform, these generally focus on the need for more collaborative partnership working between ITE providers and schools. In England, policy has been driven predominantly by the need to open up the market of teacher education and a view by policy makers that '[t]eaching is a craft and it is best learnt as an apprentice observing a master craftsman or woman' (Gove, 2010). The necessity for ITE providers to re-conceptualise their relationship with their school partners through the development of the School Direct initiative has, it could be argued, brought an end to the dominance of the HEI-led model and given schools a much greater role in determining the nature and content of ITE programmes; but this could also be seen in many respects as encouraging an approach whereby partnership working is reduced to a set of prescriptive indicators against which the performance of individual programmes can be 'audited'. Partnership policy in England has therefore focused primarily on the logistical aspects of partnership and the requirement for more collaborative working, with the distribution of resources being a significant focus in terms of the arrangement between partners. The proposals for reform following recent reviews of teacher education in the other four jurisdictions have, by contrast, focused less on the logistical aspects and more on partnership as the context for beginning teachers' learning. The final recommendations of these reviews reflect a stronger sense that partnership is primarily an 'epistemological and pedagogical concept' (Furlong et al, 2008) and highlight the contribution that respective partners can make through the potentially integrated and collaborative partnership models that are proposed.

Partnership as a pedagogical concept

In defining what partnership in ITE actually means, Brisard et al (2005) highlight two distinct ways in which the term is used, reflected in many ways in the differing approaches to partnership described above. The first, drawing on theories relating to the nature of teachers' professional learning, focuses on the 'pedagogy and curriculum of ITE' whereas the second describes the more logistical aspects of an ITE programme such as 'the resourcing of initial teacher education, particular balances of responsibility between different roles or the placing of and arrangements for particular forms of school experience' (2005, p 5). Both, it could be argued, give rise to some of the 'intractable issues' to which Alexander (1984) refers. Ideally, one would expect the first to be the essence of partnership working (that is to say, a shared understanding of what teachers need to learn and how they might best learn these things) and that the details of the arrangements for delivering the ITE curriculum would then follow, in line with any pedagogical principles already established between the respective partners. All too often, however, partnership working has, over much of the previous 30 years, been characterised by the over-dominance of one of the partners, namely the HEI (Furlong et al, 2000), or by an over-emphasis on the logistical aspects of partnership, which ignores the underlying complexity (Furlong et al, 2008).

Perhaps this is nowhere more evident than in the debates around the nature of the school-based experiences of trainee teachers, a key aspect of any partnership arrangement. A significant shift in emphasis in teacher education programmes over the last 30 years, both in the UK and internationally, has resulted in an increased focus on the school-based experience within ITE programmes, a shift that has been characterised variously as the 'practicum turn in teacher education' (Mattsson et al, 2011, p 17), the 'return to the practical' (Beauchamp et al, 2013, p 1) and 'the turn toward practice' (Zeichner and Bier, 2014, p 103). The way in which the period of school-based experience is conceptualised in terms of the opportunity that it provides for professional learning within a partnership is likewise reflected in the range of names given to this particular aspect of the programme, which may be referred to, inter alia, as 'teaching practice', 'the school placement', 'block placement', 'the practicum', 'internship', 'clinical practice or' 'field experiences'. At one level, much of the focus of partnership over the last 30 years has been on the practical arrangements for this period of school-based experience, such as the securing of a sufficient number of school placements, the length of individual placements (within an overall prescribed amount of days) and the arrangements for assessing beginning teachers' classroom competence during the time they spend in school. Along with this have been regular calls from policy makers around the world for more time within an ITE programme to be spent in school, reflected particularly in recent reforms in England aimed at ensuring 'that more training is on the job' (DfE, 2010, section 2.6), with the training in question premised upon an apprenticeship model. It is not necessarily the case, however, that a greater emphasis on school-based experience and more time spent learning 'on the job' will, of themselves, lead to more effective teacher education. Hagger and McIntyre (2006) argue for the potential of a school-based programme of ITE but this is not a model based on the view that an increased amount of time spent in schools is sufficient in itself; rather, they argue for a model that is broad enough to incorporate professional learning that draws on a range on different sources. In such a model, the valuable contribution of research-based understandings is acknowledged and promoted, and furthermore is one in which partnership between the school and the university, based on pedagogic principles, has a distinctive role to play.

All too often, however, the discourse around beginning teachers' professional learning reflects the unhelpful theory/practice binary, with partnership working exemplifying more the 'disconnect' between school and university or college settings (Zeichner, 2011; Zeichner and Bier, 2014) than a model of integration. It is greater integration that is called for in the reviews of ITE carried out in the RoI (Sahlberg et al, 2012), in Northern Ireland (DEL, 2014), in Wales (Furlong et al, 2006a) and in Scotland (Donaldson, 2011) discussed above, whose authors recognise the value of collaborative partnerships in which there is clear synergy between the various elements of the ITE programme. In the case of the reviews in Northern Ireland and the RoI, there is specific reference to the need for models of 'clinical practice' (DEL, 2014, p 11; Sahlberg et al, 2012, p 25, respectively), a term used widely in the international literature to designate school-based experience but here used specifically to indicate the nature of the integration of different aspects of the ITE curriculum. It is not insignificant that the same phrase is also taken up by the more recent Carter review of ITE (DfE 2015), carried out in England, which recommends that ITE programmes 'should be structured so there is effective integration between the different types of knowledge and skills trainees need to draw on in order to develop their own teaching' (2015, p 21). Carter goes on to emphasise the role that effective partnerships have in providing 'seamlessly integrated rather than disjointed or fragmented' programmes (DfE, 2015, p 42). Likewise the British Educational Research Association and Royal Society of Arts inquiry into research in teacher education (BERA and RSA, 2014b, pp 18-19), in advocating the development of a 'research-literate' teaching profession, identified 'the benefits of clinical preparation, through carefully designed programmes of initial teacher education, which allow trainee teachers to integrate knowledge from academic study and research with practical experience in the school and classroom'.

Established teacher education partnerships that make claims to such integration by developing models of 'research-informed clinical practice' are to be found both in the UK and internationally (Burn and Mutton, 2013). One such well-established partnership is the Oxford Internship Scheme (Benton, 1990), which was recognised by the MOTE researchers as being the only example of a truly 'collaborative' partnership in England and Wales at the time (Furlong et al, 2000). One key feature of the scheme was that it was built around a set of clear principles, which were developed over a period of time with both school and local authority partners (McIntyre, 1990). Many of these principles, drawn themselves from teacher education research, reflect the integration of the university and the school-based components of the programme as well as the collaborative nature of the partnership in terms of joint planning, delivery and evaluation of the programme. Furthermore, these principles embody a clear rejection of the 'apprenticeship' model or 'theory into practice' paradigms. In more recent years there have been specific attempts to develop 'clinical practice' models elsewhere in the UK, most notably in Scotland, through the Scottish Teachers for a New Era programme (Livingston and Shiach, 2010) and the Glasgow West Teacher Education Initiative (Conroy et al, 2013) but, notwithstanding these exceptions, it could be argued that much of the partnership development work in the UK in recent years has actually not addressed fundamental epistemological and pedagogical issues within ITE programmes.

Partnership as a teacher education practice

If teacher education partnerships are to function effectively then they have to operate within agreed frameworks and with a high level of consensual understanding. Such frameworks are constantly under review within the UK and RoI but policy change, when it occurs, appears to address more the bureaucratic aspects of partnership working than the underlying philosophies and practices. As a result, much of the 'comfortable language' endures while many of the 'intractable issues' remain unresolved. While the most intractable of these issues is perhaps the unhelpful theory/practice binary discussed above, there are further tensions that emerge from conceptual understandings of the nature of partnership working, the current policy landscape or the more practical aspects of partnership working, including the following:

Teacher education is not the primary focus of a school's activity

Schools are not statutorily required to work in partnership with specific teacher education providers and, where a school does choose to do so, teacher education remains a secondary focus of the school's activity, since its primary focus remains the learning of its own pupils. Many schools nevertheless do see the advantages to be gained from involvement in ITE (beyond immediate benefits relating to the recruitment of teachers), including:

- the opportunity that it affords for supporting the learning of its pupils (often through the introduction of more innovative ideas for practice);
- the opportunity for CPD among those teachers involved in mentoring and supporting the learning of the trainee teachers; the opportunity to engage in a professional discourse in relation to teacher education and development (Mutton and Butcher, 2008).

Furthermore, teacher education (and ITE in particular) does not have to be seen as being a disruption to the ongoing work of schools but can rather be seen as providing opportunities to enhance pupil learning. This might be achieved through an inquiry-focused approach to teaching and learning that involves collaborative working between beginning and more experienced teachers around an agreed research focus (Childs et al, 2013).

Teacher education partnerships lack adequate resources

Partnerships across the five jurisdictions clearly rely on a great deal of goodwill from those involved in partnership working and although funding arrangements are a necessary part of local partnership agreements there is an overall sense that the money available is limited and that partnerships therefore have to make the most efficient use of the resources available. With the 'practicum turn' in teacher education (see above) and the introduction of programmes such as School Direct in England, partnerships inevitably have to consider what constitutes a fair distribution of these limited resources when both schools and universities may see the funding they receive as being inadequate. School Direct is, furthermore, 'extremely resource-intensive in terms of administration for both universities and schools' (McNamara and Murray, 2013, p 16) because of the greater number of smaller-sized partnerships currently operating within this model.

Teacher education partnerships have to reconcile competing demands

While teacher education programmes need to be underpinned by specific pedagogic principles (many of which are highlighted by the reviews of teacher education discussed above), they also have to take account of the need to adhere to statutory measures of accountability, including the requirement to assess teachers' competence in relation to designated professional standards (see Chapter Nine, this volume). This inevitably gives rise to tensions as an increased focus on performativity further reduces the opportunity for teachers (and beginning teachers in particular) to engage in the process of what has been referred to as 'practical theorising' (Hagger and McIntyre, 2006), that is to say, developing professional knowledge and understanding through an informed critique of both 'the practical, contextualised perspectives of teachers and also the idealised, theoretical and research-based perspectives of university staff' (McIntyre, 2009, p 605). McIntyre (2009, p 603) argues further that, in England, partnership models are 'aimed only at preparing beginning teachers for the status quo, and very deliberately being planned to avoid them being encouraged to think critically of that status quo.'

One further manifestation of this tension is the tendency, identified by Edwards and Collinson (2004), for mentors to emphasise the need for trainee teachers to deliver the planned curriculum in a particular way – what the authors refer to as 'teaching by proxy'. Such a tendency reduces the capacity for beginning teachers to evaluate for themselves what they might consider to be the best approach, drawing on all the evidence available to them, but rather directs them to plan and teach in particular ways favoured by an individual teacher or the school in which they are working.

Schools often work in partnership with a number of different ITE providers, each requiring individual arrangements for partnership working.

Although arrangements between schools and colleges or universities in many parts of the UK and RoI reflect what might be called a 'traditional' approach to partnership, with schools working with just one provider (a model that is also, perhaps, more prevalent in primary teacher education than secondary), it is not unusual for secondary schools, particularly in England, to be working with a relatively large number of different providers across a range of curriculum subjects. Such arrangements give rise to 'complex relationships at work within multiple partnerships' (Mutton and Butcher, 2008, p 60) and while schools may manage such arrangements effectively, this nevertheless gives rise to a number of issues. First, at a practical level, for example, the maintenance of multiple teacher education partnerships is administratively demanding and time-consuming. Second, in relation to the ITE curriculum itself schools will inevitably wish to identify the common elements between programmes and, where possible, standardise approaches, but this may risk reducing further the 'epistemological and pedagogical' nature of partnership working and leading potentially to a situation where '[t]he complexity and contestability of professional knowledge is therefore no longer seen to be at the heart of what partnership is about; professional knowledge becomes simplified, flattened, it is essentially about contemporary practice in schools' (Furlong et al, 2006b, p 41).

There is variability in the quality of mentoring within teacher education partnerships

It is recognised in the international literature that one of the key 'intractable' issues within ITE programmes and programmes of induction is the variability in the support provided to beginning teachers, and in particular in the quality of mentoring (see Hobson et al, 2009). Zeichner and Bier (2014, p 107) identify the 'underresourcing of clinical experiences' as being a key factor in issues of quality but other issues have been identified, such as:

- an over-reliance on the personal, practical experience of the mentor in guiding new teachers in their development; an over-reliance on the idiosyncratic nature of the particular school context in question;
- too heavy a focus on the performance of trainee teachers in relation to meeting the prescribed professional standards; issues in terms of the relationship between mentor and mentee; the need for mentors to acquire a more developed understanding of theoretical approaches to mentoring and of the needs of teachers as learners (Jones and Straker, 2006).

While the development of mentoring (both in relation to ITE and teacher induction) has been one of the key features of partnership working across the UK and RoI in recent years, it could also be argued that the characteristics identified by McIntyre and Hagger (1993) as representing a 'developed' or 'extended' model of mentoring have not necessarily been met consistently either within or across teacher education partnerships.

In sociocultural terms, the above issues might be seen as aspects of two separate communities of practice (namely schools and universities or colleges), which overlap in the context of teacher education partnerships. While the complexity of the relationships within them, particularly when schools are often working simultaneously within multiple partnerships of this kind, can lead to tensions, they can nevertheless also be seen to offer opportunities for 'expansiveness' within the system (Wenger, 2000, p 240) – that is to say, opportunities for the development of 'mutual understanding of shared tasks and problems; and the development of expertise in negotiating meanings and the responses to those meanings' (Edwards and Mutton, 2007, p 509). There is, however, a difficulty in embracing such a positive view of the potential of partnership working as a professional learning opportunity when the capacity of those engaged in such work, both to identify and to realise this potential, is constrained by policy approaches that reduce partnership working to a 'technical-rationalist' approach (Furlong et al, 2006b, p 32).

Conclusion

This chapter has attempted to trace teacher education partnership development over the last 30 years and to highlight some of the key issues for both policy makers and practitioners. Central to all effective partnership working is a shared conceptualisation of the nature of the professional knowledge that teachers require, both in their initial training and subsequently as they become more experienced in the classroom, and a shared agreement as to what sort of qualities a teacher needs. Where there is not such agreement between partners then day-to-day teacher education practices will be affected by such tensions to the detriment of those engaged in the process of professional learning. Unnecessary and unhelpful barriers will emerge between those working in schools and those working in universities and colleges and trainee teachers will experience more segregation than integration. Likewise, when teacher education policy reflects a narrow ideological view of what teaching (or the process of learning to teach) entails, tensions will arise. Furthermore, reductive guidelines as to what constitutes effective partnership working, which focus on bureaucratic procedures rather than important pedagogical concerns, only serve to mask the complexities of partnership working with 'comfortable' language. As each of the four nations of the UK and the RoI still struggle, to some extent, to establish effective models of teacher education partnership within policy contexts that reflect, in some cases, relative stability or, in other cases, high levels of instability and change, there is clearly the need for both policy makers and practitioners to engage more fully with this complexity.

Part Four:
Conclusion

THIRTEEN

Insights from the five nations and implications for the future

Moira Hulme, Ian Menter, Jean Murray and Teresa O'Doherty

Introduction

In this final chapter we review all of the earlier work and ask what lessons may be drawn from the cases and themes that have been discussed. In particular, consideration is given to the respective evidence for convergence and/or divergence in teacher education policy across the five jurisdictions. The influence of globalisation and the significance of wider social and political change are also reviewed.

A sociocultural and historical perspective is adopted to review these questions, so that questions about national identity, the positioning of education systems as 'nation builders' and the particular role of teachers within these processes are critically examined. This raises issues of values, citizenship and democracy.

The final section considers possible scenarios for the future – as schooling changes its shape and organisation, how will the education and preparation of teachers need to respond?

Convergence or divergence?

Our analysis here indicates some policy convergence, particularly across Scotland, Northern Ireland and the Republic of Ireland (RoI), all of which seem to be following Continental European models of teacher education at least in part. Policy in Wales, where initial teacher education (ITE) provision followed English models closely until after devolution in 1999, is also increasingly distinctive. England emerges from this analysis as a definite outlier in terms of its 'marketised' and increasingly school-led system, although as we indicate later in this chapter, there may be dangers to arguing for English 'exceptionalism' in this way.

The 'practice turn' (Reid, J., 2011) in teacher education, found in many international policies in the last decade, has played out differently across the five nations. As discussed in several chapters here, especially Eleven and Twelve, common trends are to place more emphasis on 'practical' and 'relevant' aspects of ITE, particularly the practicum, but the discourses and practices in use here vary considerably. As Beauchamp et al (2013) identify, the language and rhetoric employed to discuss 'relevance', for example, reflect differing views of teaching and teacher education. In England, the 'turn to the practical' (Furlong and Lawn, 2010, p 6, quoting Hoyle, 1982) has seen the re-emergence of simplified craft models of teaching in which expertise can be acquired through apprenticeship modes of learning in the school workplace. The teacher standards, competences or codes of professional conduct currently in operation in each of the five nations now also differ in many key respects, indicating underlying variations in underpinning values and visions of teaching as a profession, but this divergence is discussed in more detail later in the chapter.

Partnership between universities and schools is a core tenet of teacher education provision in the three smaller nations of the UK and in the RoI as each of those countries moves towards more collaborative models of working between higher education institutions (HEIs) and schools, often positioning partnership as an 'epistemological and pedagogical concept' (Furlong et al, 2008). In England, more than 20 years after partnership legislation was introduced in 1992, the School Direct scheme is reconfiguring longstanding models of working, in many cases re-emphasising the logistical aspects of resourcing and management at the cost of those key epistemological and pedagogical concepts; this is a policy that many see as propelled by the ideological drive to open up the market of ITE provision.

One common higher education factor affecting teacher education provision in all five countries – and indeed most European Union states – was the Bologna Accord of 1999, which formed a European Higher Education Area with a common qualifications framework. This meant that many one-year postgraduate ITE programmes in the UK and RoI were re-validated to give credits towards the attainment of a Masters-level qualification. But, in general, across the five nations, the ways in which teacher education is embedded in the higher education sector have become increasingly diversified over the last 30 years. This can be seen in the basic patterns of provision, with ITE programmes in Scotland and Northern Ireland offered only through HEIs, provision in the RoI now also heavily dominated by universities, but entry into teaching in both Wales and England possible through both university-based and alternative routes. The latter type of provision is rapidly proliferating in England at the time of writing.

Diversity across the five nations can also be seen in the range of policy changes around the place of teacher education in the university sector (see Chapter Eleven). Influenced by Continental European policy, ITE provision in the RoI has made a distinct 'university turn' with ITE provision increasingly validated at Masters level. Teacher education policy in Northern Ireland seems to be evolving in the same European-influenced direction, with recent policy statements (DEL, 2014) recommending the extension of the Post Graduate Certificate of Education (PGCE) to Masters level. In Scotland, after the Donaldson Review (2011), ITE policy has also taken a 'university turn', albeit of a different kind, with teacher education programmes drawing on the strengths of disciplines outside schools of education. In these three countries, then, there is clear intent for ITE 'to be strengthened academically and cognitively' and for provision to be 'infused with the intellectual power which university involvement in teacher education makes possible' (DEL, 2014, p 44).

In Wales, the recent Tabberer Review (2013) (and more recently, the second report by Furlong, 2015) echoed something of this sentiment by recommending that the research element of ITE within universities be strengthened (pp 24-5). Yet the future of the Masters in Educational Practice (MEP) for newly qualified and early career teachers remains uncertain. England has not made the kinds of clear and consistent 'university turns' for Masters-level study found in the other four nations. Although elements of the PGCE have now been validated at Masters level, repeated calls for the course to become a two-year full Masters qualification have gone unanswered, and a recent review of teacher education has now attempted to disconnect the PGCE from attaining qualified teacher status (DfE, 2015 – the Carter Review). This report curiously emphasises the importance of research in ITE, while de-emphasising the importance of universities as major locations for the generation of such knowledge. Overall, the 'pendulum swing' of ITE (Gardner, 1993) in England has swung away from the dominance of higher education in earlier parts of the 20th century and towards schools as the more influential stakeholders now.

Growing research intensivity and 'selectivity' – and particularly the widespread practices of auditing research outputs and academic performativity – has had broadly similar effects on teacher education and its underpinning research across the five nations (see Chapter Eleven). In summary, these effects have been to:

- increase tensions around teacher educator involvement in teaching, research and academic management;
- increase the differential degrees of esteem attached to those activities;
- reinforce the status quo in terms of institutional hierarchies in the subject (Gilroy and McNamara, 2009);
- redefine 'what counts' as valued and legitimised knowledge in the higher education sector and schools of education.

Cumulatively, these factors have undermined the development of the 'young' field of teacher education research (Menter et al, 2010b) and limited the development of research-informed ITE.

Our analysis here indicates considerable policy divergence across the five nations, particularly between the school-led and 'marketised' system in England and the university-embedded models found in Scotland, Northern Ireland and the RoI, and perhaps increasingly in Wales too. Yet in the practices followed by student teachers, partnership teachers and mentors and university-based teacher educators, teacher education in the five nations may not differ as much as this analysis of policy might suggest. For example, in England, many providers have maintained commitments to providing research-rich programmes, alongside current official prescriptions for courses to be relevant and practical. This policy/practice gap is in large part due to the differentiated ways in which policy mediation takes place.

Teacher education, national education systems and social justice

It is evident from our review of the five nations that education and the economy are inextricably linked and that as the global recession intensified post-2007, increased focus was placed on teachers and the quality of teaching in our schools. Publications such as *Teachers matter: Attracting, developing and retaining effective teachers* (OECD, 2005), and *How the world's best-performing schools come out on top* (Barber and Mourshed, 2007) have valorised the pivotal role played by teachers in creating 'world-class' schools. The availability of objective data, in the form of 'Education at a Glance' statistics and more recently the triennial Programme for International Student Assessment (PISA) results, have raised public and political awareness of teaching and created a global discussion on the comparative performance of school systems. In a recent survey of the impact of PISA results on national/federal education policy making, processes in Wales and the RoI were deemed to be 'very influenced' by PISA results, while England was rated to be 'extremely' influenced by PISA, and Scotland only 'moderately' so (Breakspear, 2012, p 14). The reaction to disappointing results and a slippage in the international education league has spurred politicians, such as UK Prime Minister David Cameron, into action and priority is being placed on 'excellence, with a complete intolerance of failure.... We've got to be ambitious if we want to compete in the world. When China is going through an educational renaissance, when India is churning out science graduates, any complacency right now would be completely fatal to our economic prospects' (Cameron, 2011). Cameron continued his speech to refer to his ambition to 'mend our broken society. Because education doesn't just give people the tools to make a good living – it gives them the character to live a good life, to be good citizens'. The parallels between this speech and the views of the RoI Minister for Education some six months later are notable: 'The rise of China has been relentless ... India and Japan, along with South-East Asia, are now matched by the rise of Brazil and other countries in Latin America.... They are looking to their education systems to give them competitive advantage especially in high-tech, pharmaceutical and other growth areas' (Quinn, 2012). The Minister continued: 'Of course educational reform is not just about boosting economic growth. It is also about helping students reach their potential and prepare for citizenship in a rapidly changing society.' The prioritisation of education as an engine for economic growth to be harnessed to build a nation's capacity to compete within a global economy is not new, nor is the external legislation and imposition of educational reform for commercial ends. What is more novel is that inequity is not viewed as an issue to be tackled within a broad socioeconomic landscape, but one that can be identified and coded according to attainment on a standardised test. Given the 'right' education policies, based on evidence rather than values, inequity can be quantified by differential student outcomes, irrespective of processes and resources, and the problem of inequity has become the problem of teachers (Zeichner, 2009; and Chapter Nine, this volume).

The articulation of standards across the five nations illustrates varying approaches to how accountability for student performance is defined and translated; Northern Ireland standards are situated within the discourse of democratic professionalism (Whitty, 2008) while those from the RoI and Scotland straddle both democratic and managerial professionalism domains. Standards in Wales and England offer a more restricted view of teacher professionalism, with responsibility for student achievement being placed squarely on teachers' shoulders. Reflecting the consensus across jurisdictions that a 'teacher' problem also constitutes a 'teacher education' problem, recent reforms of teacher education mirror distinctive national standards. Where teacher competence is delineated as technical knowledge and skill, then School Direct and alternative and for-profit teacher preparation (eg, Hibernia College in the RoI) approaches are deemed appropriate. A teacher education curriculum where teachers are provided with a 'weak and intellectually uncritical base in educational theory' (Sockett, 2008, p 45) reduces the capacity of teachers to engage in their work as activists, who are autonomous and able to exercise agency. If those who regulate and accredit teacher education programmes (governments and teaching councils) value and promote social justice, then one would expect that they would promote a curriculum that ensures teachers have the conceptual tools and disposition to interrogate the social complexities in which they work and to make adjudications between actions on the basis of one being more just than another (Walker, 2003, cited in Grant and Agosto, 2008, p 184). Teacher education programmes that seek to promote social justice include a number of characteristic practices as outlined by Nieto (2000, cited in Grant and Agosto, 2008, p 188), namely:

- critical pedagogy;
- community and collaboration;
- reflection;
- social (critical) consciousness;
- social change and change agents;
- culture and identity;
- analyses of power.

The emphasis on developing teachers' criticality through investment in processes, resources, time and collective dialogue, which would promote teacher autonomy and agency and are the basis for teaching for social justice, is at odds with the dominant requirement that programmes be evaluated on their outcomes and that they conform to and comply with the requirements for accreditation as prescribed. It is difficult to assess the latent potential of student teachers for social justice; in an era of increased managerialism and accountability, standards prioritise knowledge that is measurable and relevant, while they are frequently silent on the fundamental issues of equality and equity, social justice and citizenship.

Citizenship and identity in a globalising world

The system or 'systems' of teacher preparation within national jurisdictions reflect the influence of dominant political ideologies, the traditions or 'shaping myths' of education (Raffe, 2004) and arrangements for the governance of teacher education. Since 2010, teacher education across the UK and RoI has attracted critical attention as teacher quality is coupled to national economic competitiveness. Government-commissioned reviews of teacher education have been undertaken in the RoI (Sahlberg et al, 2012), Northern Ireland (DEL, 2014), Scotland (Donaldson, 2011), Wales (Tabberer, 2013; Furlong, 2015) and England (DfE, 2015). It is clear that teacher education faces challenging times as national administrations recalibrate provision in a climate of austerity. Variation in intra-UK policy outcomes reflects, in part, the uneven pace and reach of devolution, the different voting systems (proportional representation outside England), party political composition and policy styles of the devolved legislatures – the Scottish and Welsh Governments, and the Northern Ireland Assembly. Education is a particularly significant portfolio in devolved government. In these smaller policy communities it is possible for political intervention to be mediated through processes of consultation and the operation of significant veto players. The earlier national chapters (Chapters Four to Eight) record differences in terms of routes and providers, the scale and structure of provision, forms of governance, the pace and direction of change, and rate of innovation.

As we have noted, different conceptualisations of teaching are signalled in the teachers' standards produced in different systems (see Chapter Nine). Revised standards/competences have been introduced in England (DfE, 2013a), Scotland (GTCS, 2012a, 2012b), Wales (Welsh Government, 2011), Northern Ireland (GTCNI, 2007) and the RoI (Teaching Council, 2012). It matters how these frameworks are developed and the range of actors involved in deliberation. Of significance here is the longevity, role and influence of teaching councils and the power and unity of purpose of professional associations/teacher unions, local authorities and higher education. The standards are aligned with accountability, but vary in the extent to which they can be seen to represent forms of professional or managerial accountability, or indeed, in the case in Chapter Nine of the Scottish 'suite' of standards, as Kennedy notes, the extent to which they can be described as internally consistent. The standards vary in how far they represent baseline thresholds for competence (England) or promote career-long professional learning (Scotland), or seriously engage with the ethical and moral dimensions of professional conduct (Northern Ireland).

Of significance too is the extent to which it is possible to talk of a national system of schooling with which teacher education is inextricably aligned. In Scotland and Wales there is continuing support for community comprehensive schools and local democratic accountability. In contrast, diversification of public education has been aggressively pursued in England through the creation of free schools and academies and the expansion of fast-track and school-based routes into teaching. Chapters Four and Twelve provide an account of the rapidly changing landscape of teacher education in England as a result of recent structural reform. In this emerging context, Whitty (2014) has questioned whether decentralisation and deregulation are producing 'multiple professionalisms' within 'a system of small systems'. He notes possibilities for 'branded professionalisms' to emerge as new 'providers' – academy chains and training schools – enter a 'market' for the provision of teacher education as a tradeable service. The displacement of the idea of the common school in this expression of localism in England fractures relations across sectors of education and may further diminish the capacity of public education to serve the common good.

This book has sought to challenge some aspects of 'Anglo-British' narratives of teacher education and to acknowledge teacher education as an area of public policy. How best to prepare teachers for publicly funded schools is a political, economic and ethical issue linked to systems of welfare and wellbeing that reflect what society values. Accounts of policy divergence strengthen the rationale for further work. In the past, policy studies of teacher education have tended to be Anglo-centric. The report entitled *The reform of teacher education in the United Kingdom* (Lynch, 1979) devoted just three pages to Scotland, less to Northern Ireland and had no separate section for Wales. The report entitled *The education of teachers in Britain* (Lomax, 1973) gave a single page to Northern Ireland (in the context of in-service provision). In a review of the first 40 volumes of the journal *History of Education*, Crook (2012, p 71) concludes that 'it must be noted with disappointment that the research on teacher education published in this journal has been exclusively English, with nothing on Northern Ireland, Scotland or Wales'. Political devolution has opened up new spaces for policy divergence and stimulated renewed interest in cross-national policy research. While noting that capacity in educational research continues to vary markedly across the UK, the Research Excellence Framework education subject panel report recently acknowledged, 'growing strength' in 'home international' comparative research, which uses the increasingly divergent policy approaches to education in England, Northern Ireland, Scotland and Wales to understand the differential impact of policy and provision' (HEFCE, 2015, p 106).

Developments in the UK need to be located within a strong transnational frame to contribute to the 'de-parochialisation' of research on policy (Lingard, 2006). Part One of this book (in Chapters Two and Three) noted how the relationship between national and international, public and private actors, in education policy networks has shifted over the last 30 years. Many commentators have noted the declining significance of the nation state as a result of economic globalisation and the increasing importance of de-territorialised political spaces. At the same time, place has achieved greater prominence in a global trend towards devolution. As Keating (2004, p 241) observes, 'states in Europe and elsewhere are being transformed, losing power upwards to global and European institutions, downwards to regions and localities and outwards to the market and civil society'. These movements are important in areas of public policy that have traditionally been nationally anchored. Robertson (2012, p 584) describes processes of individualisation whereby 'the mechanisms of global governance of teachers are being transformed from 'education as (national) development' and 'norm setting' to 'learning as (individual) development' and 'competitive comparison'. While the construction of the good (or good enough) teacher is necessarily context-dependent, our accounts of divergence within the UK clearly connect with globally mobile ideas on teacher accountability and professionalism (Sahlberg, 2012).

In terms of political culture, it is perhaps unwise to embrace accounts that exaggerate the 'exceptionalism' of English individualism. A historical perspective enables the recovery of traditions of collectivism and communitarianism. Anglo-British narratives have been rightly challenged but equally claims to homogeneity, distinctiveness and exceptionalism that equate society with nation should be approached with caution. A desire for decentralisation is evident in calls for devolution in local government in Scotland (including Scotland's islands) and the cities and sub-regions of (northern) England, Wales and Northern Ireland. If one accepts that Britishness is a 'cultural artefact' (Anderson, 1991, p 4) forged through time and struggle, then similarly there are 'varieties of Irishness' (Foster, 1989) and cultural variants of Scottishness, Welshness and Englishness (that are independent of political institutions). As parties across the UK vie for attention within a congested centre-ground, '[t]he belief that values are distinctly national may be more important than any objective evidence to the contrary' (Henderson and McEwen, 2005, p 177). As emphasised in the introduction to this work (Chapter One), divergence at the level of national policy should not be naively equated with divergent principles and practices 'on the ground'.

Teaching in the Global North is rendered more complex through emergent tensions between the espousal of national and pan-European core values, and a heightened sense of risk. Anxieties in Europe around a perceived threat of extremism have drawn education into counter-terrorism strategies. Recent non-statutory advice for schools in England (DfE, 2014, p 5) has its origins in the Prevent Strategy. Enacted with a 'different style and emphasis', the Prevent Strategy operates across the UK (HM Government, 2011, p 103). Following a series of no-notice inspections conducted in the autumn of 2014, the English schools inspectorate, Ofsted, generated a controversial 'blacklist' of schools judged to have failed to actively promote British values through spiritual, moral, social and cultural education (SMSC). The inspections followed a so-called 'Trojan horse' plot to 'take over' some schools in Birmingham and run them on 'strict Islamic principles (Clarke, 2014, p 5). The new *School inspection handbook* (Ofsted, 2015, pp 35-36) outlines how schools and teachers will be held to account for the social development of pupils in terms of their

> acceptance and engagement with the fundamental British values of democracy, the rule of law, individual liberty and mutual respect and tolerance of those with different faiths and beliefs; the pupils develop and demonstrate skills and attitudes that will allow them to participate fully in and contribute positively to life in modern Britain.

In cultures of accountability, such guidance encourages activity to embed, to 'evidence' or render visible values in education. In the context of diversity, this creates new dilemmas for educators. The nation returns as an ideological grand narrative erasing or subjugating a multitude of small narratives (Rutten et al, 2010). Values education here is subject to regulation rather than open democratic argumentation. The promotion of individual liberty and freedom of expression through decisively *il*liberal acts that construct 'anti-citizens' or 'problem communities' is a characteristic of advanced liberalism and processes of responsibilisation underpin the construction of the teacher and teacher educator in such readings. The educator is a conduit in the 'enfolding of authority' (Dean, 1996). The controversy around values education brings to the fore the normative basis of education and connects with concurrent debate on the location and content of teacher education. Mahony (2009), among others, has drawn attention to the notable omission of ethical education from teacher education curricula. There is much debate to be had on the extent to which deliberative agency is a characteristic of the new professionalism(s) in an age of 'precarity'.

Following Jones (2013), it is important that educational politics are not evacuated from deliberation in/on a European education space. Deliberation on 'what teachers are expected to know and be able to do' (OECD, 2005, p 9) might also include the role of public universities in the early 21st century (Collini, 2012). This is not to romanticise a pre-marketised era, but to draw attention to the role of critical enquiry as integral to both citizenship and professionalism. The university connection potentially strengthens expansive views of education, and understandings of what it means to be educated (Furlong, 2013a). The British Educational Research Association (BERA) and Royal Society of Arts (RSA) inquiry (BERA and RSA, 2014b) called for the promotion and development of research literacy among practitioners. While the direction of travel across the UK and RoI is in some ways similar – particularly through different expressions of a '(re)turn to the practical' – prospects for the active cultivation of a researcherly disposition are enhanced where the university connection is strong. Engagement *with* educational research and engagement *in* professional enquiry are highly visible in policy discourse in Scotland. In contrast to the craft model advanced in England, teaching is officially positioned as a complex activity demanding adaptive expertise. If one accepts Lingard and Gale's (2010, p 4) argument that a 'researcherly disposition should be conceptualised as a basic human right' that is 'central to active citizenship', then the possible erasure of deliberative enquiry from teacher education is all the more significant.

This book has considered national cases and themes that transcend geographical borders. The volume highlights areas of divergence in the post-devolution context but also a degree of interconnectedness and interdependence – or 'entanglement' (Sobe, 2013a) – in the policy-making field. Of course, the nation remains important, especially in teacher education with its long association with the political project of nation building. Identity politics create powerful attachments and these are often mobilised in national monologues about what it means to be a teacher in different jurisdictions. The degree to which national jurisdictions are able to mediate global policy influence reflects different levels of 'national capital' (Lingard, 2006). Cross-national comparison helps to disturb national monologues, to de-parochialise research, and to identify alternatives. Home international studies have an important contribution to make in exploring processes of 'glocalisation' and making sense of the many professionalisms to emerge from the interaction of the local, national and global in the reform of teacher education. Comparison can be deployed not only to account for how things are done but also to consider how things might be done differently.

Looking to the future

Where now for teacher education in these islands, our five nations? In this book we have seen how there are strong elements of both convergence and divergence in policy and practice. The RoI and the smaller UK nations are increasingly aligning themselves – at least politically – with Europe, although there appear to be greater similarities in the teacher education systems between each other than there are with the very different approaches on the European 'mainland'. However, in teacher education, even in England, which as we have noted has at times seemed to be 'going it alone', there is still perhaps greater similarity with the RoI and the other three UK jurisdictions than there is with Europe, in spite of the influence of the Bologna process – although we can detect greater affinity in England with some of the developments in the United States.

The extent to which continuing political developments, including the continuing possibility of Scottish independence (many would say likelihood), will bring about changes in teacher education is not at all clear. It could well be argued that with the extent to which global forces are now influencing all education systems, the main factors affecting teacher education are transnational – and therein lies the main force for greater 'convergence'.

But there is a key underlying question that is also very significant here. That is, how is schooling itself likely to develop in the 21st century? Is the notion of the local publicly funded school with classrooms for 20 to 35 pupils and one teacher, albeit supported by some assistants, likely to continue as the dominant form of educational provision for the future? In higher education we see some evidence of major expansions of online learning through 'MOOCs' (Massive Open Online Courses). Will new technologies have a significant impact on the ways in which compulsory schooling is provided? Some schools in the UK and RoI are already experimenting with the introduction of tablets for every child. How will this affect teaching and learning? How will this affect the role of the teacher? What will be the implications for teacher education?

What forms of knowledge will emerge in the reformed curricula of schools and of teacher education (Young and Lambert, 2014)?

Whatever the answers to these questions, our analysis of teacher education in these five nations certainly leads us to conclude that there is much to be learned from greater cooperation and collaboration between researchers, policy makers and practitioners across 'national' boundaries. Indeed, the BERA and RSA inquiry noted the missed opportunities for intra-UK learning and recommended much closer working than has been the case hitherto (BERA and RSA, 2014b). But we can also learn much more through comparing and sharing experiences with the wider world. As we have seen, 'the quality of teaching' is a worldwide concern at present and there are very few, if any, contexts where teacher education is now not under review and/or going through processes of reform (Townsend, 2011b; Darling-Hammond and Lieberman, 2012).

One of the lessons of the analysis in this book, though, is that 'simply' tinkering with teacher education itself is unlikely to bring about very significant change in the quality of teaching and teachers. At present, the working conditions for those employed in higher education sites for teacher education are far from propitious (Menter et al, 2012; Ellis and McNicholl, 2015).

Changing employment practices in higher education have brought a 'casualisation' of part of the academic workforce and the introduction of 'teaching-only' contracts across all disciplines, but because of institutional and sector reforms, teacher education has been hit particularly hard. As this book indicates, in some parts of the UK, this has resulted in the fragmentation of the occupational group, the emergence of new roles and work patterns and significant changes to professional knowledge bases and identities. Long portrayed as doing 'the impossible job' (Maguire and Weiner, 1994, p 15), teacher educators now face new pressures and demands (Brennan et al, 2014; Ellis and McNicholl, 2015).

In those instances where teaching and teacher education are judged to be of high quality and effective, we see that the teaching profession itself is of high standing within the national culture. Finland is probably the best example of this (Sahlberg, 2011a, 2011b), but the same can be said of Singapore (Tatto, 2013). In our five nations, the whole profession – including teachers and university-based teacher educators – must continue to work together through their professional organisations, such as teaching councils and colleges of teaching, to promote the profession as a whole and to demonstrate to parents and politicians that these are matters of huge social significance.

As well as this sociocultural agenda, which focuses on influencing hearts and minds throughout our communities, there is also a critical research agenda. It is crucial that at local, regional, national and international levels, there is more and better research on and in teacher education. It was the view of the sub-panel evaluating educational research in the UK that teacher education research significantly improved between 2008 and 2014 (HEFCE, 2015). But yet we still lack studies that really assess the strengths or weaknesses of different approaches, that really do seek to identify what kinds of programmes, what kinds of experiences, what kinds of structure and institutional relationships lead to improved educational outcomes. These, as we have noted, are very complex questions to investigate. We need research that is *in* teacher education, *on* teacher education and *about* teacher education (Menter, 2011a). At present, we have a fair amount of mainly small-scale research *in* teacher education, but it is all too rare for research to be carried out *on* or *about* teacher education (Menter et al, 2010b). The significant steps being taken at present towards the adoption of 'enquiry-based' or 'evidence-based' teaching are part of this picture as well and can certainly play a major part in the improvement of policy and practice, but these approaches will need to be complemented by more sustained, large-scale, critical and independent studies.

It is our hope that this book has provided some evidence of the need for these agendas to be pursued. There are agendas respectively for research, for policy and for practice. Most critically, of course, these three domains need to interact in a mutually beneficial way. Teacher education is too important an area of public policy – and spending – for ideology or prejudice to prevail. In raising the wider political significance of teacher education, paradoxically we are urging that teacher education (and indeed education more broadly) should actually be depoliticised and become much more influenced by well-informed deliberations among and between parents, students and professionals. As Furlong (2013a) argued in his analysis of the university contribution to education, what is needed is 'a maximisation of reason'. Research of the best quality will contribute towards that process and make a major contribution to the improvement of education.

Writing more than 30 years ago, Alexander et al (1984, p xviii) commented on the preceding 'two decades of organisational change' but noted that this had been within 'a context of cultural and epistemological continuity'. In some parts of these islands more than others, there has been some serious disruption to that continuity, both cultural and epistemological, since 1984. It is to be hoped that through research and dialogue over the next 20 or indeed 40 years, we can build new cultural and epistemological strengths for our important endeavours in preparing future teachers.

References

AACTE (American Association of Colleges for Teacher Education) (2010) *The clinical preparation of teachers: A policy brief*, Washington DC: American Association of Colleges for Teacher Education.

Abbott, A. (1988) *The system of professions. An essay on the division of expert labour*, Chicago: University of Chicago Press.

Abbott, A. (2005) 'Linked ecologies: States and universities as environments for professions', *Sociological Theory*, 23(3): 245-72.

Adams, R. (2013, December 4) 'Gove stands by school reforms despite Britain's failure to close gap with Asia: Change needed to improve UK rankings, says minister', *The Guardian, n.pag.* Retrieved 8 December 2013, from NewsBank online database (Access World News).

Advisory Council on Education in Scotland (1946) *Training of teachers*, Edinburgh: Advisory Council on Education in Scotland.

Ahlstrom, D. (2013, December 4). 'Teacher verdict would be: 'Satisfactory progress, but could do better' Irish Times n.pag. Retrieved 8 December 2013, from NewsBank on-line database (Access World News).

Aitken, G., Sinnema, C. and Meyer, F. (2013) *Initial teacher education outcomes: Standards for graduating teachers. A paper for discussion*, University of Auckland. Retrieved from: http://www.educationcounts.govt.nz/__data/assets/pdf_file/0014/120155/Initial-Teacher-Education-Outcomes-Standards-for-Graduating-Teachers.pdf

Aldrich, R. (2002) *The Institute of Education 1902-2002: A centenary history*, London: Institute of Education.

Aldrich, R. (2004) 'The training of teachers and educational studies: The London day training college, 1902–1932', *Paedagogica Historica*, 40(5-6): 617-31.

Alexander, R. (2012) 'Moral panic, miracle cures and education policy: What can we really learn from international comparison?', *Scottish Educational Review*, 44(1): 4-21.

Alexander, R., Craft, M. and Lynch, J. (eds) (1984a) *Change in teacher education: Context and provision since Robbins*, London: Holt, Rinehart and Winston.

Alexander, R., Craft, M. and Lynch, J. (1984b) 'Introduction', in R. Alexander, M. Craft and J. Lynch (eds) *Change in teacher education. Context and provision since Robins*, London: Holt, Rinehart and Winston, pp xiii-xviii.

Alter, J., and Coggshall, J. (2009) *Teaching as a clinical practice profession: Implications for teacher preparation and state policy*, New York: National Comprehensive Center for Teacher Quality.

Altrichter, H., Feldman, A., Posch, P. and Somekh, B. (2006) *Teachers investigate their work: An introduction to action research across the professions*, London: Routledge.

Anderson, B. (1991) *Imagined Communities*, London: Verso.

Andrews, L. (2011) 'Teaching makes a difference', Speech on 2 February 2011, Reardon Smith Theatre, Cardiff. Available at: http://gov.wales/topics/educationandskills/allsectorpolicies/ourevents/teachingmakesadifference/?lang=en

Andrews, L. (2014) *Ministering to education: A reformer reports*, Cardigan: Parthian.

Appadurai, A. (1996) *Modernity at large: Cultural dimensions of globalization*, Minneapolis, MN: University of Minnesota Press.

Apple, M. (1986) *Teachers and texts*, London: Routledge.

Apple, M. (2005). *Educating the 'Right' way: Market, standards, God, and inequality*, New York, NY: Routledge.

Arnott, M. and Ozga, J. (2010) 'Nationalism, governance and policy-making in Scotland: The Scottish National Party in power', *Public Money and Management*, 30(2): 91-6.

Asia Society (2013) *Teacher quality: The 2013 International Summit on the Teaching Profession*. Retrieved from: http://asiasociety.org/files/teachingsummit2013.pdf

ATL (Association of Teachers and Lecturers) (2013) *Select committee inquiry on School Direct and College of Teaching*, July 2013. Retrieved from: https://www.atl.org.uk/Images/atl-response-select-committee-school-direct.pdf

ATL (2014) 'Learning lessons', *Report*, March 2014, p 10..

Bailyn, B. (1963) 'Education as a discipline: Some historical notes,' in J. Walton and J.L. Kuethe (eds) *The Discipline of Education*, Madison, Wisconsin: University of Wisconsin Press, pp 125-39.

Bain, A. (1879) *Education as a science*, London: Kegan, Trench and Tubner.

Baker, P. (2006) 'Developing standards, criteria and thresholds to assess fitness to practise', *British Medical Journal*, 332(7235): 230-32.

Ball, S.J. (1990) *Politics and policy making in education: Explorations in policy sociology*, London: Routledge.

Ball, S.J. (1994) *Education reform: A critical and post-structural approach*, Buckingham: Open University Press.

Ball, S.J. (2003) *Class strategies and the education market*, London: Routledge/Falmer.

References

Ball, S.J. (2012) *Global education inc.*, London: Routledge.

Ball, S. J., and Goodson, I. F. (eds) (2002) *Teachers' lives and careers*, East Sussex: The Falmer Press.

Ball, S.J. and Junemann, C. (2012) *Networks, new governance and education*, Bristol: Policy Press.

Ball, S.J., Maguire, M., and Braun, A. (2012) *How schools do policy: Policy enactments in secondary schools*, Abingdon: Routledge.

Barber, M. and Mourshed, M. (2007) *The McKinsey report: How the world's best performing school systems come out on top*, London: McKinsey and Co.

Barnett, R. (2000) *Realising the university in an age of super-complexity*, Buckingham: Open University Press.

Barnett, R. (2003) *Beyond all reason: Living with ideology in the university*, Buckingham: Open University Press.

Bassett, P. (2003) 'Initial teacher education and training: A new opportunity for partnership in Wales', *Welsh Journal of Education*, 12(3): 4-12.

Bassey, M. and Constable, H. (1997) 'Higher education research in education 1992-1996', *Research Intelligence,* 6(1): 6-8.

Baumfield, V., Hall, E. and Wall, K. (2013) *Action research in education* (2nd edn), London: SAGE.

Beauchamp, G. (2003) 'From Hadow to Gittins: A music education framed by the people or for the people – cultural aspirations and official validation of primary school music in Wales', *Journal of Educational Administration and History*, 35:2, 127-35.

Beauchamp, G., Clarke, L., Hulme, M. and Murray, J. (2013) *Policy and practice within the United Kingdom (Research and Teacher Education: The BERA-RSA Inquiry*, London: BERA. Retrieved from: https://www.bera.ac.uk/wp-content/uploads/2013/12/BERA-Paper-1-UK-Policy-and-Practice.pdf

Beauchamp, G., Clarke, L., Hulme, M. and Murray, J. (2015) 'Teacher education in the United Kingdom post devolution: Convergences and divergences', *Oxford Review of Education*, 41(2): 154-70.

Becher, T. and Trowler, P. (2002) *Academic tribes and territories: Intellectual enquiry and the culture of disciplines*, Buckingham: SRHE and OUP.

Beck, A. (2013) *Tracing the implementation of Teaching Scotland's Future (Donaldson Report): Identifying forces at play in Scottish education policy-making*, Australian Association for Research in Education (AARE) 4/12/2013: Adelaide: SA.

Beech, J. (2006) 'The theme of educational transfer in comparative education: A view over time', *Research in Comparative and International Education*, 1(1): 2-13.

Beech, J. (2011) *Global panaceas, local realities. International agencies and the future of education,* Frankfurt: Peter Lang.

Bell, A. (1981) 'Structure, knowledge and social relationships in teacher education', *British Journal of Sociology of Education,* 2(1): 21-32.

Bennetot Pruvot, E.B., Estermann, T. and Mason, P. (2015) *Designing Strategies for Efficient Funding of Higher Education in Europe (DEFINE) Thematic Report 2; University Mergers in Europe.* Brussels: European University Association.

Bennett, T. (2013) *Teacher proof,* London: Routledge.

Benton, P. (ed) (1990) *The Oxford internship scheme: Integration and partnership in initial teacher education,* London: Calouste Gulbenkian.

BERA (British Educational Research Association) (2014) *40@40 – A portrait of educational research over forty years through forty studies.* Retrieved from: https://www.bera.ac.uk/project/40at40

BERA and RSA (Royal Society for the encouragement of Arts, Manufactures and Commerce) (2014a) *The role of research in teacher education. Reviewing the evidence. interim report of the BERA–RSA inquiry,* Author: London. Retrieved from: https://www.bera.ac.uk/wp-content/uploads/2014/02/BERA-RSA-Interim-Report.pdf

BERA and RSA (2014b) *Research and the teaching profession. Building the capacity for a self-improving education system. Final report of the BERA–RSA Inquiry into the role of research in teacher education,* Author: London. Retrieved from: https://www.bera.ac.uk/wp-content/uploads/2013/12/BERA-RSA-Research-Teaching-Profession-FULL-REPORT-for-web.pdf

BERA and UCET (Universities' Council for the Education of Teachers) Working Group on Education Research) (2012) *Prospects for education research in education departments in higher education institutions in the UK,* London: BERA and UCET.

Berg, L. (1969) *Risinghill: Death of a comprehensive school,* Harmondsworth: Penguin.

Berliner, D. (1994) 'Teacher expertise', in B. Moon and A.S. Mayes (eds) *Teaching and learning in the secondary school,* London: Routledge, pp 107-13.

Bestor, A.E. (1953) *Educational wastelands,* Urbana, IL: University of Illinois Press.

Bill and Melinda Gates Foundation (2010) *Working with teachers to develop fair and reliable measures of teaching.* Retrieved from: http://www.metproject.org/downloads/met-framing-paper.pdf

Birrell, D. (2013) 'Qualitative research and policy-making in Northern Ireland: Barriers arising from the lack of consensus, capacity and conceptualisation', *Innovation: The European Journal of Social Science Research*, 27(1): 20-30.

Birrell, D. and Heenan, D. (2013) 'Policy style and governing without consensus: devolution and education policy in Northern Ireland', *Social Policy and Administration*, 47(7): 765-82.

Blake, D. (1982) 'The purposes and nature of comparative education: the contribution of I.L. Kandel', *Comparative Education*, 18(1): 3-13.

Borko, H., Liston, D., and Whitcomb, J.A. (2007) 'Genres of empirical research in teacher education', *Journal of Teacher Education*, 58(1): 3-11.

Bourdieu, P. (1987) 'What makes a social class?' *Berkeley Journal of Sociology*, 32: 32-45.

Boxall, W. and Burrage, H. (1989) 'Recent relevant experience: how CATE legitimates narrowly defined concepts of teacher education', *Journal of Further and Higher Education*, 13(3): 30-45.

Boyd, W. and Rawson, W. (1965) *The story of the new education*, London: Heinemann.

Breakspear, S. (2012) 'The policy impact of PISA: An exploration of the normative effects of international benchmarking in school system performance', *OECD Education Working Papers,* No 71, OECD Publishing. Retrieved from: http://dx.doi.org/10.1787/5k9fdfqffr28-en

Brennan, C., Murray, J. and Read, A. (2014) *Creating the new, whilst maintaining the old? The School Direct programme and its effects on teacher education*, presentation at the BERA Conference, Institute of Education: London, September 2014.

Brisard, E., Menter, I. and Smith, I. (2005) *Models of partnership in programmes of initial teacher education. Full report of a systematic literature review commissioned by the General Teaching Council for Scotland*, GTCS Research, Research Publication No 2, Edinburgh: General Teaching Council for Scotland.

Brookfield, S. D. (2002) 'Using the lenses of critically reflective teaching in the community college classroom', *New Directions for Community Colleges*, 118: 31-8.

Brown, T., Rowley, H. and Smith, K. (2014) 'Rethinking research in teacher education', *British Journal of Educational Studies*, 62(3): 281-96.

Browne, L. (2013) 'Challenges facing HE: Teacher education provision under the microscope and what next for the academy', *Learning and Teaching*, 5(2): 1-7. Retrieved from: http://bejlt.brookes.ac.uk/issue/volume-five-issue-two/

Bruner, J. (1963) *The process of education*. New York: Random House.

Bruner, J. (1968) *Towards a theory of instruction*. New York: W.W. Norton.

Bruns, B., Filmer, D. and Patrinos, H.A. (2011) *Making schools work: New evidence on accountability reforms,* Washington DC: World Bank.

Bryce, T. G. K., Humes, W.M., Gillies, D. and Kennedy, A. (eds) (2013) *Scottish education. Fourth edition: Referendum,* Edinburgh: Edinburgh University Press.

Burke, A. (2000) 'The devil's bargain revisited: The BEd degree under review', *OIDEAS*, 48: 1-46.

Burke, A. (2009) 'The BEd degree: Still under review', *OIDEAS*, 54: 30-67.

Burn, K. and Mutton, T. (2013) *Review of 'research-informed clinical practice' in initial teacher education. Research and teacher education: The BERA–RSA Inquiry*. Retrieved from: https://www.bera.ac.uk/wp-content/uploads/2014/02/BERA-Paper-4-Research-informed-clinical-practice.pdf

Burton, N., Brundrett, M., and Jones, M. (2014) *Doing your education research project*, London: Sage.

Byrne, K.R. (2002) *Advisory group on post-primary teacher education*, Dublin: Department of Education and Science.

Cairney, P. and McGarvey, N. (2013) *Scottish politics* (2nd edn), Basingstoke: Palgrave Macmillan.

Calderhead, J. and Gates, P. (eds) (2003) *Conceptualising reflection in teacher development*, London: The Falmer Press.

Cameron, D. (2011) 'Prime Minister David Cameron has outlined his vision for the education system at a visit to a newly-opened free school in Norwich', 9 September. Retrieved from: https://www.gov.uk/government/speeches/pms-speech-on-education--2

Cannon, P. (2004) 'Teaching practice in colleges of education in the Republic of Ireland', in A. Burke (ed) *Teacher education in the Republic of Ireland: Retrospect and Prospect*, Standing Conference on Teacher Education, North and South (ScoTENS), Armagh: Centre for Cross Border Studies, pp 26-28.

Carr, W. (1987) 'What is an educational practice?', *Journal of Philosophy of Education*, 21(2): 163-75.

Carroll, J.B. (1963) 'The place of educational psychology in the study of education' in J. Walton, J. and J. L. Kuethe (eds) *The discipline of education*, Madison, Wisconsin: University of Wisconsin Press, pp 101-19.

Caul, L. and McWilliams, S. (2002) 'Accountability in partnership or partnership in accountability: Initial teacher education in Northern Ireland', *European Journal of Teacher Education*, 25(2): 187-97.

Chiesa, M. and Robertson, A. (2000) 'Precision teaching and fluency training: Making maths easier for pupils and teachers', *Educational Psychology in Practice*, 16(3): 297-310.

Childs, A., Edwards, A. and McNicholl, J. (2013) 'Developing a multi-layered system of distributed expertise: what does cultural historical theory bring to understanding workplace learning in school-university partnerships?' in O. McNamara, J. Murray, and M. Jones (eds) *Workplace learning in teacher education. Professional learning and development in schools and higher education, volume 10*, Dordrecht: Springer, pp 29-47.

Chilver Review Group (1980) *The future of higher education in Northern Ireland: An interim report of the higher education review group for NI*, Belfast: HMSO.

Chitty, C. (2014) *Education policy in Britain* (3rd edn), London: Palgrave.

Christie, D. (2008) 'Benchmarks and standards in teaching,' in T. Bryce and W. Humes (eds) *Scottish education* (3rd edn), Edinburgh: Edinburgh University Press, pp 245-54.

Christie, D., Donoghue, M., Kirk, G., McNamara, M., Menter, I., Moss, G., Noble-Rogers, J., Oancea, A., Rogers, C., Thomson, P. and Whitty, G. (2012) *BERA–UCET working group on education research. Prospects for education research in education departments in higher education institutions in the UK*, London: BERA/UCET.

Christodoulou, D. (2013) *Seven myths about education*, London: Routledge.

Clarke, P. (2014) *Report into allegations concerning Birmingham schools arising from the 'Trojan Horse' letter*. Retrieved from: https://www.gov.uk/government/uploads/system/uploads/attachment_data/file/340526/HC_576_accessible_-.pdf

Clarke, M. and Killeavy, M. (2012) 'Charting teacher education policy in the Republic of Ireland with particular reference to the impact of economic recession', *Educational Research*, 54(2): 125-36.

Clarke, M. and Killeavy, M. (2013) 'Pre-service teacher education policy and practice in an economic recession: Perspectives from the Republic of Ireland', in J. Stephenson and L. Ling (eds) *Economic challenges to teacher education in difficult economic times: International perspectives*, London: Routledge, pp 113-26.

Clarke, M. and Moore, A. (2013) 'Professional standards, teacher identities and an ethics of singularity', *Cambridge Journal of Education*, 43(4): 487-500.

Clifford, G.J. and James W. Guthrie, J.W. (1988) *Ed school: A brief for professional education*, Chicago: Chicago University Press.

Cochran-Smith, M. (2002a) 'The research base for teacher education: Metaphors we live (and die)', *Journal of Teacher Education*, 53(4): 283-85.

Cochran-Smith, M. (2002b) 'Reporting on teacher quality: The politics of politics', *Journal of Teacher Education*, 53(5): 379-82.

Cochran-Smith, M. (2004) *Walking the road – Race, diversity and social justice in teacher education,* New York: Teachers' College Press.

Cochran-Smith, M. (2005a) 'Studying teacher education what we know and need to know', *Journal of Teacher Education*, 56(4): 301-6.

Cochran-Smith, M. (2005b) 'The new teacher education: for better or for worse?', *Educational Researcher,* 34(3): 3-17.

Cochran-Smith, M. (2012) 'Trends and challenges in teacher education: National and international perspectives', in F. Waldron, J. Smith, M. Fitzpatrick and T. Dooley (eds) *Re-imagining initial teacher education: Perspectives on transformation,* Dublin: Liffey Press, 29-53.

Cochran-Smith, M. (in press) 'Keeping teaching complex: policy, research and practice', *Venue exchange of thoughts and knowledge about pre-school and school,* Linkoping, Sweden: Linkoping University.

Cochran-Smith, M. and Fries, K. (2011) 'Teacher quality, teacher education and diversity: policy and politics', in A. Ball and C. Tyson (eds) *Studying diversity in teacher education,* New York, NY: Roman and Littlefield, 337-59.

Cochran-Smith, M. and Lytle, S. L. (1993) *Inside out: Teacher research and knowledge,* New York: Teachers College.

Cochran-Smith, M. and Lytle, S. L. (1999) 'Relationships of knowledge and practice: Teacher learning in communities', *Review of Research in Education,* 24(1): 249-305.

Cochran-Smith, M., and Lytle, S. L. (2009) *Enquiry as stance: Practitioner research for the next generation,* NY: Teachers College Press.

Cohen-Vogel, L. and Ingle, K. (2007) 'When neighbors matter most: Innovation, diffusion and state policy adoption in tertiary education', *Journal of Education Policy,* 22 (3):241-62.

Collini, S. (2012) *What are universities for?,* London: Penguin.

Conle, C. (2000) 'Narrative enquiry: Research tool and medium for professional development', *European Journal of Teacher Education,* 23(1): 49-63.

Conroy, J.C., Hulme, M, and Menter, I. (2013) 'Developing a 'clinical' model for teacher education', *Journal of Education for Teaching: International Research and Pedagogy,* 39(5): 557-73.

Conway, P. F. (2013) 'Cultural flashpoint: The politics of teacher education reform in Ireland', *The Educational Forum,* 77(1): 51-72.

References

Conway, P.F. and Murphy, R. (2013) 'A rising tide meets a perfect storm: New accountabilities in teaching and teacher education in Ireland', *Irish Educational Studies*, 32(1): 11-36.

Conway, P.F, Murphy, R. and Rutherford, V. (2013) "Learning place' practices and pre-service teacher education in Ireland: Knowledge generation, partnerships and pedagogy' in O. McNamara, J. Murray, and M. Jones (eds) *Workplace learning in teacher education: International practice and policy*, Amsterdam: Springer/Verlag, pp 221-41.

Conway, P.F., Murphy, R., Rath, A. and Hall, K. (2009) *Learning to teach and its implications for the continuum of teacher education: A nine country cross-national study*, Teaching Council of Ireland: Maynooth. Retrieved from: http://www.teachingcouncil.ie/_fileupload/Research/Commisioned%20Research/LearningToTeach-ConwayMurphyRathHall-2009_10344263.pdf

Coolahan, J. (2003) *Attracting, developing and retaining effective teachers: Country background report for Ireland*, Dublin: Department of Education and Science.

Coolahan, J. (2004a) 'The historical development of teacher education in the Republic of Ireland', in A. Burke (ed) *Teacher education in the Republic of Ireland: Retrospect and prospect*, Armagh: Centre for Cross-Border Studies.

Coolahan, J. (2004b) 'The development of education studies and teacher education in Ireland', *Education Research and Perspectives*, 31(2): 30-47.

Coolahan, J. (2007) *A review paper on thinking and policies relating to teacher education in Ireland*, Paper prepared for the Teaching Council, Ireland. Retrieved from: www.theteachingcouncil.ie

Coolahan, J. (2013) 'Towards a new era for teacher education and the engagement of the teaching profession', *Irish Teachers' Journal*, 1(1): 9-27.

Coolahan, J., Hussey, C. and Kilfeather, F. (2012) *Forum on patronage and pluralism in the primary sector: Report of the forum's advisory group*, Dublin: Government Publications.

Cordingley, P. (2013) *The contribution of research to teachers' professional learning and development. Research and teacher education: The BERA–RSA Enquiry*. Retrieved from: https://www.bera.ac.uk/wp-content/uploads/2013/12/BERA-Paper-5-Continuing-professional-development-and-learning.pdf

Counsell, C. (2013) 'The other person in the room: a hermeneutic-phenomenological inquiry into mentors' experience of using academic and professional literature with trainee history teachers' in M. Evans (ed) *Teacher education and pedagogy: theory, policy and practice,* Cambridge: Cambridge University Press, pp 134-82.

Cox, C.B. and Dyson, A.E. (eds) (1969) *Fight for education: A black paper*, London: Critical Quarterly Society.

CPPR (Centre for Public Policy for Regions) (2012) *Scottish government's draft budget 2013-14, briefing No. 1. CPPR pre-budget briefing*. Retrieved from: http://www.cppr.ac.uk/media/media_241748_en.pdf

Craft, M. (1984) 'Change and continuity in teacher education', in R. Alexander, M.Craft, and J. Lynch (eds) *Change in teacher education. Context and provision since Robbins*, London: Holt, Rinehart and Winston, pp 332-41.

Cromien, S. (2000) *Department of Education and Science: Review of Department's operations, systems and staffing needs report*, Dublin: Department of Education and Skills.

Crook, D. (2012) 'Teacher education as a field of historical research: Retrospect and prospect', *History of Education*, 41(1): 57-72.

Crozier, G., Menter, I., Pollard, A. (1990) 'Changing partnerships', in M. Booth, J. Furlong, and M. Wilkin (eds), *Partnership in initial teacher training*, London: Cassells, pp 44-56.

Cruickshank, M. (1970) *A history of the training of teachers in Scotland*, London: University of London Press.

Cullingford, C. (1999) *An inspector calls: Ofsted and its effect on school standards*, London: Routledge.

Czarniawska, C. and Sevon, G. (eds) (2005) *Global ideas. How ideas, objects and practices travel in the global economy*, Malmo: Liber and Copenhagen Business School Press.

Daily Mail (2012). Retrieved from: http://www.dailymail.co.uk/news/article-2159031/Top-graduates-handed-25-000-learn-teach-tough-inner-city-schools.html

Daly, C., Pachler, N., and Lambert, N. (2004) 'Teacher learning: Towards a professional academy', *Teaching in Higher Education*, 9(1): 99-111.

Darling-Hammond, L. (1999) 'Reforming teacher preparation and licensing: debating the evidence', *Teachers College Record*, 102(1): 28-56.

Darling-Hammond, L. (2012) 'Foreword', in M.S. Tucker (ed) *Surpassing Shanghai. An agenda for American education built on the world's leading systems*, Cambridge, MA: Harvard University Press, pp ix-xii.

Darling-Hammond, L. and Lieberman, A. (eds) (2012) *Teacher education around the world*, London: Routledge.

Daugherty, R. and Davies, S.M.B. (2011) 'Capacity and quality in education research in Wales: A stimulus report for the SFRE – August 2008', *Welsh Journal of Education*, 15(1): 4-23.

Daugherty, R. and Jones, G.E. (2002) 'Research note: The learning country', *The Welsh Journal of Education*, 11(1): 107-13.

Davie, G. (1961) *The democratic intellect*, Edinburgh: Edinburgh University Press.

Davies, S. and Salisbury, J. (2007) 'Building educational research capacity through inter-institutional collaboration: An evaluation of the first year of the Welsh Education Research Network (WERN)', *The Welsh Journal of Education*, 14(2): 78-94.

Day, C. (1999) *Developing teachers*, London: Routledge.

Day, C., Sammons, P., Stobart, G., Kington, A. and Gu, Q. (2007) *Teachers matter*, Buckingham: Open University.

DCELLS (Department for Children, Education, Lifelong Learning and Skills) (2008) *Framework for children's learning for 3 to 7-year-olds in Wales*, Cardiff: Welsh Assembly Government.

DCSF (Department for Children, Schools and Family) (2008) *Being the best for our children*, Green Paper, London: DCSF.

DE (Department of Education) (2010) *The teacher education partnership handbook*, Bangor: DE. Retrieved from: http://www.deni.gov.uk/the_teacher_education_partnership_handbook_-_august_2010.pdf

DE (2013) 'Approved intakes to initial teacher education courses'. Retrieved from: http://www.deni.gov.uk/index/school-staff/teachers-teachinginnorthernireland_pg/teachers_-_teaching_in_northern_ireland-4_approved_intakes.htm

DE (2015) *Integrated schools*. Retrieved from: http://www.deni.gov.uk/16-schools-integratedschools_pg.htm

Dean, M. (1996) 'Foucault, government and the enfolding of authority', in A. Barry, T. Osborne and N. Rose (eds) *Foucault and political reason: Liberalism, neo-liberalism and rationalities of government*, Chicago: Chicago University Press, pp 209-230.

Dean, M. (1999) *Governmentality: Power and rule in modern society*, London: Sage.

Deegan, J. (2012) 'Bridging being and becoming: Teacher education programmes in the Republic of Ireland', in F. Waldron, J. Smith, M. Fitzpatrick and T. Dooley (eds) *Re-imagining initial teacher education: Perspectives on transformation*, Dublin: Liffey Press, pp 179-200.

DEL (Department of Employment and Learning) (2010) *Teacher education in a climate of change: The way forward*, Belfast: DEL. Retrieved from: http://www.deni.gov.uk/teacher_education_in_a_climate_of_change_-_the_way_forward_-_english_version.pdf

DEL (2014) *Aspiring to Excellence: Final report of the International Review Panel on the Structure of Initial Teacher Education in Northern Ireland*, Belfast: DEL. Retrieved from: http://www.delni.gov.uk/aspiring-to-excellence-review-panel-final-report.pdf

Dent, H. (1977) *The training of teachers in England and Wales 1800–1975*, London: Hodder and Stoughton.

Depaepe, M. (2012) *Between educationalization and appropriation: Selected writings on the history of modern educational systems*, Verlag: Leuven University Press.

Department of Education and Skills (2011) *Literacy and numeracy for learning and for life: The national strategy to improve literacy and numeracy among children and young people, 2011–2020*, Dublin: DES.

Department of Education and Skills (2012) *Report of the International Review Panel on the Structure of Initial Teacher Education Provision in Ireland*, Dublin: DES. Retrieved from: http://www.education.ie/en/Press-Events/Press-Releases/2012-Press-Releases/Report-of-the-International-Review-Panel-on-the-Structure-of-Initial-Teacher-Education-Provision-in-Ireland.pdf

Dent, H. (1977) *The training of teachers in England and Wales 1800–1975*, London: Hodder and Stoughton.

DES (1983) *Teaching quality*, White Paper, London: HMSO.

DES (1984) *Initial teacher training: Approval of courses* (Circular 3/84), London: DES.

DES (1987) *Higher education: Meeting the challenge*, London: HMSO.

DES (1989) *Initial teacher training: approval of courses* (Circular 24/89), London: HMSO.

DfE (Department for Education) (1992) *Initial teacher training (secondary phase)* (Circular 9/92), London: DFE.

DfE (1993) *The initial training of primary school teachers: New criteria for course approval* (Circular 14/93), London: DFE.

DfE (2010) *The importance of teaching*, White Paper, London: DfE.

DfE (2011) *Training our next generation of outstanding teachers: Implementation plan*. Retrieved from: https://www.gov.uk/government/publications/training-our-next-generation-of-outstanding-teachers-implementation-plan

DfE (2013a) *Teachers' standards*, Department for Education: UK Government.

DfE (2013b) *New randomised controlled trials will drive forward evidence-based research*. Retrieved from: https://www.gov.uk/government/news/new-randomised-controlled-trials-will-drive-forward-evidence-based-research

DfE (2014) *Promoting fundamental British values as part of SMSC in schools. Departmental advice for maintained schools.* Retrieved from: https://www.gov.uk/government/uploads/system/uploads/attachment_data/file/380595/SMSC_Guidance_Maintained_Schools.pdf

DfE (2015) *Carter review of initial teacher training (ITT)*, London: DfE. Retrieved from: https://www.gov.uk/government/publications/carter-review-of-initial-teacher-training

DfEE (Department for Education and Employment) (1997) *Teaching: high status, high standards* (Circular 9/97), London: DfEE.

DfEE (1998) *Teachers: Meeting the challenge of change*, Green Paper, London: DfEE.

Dickson, B. (2011) 'Beginning teachers as enquirers: m-level work in initial teacher education', *European Journal of Teacher Education*, 34(3): 259-76.

Dolowitz, D. with Hulme, R., Nellis, M. and O'Neal, F. (2000) *Policy transfer and British social policy*, Buckingham: Open University Press.

Dolowitz, D.P. and Marsh, D. (2000) 'Learning from abroad: The role of policy transfer in contemporary policy-making', *Governance*, 13: 5-23.

Donaldson, G. (2010) *Teaching Scotland's future: A report of the review of teacher education in Scotland*, Edinburgh: Scottish Government.

Donaldson, G. (2015) *Successful futures: Independent review of assessment and the national curriculum for Wales.* Retrieved from: http://wales.gov.uk/docs/dcells/publications/141009-update-to-minister-en.pdf

Donnelly, C., McKeown, P. and Osborne, R. (eds) (2006) *Devolution and pluralism in education in Northern Ireland*, Manchester: Manchester University Press.

Drakeford, M. (2007) 'Progressive universalism', *Agenda*, Winter, 4–7.

Education Scotland (2013) *Transforming lives through learning, Corporate Plan 2013–2016*, Glasgow: Education Scotland.

Edwards, A. and Collison, J. (1996) *Mentoring and developing practice in primary schools*, Buckingham: Open University Press.

Edwards, A. and Mutton, T. (2007) 'Looking forward: Rethinking professional learning through partnership arrangements in initial teacher education', *Oxford Review of Education*, 33(4): 503-19.

Edwards, A., Tanner, D. and Carlin, P. (2011) 'The Conservative governments and the development of Welsh language policy in the 1980s and 1900s', *The Historical Journal*, 54(2): 529-51.

Ellis, V. and McNicholl, J. (2015) *Transforming teacher education*, London: Bloomsbury.

Ellis, V., McNicholl, J. and Pendry, A. (2012) 'Institutional conceptualisations of teacher education as academic work in England', *Teaching and Teacher Education* 28(5): 685-93.

Equality and Human Rights Commission (2011), *An anatomy of economic inequality in Wales*, Wales Institute of Social and Economic Research, Data and Methods (WISERD) Retrieved from: http://www.equalityhumanrights.com/sites/default/files/documents/Wales/an_anatomy_of_economic_inequality_in_wales.pdf

Eraut, M. (2014) 'Developing knowledge for qualified professionals' in O. McNamara, J. Murray, and M. Jones (eds) (2014) *Workplace learning in teacher education. Professional learning and development in schools and higher education,* volume 10, Dordrecht: Springer, pp 47-72.

European Commission, (2013) *Supporting teacher competence development for better learning outcomes*, European Commission Education and Training. Retrieved from: http://ec.europa.eu/education/policy/school/doc/teachercomp_en.pdf

Evans, L. (2011) 'The "shape" of teacher professionalism in England: Professional standards, performance management, professional development and the changes proposed in the 2010 White Paper', *British Educational Research Journal,* 37(5): 851-70.

Fairclough, N., Mulderrig, J. and Wodak, R. (2011) 'Critical discourse analysis', in T.A. van Dijk (ed) *Discourse studies: A multidisciplinary introduction* (2nd edn), Sage: London, pp 357-78.

Feiman-Nemser, S. (2008) 'Teacher learning: How do teachers learn to teach' in M. Cochran-Smith, S. Feiman-Nemser, D. McIntyre, and K. Demers (eds) *Handbook of research on teacher education: Enduring questions in changing contexts*, NY: Routledge, pp 697-705.

Fish, D. (1995) *Quality learning for student teachers: University tutors' educational practices*, London: David Fulton Publishers.

Flesch, R. (1955) *Why Johnny can't read*, New York: Harper.

Forbes, J. and Watson, C. (eds) (2012) *The transformation of children's services,* London: Routledge.

Forde, C., McPhee, A., McMahon, M. and Patrick, F. (2006) *Professional development, reflection and enquiry,* London: Paul Chapman.

Foster, R.F. (1989) *Cultural traditions in Northern Ireland: varieties of Irishness*, Chester Springs PA: Dufour Editions.

Freire, P. (1971) *Pedagogy of the oppressed,* Harmondsworth: Penguin.

Fullan, M. (2013) *Great to excellent: Launching the next stage of Ontario's education agenda.* Retrieved from: http://www.michaelfullan.ca/media/13599974110.pdf

Furlong, J. (1996) 'Do student teachers need higher education?', in J. Furlong, and R. Smith (eds) *The role of higher education in initial teacher education,* Abingdon: Kogan Page, pp 150-65.

Furlong, J. (2013a) *Education – an anatomy of the discipline: Rescuing the university project?* Oxon: Routledge.

Furlong J. (2013b) 'Globalisation, neoliberalism, and the reform of teacher education in England', *The Educational Forum*, 77(1): 28-50.

Furlong, J. (2015) *Teaching Tomorrow's Teachers: Options for the future of initial teacher education in Wales,* Oxford: University of Oxford Department of Education.

Furlong, J. and Lawn, M. (2011) *Disciplines of education: Their role in the future of education research,* Abingdon: Routledge.

Furlong, J., Hirst, P., Pocklington, K. and Miles, S. (1988) *Initial teacher training and the role of the school,* Milton Keynes: Open University Press.

Furlong, J., Whitty, G., Whiting, C., Miles, S., Barton, L., and Barrett, E. (1996) 'Re-defining partnership: revolution or reform in initial teacher education?, *Journal of Education for Teaching: International research and pedagogy*, 22(1): 39-56.

Furlong, J., Barton, L., Miles, S., Whiting, C. and Whitty, G. (2000) *Teacher education in transition: Reforming professionalism,* Buckingham: Open University Press.

Furlong, J., Hagger, H. and Butcher, C. (2006a) *Review of Initial Teacher Training Provision in Wales: A report to the Welsh Assembly Government,* January 2006, Oxford: University of Oxford Department of Educational Studies.

Furlong, J., Campbell, A., Howson, J., Lewis, S. and McNamara, O. (2006b) 'Partnership in English initial teacher education: changing times, changing definitions. Evidence from the Teacher Training Agency's National Partnership Project', *Scottish Educational Review*, 37: 32–45.

Furlong, J., Pendry, A. and Mertova, P. (2011) *SCoTENS: An evaluation of its first 8 years,* Armagh: Standing Conference on Teacher Education, North and South.

Fyne, C. (2014) 'Teacher education and training: Announcement of teacher education ministerial advisory group', 19 February. Retrieved from: http://www.pyneonline.com.au/media/transcripts/announcement-of-teacher-education-ministerial-advisory-group

Gale, T. and Densmore, K. (2003) *Engaging teachers,* Maidenhead: Open University Press.

Galvin, C. (2009) 'Public policy making: The emerging policy making modality and its challenge for education policy research in Ireland', in S. Drudy (ed) *Education in Ireland, challenge and change,* Dublin: Gill and Macmillan, pp 268-82.

Gardner, P. (1993) 'The early history of school-based teacher training' in D. McIntyre, H. Hagger, and M. Wilkin (eds) *Mentoring: Perspectives on school-based teacher education,* London: Kogan Page, pp 21-36.

Gardner, P. and Cunningham, P. (2010) 'Teacher trainers and educational change in Britain, 1876-1996: 'A flawed and deficit history'?, *Journal of Education for Teaching,* 24(3): 231-55.

Gewirtz, S., Mahony, P., Hextall, I. and Cribb, A. (eds.) (2009) *Changing teacher professionalism,* London: Routledge.

Gilroy, P. (1992) 'The political rape of initial teacher education in England and Wales: a JET rebuttal', *Journal of Education for Teaching,* 18(1): 5-22.

Gilroy, P. (2014) 'Policy intervention in teacher education: sharing the English experience', *Journal of Education for Teaching,* 40(5): 622-32.

Gilroy, P. and McNamara, O. (2009) 'A critical history of research assessment in the United Kingdom and its post-1992 impact on education, *Journal of Education for Teaching: International research and pedagogy',* 35(4): 321-35.

Gleeson, J. (2004) 'Concurrent teacher education (post-primary) in the Republic of Ireland: Some issues and trends', in A. Burke (ed) *Teacher education in the Republic of Ireland: Retrospect and prospect,* Armagh: Centre for Cross-Border Studies.

Goldacre, B. (2013) *Building evidence into education.* Retrieved from: http://media.education.gov.uk/assets/files/pdf/b/ben%20 goldacre%20paper.pdf.

Goodchild, L.F. (2006) 'The beginnings of education at American universities', in R. Hofstetter and B. Schneuwly (eds) *Passion, fusion, tension. New education and educational sciences. End 19th–middle 20th century,* Berne: Peter Lang, pp 69-105.

Goodlad, J. (1990) 'Connecting the present to the past', in J. Goodlad, R. Soder, and K.A. Sirotnik (eds) *Places where teachers are taught,* San Francisco, CA: Jossey-Bass, pp 3-39.

Goodson, I. F. (1991) 'Sponsoring the teacher's voice: Teachers' lives and teacher development', *Cambridge Journal of Education,* 21(1): 35-45.

Goodson, I.F. (2003) *Professional knowledge, professional lives,* Maidenhead: Open University.

Goodwin, A. L. (2010) 'Globalization and the preparation of quality teachers: Rethinking knowledge domains for teaching', *Teaching Education*, 21(1): 19-32.

Gove, M. (2010) Speech to the National College Annual Conference, Birmingham on 16 June 2010. Retrieved from: https://www.gov.uk/government/speeches/michael-gove-to-the-national-college-annual-conference-birmingham

Gove, M. (2012) The education secretary's speech on academies at Haberdashers' Aske's Hatcham College, 4 January 2012. Retrieved from: https://www.gov.uk/government/speeches/michael-gove-speech-on-academies

Gove, M. (2013) 'I refuse to surrender to the Marxist teachers hell-bent on destroying our schools', *Daily Mail*, 23 March. Retrieved from: http://www.dailymail.co.uk/debate/article-2298146/I-refuse-surrender-Marxist-teachers-hell-bent-destroying-schools-Education-Secretary-berates-new-enemies-promise-opposing-plans.html

Government of Ireland (1965) *Investment in education: Report of the survey team presented to the Minister for Education in October 1962*, Dublin: Stationery Office.

Government of Ireland (1967) *Report of the Commission on Higher Education 1960–67*, Dublin: Stationery Office.

Government of Ireland (1992) *Education for a changing world: Green paper on education*, Dublin: the Stationery Office.

Government of Ireland, (1995) *Charting our education future: White paper on education*, Dublin: the Stationery Office.

Government of Ireland, Department of Finance (2011) *The Irish Economy*. Retrieved from: http://www.finance.gov.ie/sites/default/files/irisheconomyjune2011.pdf.

Graham, J. (ed) (1999) *Teacher professionalism and the challenge of change*, Stoke-on-Trent: Trentham.

Graham, S. and Macaro, E. (2008) 'Strategy instruction in listening for lower-intermediate learners of French', *Language Learning*, 58(4): 747-83.

Grant, C.A. and Agosto, V. (2008), 'Teacher capacity and social justice in teacher education', in M. Cochran-Smith, S. Feiman-Nemser, D. McIntyre, D. and K. Demers (eds) *Handbook of research on teacher education: Enduring questions in changing contexts*, NY: Routledge, pp 175-200.

Grant Thornton (2013) *DEL: Study of the teacher education infrastructure in Northern Ireland*, Belfast: DEL. Retrieved from: http://www.delni.gov.uk/teacher-education-infrastructure-ni-study.pdf

Griffiths, D. (1999) 'The Welsh Office and Welsh autonomy', *Public Administration*, 77(4): 793-807. Retrieved from: http://www.walesonline.co.uk/news/local-news/ministers-view---leighton-andrews-2024801

Griffiths, M. (2000) 'Collaboration and partnership in question: Knowledge, politics and practice', *Journal of Education Policy,* 15(4): 383-95.

Griffiths, M. and Tann, S. (1992) 'Using reflective practice to link personal and public theories', *British Journal of Teacher Education*, 18(1): 69-84.

Grossman, P. and McDonald, M. (2008) 'Back to the future: Directions for research in teaching and teacher education', *American Educational Research Journal*, 45(1): 184-205.

Grossman, P., Hammerness, K. and McDonald, M. (2009) 'Re-defining teaching, re-imagining teacher education', *Teachers and Teacher Education,* 15(2): 273-89.

Groundwater-Smith, S. (2006) 'Professional knowledge formation in the Australian market place: Changing the perspective', *Scottish Educational Review,* 37 (Special edition on Teacher Education and Professional Development): 123-31.

Groundwater-Smith, S. (2011) 'Foreward,' in M. Mattsson, T. Eilertson, and D. Rorrison, (eds) *A practicum turn in teacher education*, Rotterdam: Sense, pp ix-xi.

GTCNI (General Teaching Council for Northern Ireland) (2005) *GTCNI reviews of teacher competences and continuing professional development*, Belfast: GTCNI. Retrieved from: http://www.gtcni.org.uk//publications/uploads/document/Teacher%20Education%20Report.pdf

GTCNI (2007) *Teaching: The reflective profession,* Belfast: GTCNI. Retrieved from: http://www.gtcni.org.uk/uploads/docs/gtcni_comp_bmrk%20%20aug%2007.pdf

GTCS (General Teaching Council for Scotland) (1997) *The report of the working group on partnership in initial teacher education*, Edinburgh: GTC Scotland.

GTCS (2012a) *The standards for registration: Mandatory requirements for registration with the General Teaching Council for Scotland,* Edinburgh: GTCS.

GTCS (2012b) *The standard for career-long professional learning: Supporting the development of teacher professional learning,* Edinburgh: GTCS.

GTCS (2012c) *The standards for leadership and management: Supporting leadership and management development*, Edinburgh: GTCS.

GTCNI (General Teaching Council for Northern Ireland) (2005) *GTCNI Reviews of Teacher Competences and Continuing Professional Development*, Belfast: GTCNI. Retrieved from: http://www.gtcni.org.uk//publications/uploads/document/Teacher%20Education%20Report.pdf

GTCW (General Teaching Council for Wales) (2014) *Annual statistics digest March 2014.* Retrieved from: http://www.gtcw.org.uk/gtcw/images/stories/downloads/Annual%20Statistics%20Digest/Annual_Stats_14_E.pdf

GTCW and Welsh Government (2012) *Induction, Masters in Educational Practice (MEP) and early professional development (EPD): Funding, tracking and recording arrangements,* Cardiff: GTCW / WG.

Guimond, S., Begin, G. and Palmer, D. L. (1989) 'Education and causal attributions: the development of "person-blame" and "system-blame" ideology', *Social Psychology Quarterly,* 52(2): 126-40.

Hagan, M. (2013) 'Developing teacher competence and professionalism in Northern Ireland: An analysis of 'Teaching the Reflective Profession", *Teacher Education Advancement Network Journal,* 5(1): 60-70.

Hagger, H., and McIntyre, D. (2000) 'What can research tell us about teacher education?', *Oxford Review of Education,* 26(3-4): 483-94.

Hagger, H. and McIntyre, D. (2006) *Learning teaching from teachers: Realizing the potential of school-based teacher education,* Maidenhead: Open University Press.

Hammerness, K., Darling-Hammond, L., Bransford, J., Berliner, D., Cochran-Smith, M., McDonald, M. and Zeichner, K. (2005) 'How teachers learn and develop', in L. Darling-Hammond and J. Bransford (eds) *Preparing teachers for a changing world: What teachers should learn and be able to do,* San Francisco: Jossey-Bass, pp 358-89.

Hammersley, M. (ed) (2007) *Educational research and evidence-based practice,* Buckingham: Open University Press.

Han, X. (2012) 'Big moves to improve the quality of teacher education in China', *On the Horizon,* 20(4): 324-35.

Hardy, I. and Rönnerman, K. (2011) 'The value and valuing of continuing professional development: current dilemmas, future directions and the case for action research' *Cambridge journal of education,* 41(4): 461-72.

Hargreaves, A. (2013) 'Professional capital and the future of teaching', in T. Seddon and J.S. Levin (eds) *Educators, professionalism and politics. Global transitions, national spaces and professional projects,* London: Routledge, pp 290-310.

Hargreaves, A. and Fullan, M. (2012) *Professional capital,* London: Routledge.

Harkin, S and Hazelkorn, E. (2015) 'Restructuring Irish higher education through collaboration and merger', inn Curai, A. Georghiou, L., Harper, J.C., Pricopie, R. and Ergon-Polak, E. (eds) (2015) *Mergers and alliances in higher education: international practice and emerging opportunities.* Springer.

Harris, K. (1982) *Teachers and classes,* London: Routledge and Kegan Paul.

Harrison, J., and McKeon, F. (2008) 'The formal and situated learning of beginning teacher educators in England: identifying characteristics for successful induction in the transition from workplace in schools to workplace in higher education', *European Journal of Teacher Education,* 31(2): 151-68.

Hartley, D. (2002) 'Global influences on teacher education in Scotland', *Journal of Education for Teaching,* 28(3): 251-55.

HEA (Higher Education Authority) (1967) *Report of the commission on higher education,* Dublin: The Higher Education Authority.

HEA (2012) *Towards a future higher education landscape,* Dublin: The Higher Education Authority.

HEA (2014) *What do our graduates do? The class of 2013: An analysis of the universities and colleges of education first destination of graduates survey 2014,* Dublin: HEA. Retrieved from: http://www.hea.ie/sites/default/files/final_class_of_2013_221214.pdf

HEFCE (Higher Education Funding Council for England) (1997) *The impact of the 1992 Research Assessment Exercise on higher education institutions in England.* Retrieved from: http://www.hefce.ac.uk/pubs/hefce/1997/m6_97.htm

HEFCE (2009) *RAE 2008 UOA 45 Subject Overview Report (Education),* Retrieved from: http://www.rae.ac.uk/pubs/2009/ov/

HEFCE (2015) *Research Excellence Framework 2014: Overview report by Main Panel C and Sub-panels 16 to 26.* Retrieved from: http://www.ref.ac.uk/media/ref/content/expanel/member/Main%20Panel%20C%20overview%20report.pdf

Hencke, D. (1978) *Colleges in crisis.* London: Penguin.

Henderson, A. and McEwen, N. (2005) 'Do shared values underpin national identity? Examining the role of values in national identity in Canada and the United Kingdom', *National Identities,* 7(2): 173-91.

Heward, C. (1993) 'Men and women and the rise of professional society: The intriguing history of teacher educators', *History of Education,* 22(1): 11–32.

Hill, D. (1992) 'What's happened to initial teacher education? Three ways of 'conforming' the teacher educators', *Education Review*, 6(2): 32-42.

Hillgate Group (1986) *Whose schools? A radical manifesto*, London: Hillgate Group.

Hislop, H. (2011) 'Teacher education and Ireland's national strategy to improve literacy and numeracy', Speech given at SCoTENS Annual Conference, 29 September 2011. Retrieved from: http://scotens.org/docs/2011-Hislop-speech.pdf.

HM Government (2011) *Prevent Strategy*, Cm 8092. London: Stationery Office. Retrieved from: https://www.gov.uk/government/publications/prevent-strategy-2011

HM Treasury (2013) *Public expenditure statistical analyses 2013*, Cm 8663, July, London: HM Treasury.

Hobson, A. and Malderez, A. (2005) *Becoming a teacher: Student teachers' motives and preconceptions, and early school-based experiences during initial teacher training (ITT)*, Nottingham: The University of Nottingham.

Hobson, A.J, Malderez, A., Johnson, F., and Tracey, L. (2006) *Becoming a teacher: Student teachers' experiences of initial teacher training in England*, Nottingham: The University of Nottingham.

Hobson, A.J., Ashby, P., Malderez, A. and Tomlinson, P.D. (2009) 'Mentoring beginning teachers: What we know and what we don't', *Teaching and Teacher Education*, 25(1): 207-16.

Hofstetter, R. and Schneuwly, B. (2006) 'Introduction. Progressive education and educational sciences. The tumultuous relations of an indissociable and irreconcilable couple?' in R. Hofstetter and B. Schneuwly (eds) *Passion, fusion, tension. New education and educational sciences. End 19th–middle 20th century*, Berne: Peter Lang, pp 1-16.

Horlacher, R. (2013) 'Do educational models impose standardization? Reading Pestalozzi historically', in T.S. Popkewitz (ed) *Rethinking the history of education: Transnational perspectives on its questions, methods, and knowledge*, New York: Palgrave Macmillan, pp 135-56.

House of Commons Children, Schools and Families Committee (2010) *The training of teachers: Fourth report of session 2009–10. Vol 1*, London: HCSO.

Huberman, M. (1993) *The lives of teachers*, London: Cassell.

Hulme, M. and Menter, I. (2008a) 'Learning to teach in post-devolution UK', ESRC Teaching and Learning Research Programme, Research briefing No 49, London: ESRC.

Hulme, M. and Menter, I. (2008b) 'Learning to teach in post-devolution UK: A technical or an ethical process?', *Southern Africa Review of Education*, 14(1-2): 43-64.

Hulme, M. and Menter, I. (2011) 'Teacher education policy in England and Scotland: A comparative textual analysis', *Scottish Educational Review*, 43(2): 70-90.

Hulme, M. and Menter, I. (2013) 'The evolution of teacher education and the Scottish universities', in T.G.K. Bryce, W.M. Humes, D. Gillies and A. Kennedy (eds) *Scottish education (4th edn): Referendum*, Edinburgh University Press: Edinburgh, pp 905-14.

Hulme, M., Baumfield, V. and Payne, F. (2009) 'Building capacity through teacher enquiry: the Scottish schools of ambition', *Journal of Education for Teaching*, 35(4): 409-24.

Humes, W. (1986) *The leadership class*, Edinburgh: John Donald.

Humes, W. (2013) 'The origins and development of Curriculum for Excellence: discourse politics and control', in M. Priestley and G. Biesta (eds) *Reinventing the curriculum: new trends in curriculum policy and practice*, London: Bloomsbury, pp 13-34.

Humes, W. and Bryce, T. (2013) 'The distinctiveness of Scottish education', in T.G.K. Bryce, W.M. Humes, D. Gillies, and A. Kennedy (eds) *Scottish education. Fourth edn: Referendum*, Edinburgh: Edinburgh University Press, pp 138-50.

Hyland, A. (2012) *A review of the structure of initial teacher education provision in Ireland: Background paper for the international review team*, Dublin: Department of Education and Skills.

Ingvarson, L. (1998) 'Professional development as the pursuit of professional standards: the standards-based professional development system', *Teaching and Teacher Education*, 14(1): 127-40.

Jackson, A. and Eady, S. (2012) 'Teaching as a Master's profession in England: The need for continued debate', *Professional Development in Education*, 38(1): 149-52.

James, Lord (1972) *Teacher Education and Training* (The James Report), London: HMSO.

Jeffrey, B. and Woods, P. (1998) *Testing teachers: The effects of inspections on primary teachers*, London: Routledge.

Jessop, B. (1999) 'Narrating the future of the national economy and the national state: Remarks on remapping regulation and reinventing governance', in G. Steinmetz (ed) *State/culture. State-formation after the cultural turn*, Ithaca: Cornell University Press, pp 378-405.

Jones, G.E. (1997) *The education of a nation*, Cardiff: University of Wales Press.

Jones, G.E. and Roderick, W. (2003) *A history of education in Wales*, Cardiff: University of Wales Press.

Jones, J.G. (2014) *The history of Wales* (3rd edn), Cardiff: University of Wales Press.

Jones, K. (1983) *Beyond progressive education*, London: Macmillan.

Jones, K (2003) *Education in Britain*, Cambridge: Polity.

Jones, K. (ed) (2013) *Education in Europe: The politics of austerity*, London: RadicalEd.

Jones, K. and Alexiadou, N. (2001) 'Travelling Policy: Local Spaces', Paper presented in symposium 'The Global and the national: reflections on the Experience of three European states', European Conference on Educational Research (ECER), Lille ,September.

Jones, M., Campbell, A., McNamara, O. and Stanley, G. (2009) 'Developing professional learning communities through ITE mentoring', *CPD Update*, 116, 6-9.

Jones, M., Stanley, G., McNamara, O. and Murray, J. (2011) 'Facilitating teacher educators' professional learning through a regional research capacity-building network', *Asia-Pacific Journal of Teacher Education*, 39(3): 263-75.

Judge, H., Lemosse, M., Paine, L. and Sedlak, M. (1994) *The university and the teachers*, Wallingford: Triangle Press.

Kansansen, P. (2014) 'Teaching as a master's level profession in Finland: Theoretical reflections and practical solutions', in O. McNamara, J. Murray, and M. Jones (eds) (2014) *Workplace learning in teacher education. Professional learning and development in schools and higher education*, vol 10, Dordrecht: Springer, pp 47-72.

Katz, M.B. (1966) 'From theory to survey in graduate schools of education', *Journal of Higher Education* 37(6): 325-34.

Keating, M. (2004) 'Socialism, territory and the national question', in G. Hassan (ed) *The Scottish Labour Party: History, institutions and ideas*, Edinburgh: Edinburgh University Press, pp 233-47.

Keating, M., Cairney, P. and Hepburn, E. (2009) 'Territorial policy communities and devolution in the UK', *Cambridge Journal of Regions, Economy and Society*, 2(1): 51-66.

Kellaghan, T. (2002) *Preparing teachers for the 21st century: Report of the working group on primary preservice teacher education*, Dublin: Stationery Office.

Kellaghan, T. (2004) 'Preparing teachers for the 21st century: Report of the working group on primary preservice teacher education', in A. Burke (ed) *Teacher education in the Republic of Ireland: Retrospect and prospect*, Armagh: Centre for Cross-Border Studies, pp 19-25.

Kennedy, A. (2013) 'Teacher professional learning', in T. Bryce, W. Humes, D. Gillies and A. Kennedy (eds) *Scottish education (4th edn)*, Edinburgh: Edinburgh University Press.

Kennedy, A., Barlow, W. and Macgregor, J. (2012) '"Advancing professionalism in teaching"? An exploration of the mobilisation of the concept of professionalism in the McCormac Report on the review of teacher employment in Scotland', *Scottish Educational Review,* 44(2): 3-13.

Kirk, D. (1986) 'Beyond the limits of theoretical discourse in teacher education: Towards a critical pedagogy', *Teaching and Teacher Education,* 2(2): 155-67.

Kirk, G. (2000) *Enhancing quality in teacher education,* Edinburgh: Dunedin.

Korthagen, F. A. (2004) 'In search of the essence of a good teacher: Towards a more holistic approach in teacher education', *Teaching and Teacher Education,* 20(1): 77-97.

Korthagen, F.A. and Kessels, J.P. (1999) 'Linking theory and practice: Changing the pedagogy of teacher education', *Educational Researcher,* 28(4): 4-17.

Korthagen, F.A., Loughran, J., and Russell, T. (2006) 'Developing fundamental principles for teacher education programs and practices', *Teaching and Teacher Education,* 22(8): 1020-41.

Kriewaldt, J. and Turnidge, D. (2013) 'Conceptualising an approach To clinical reasoning In the education profession', *Australian Journal of Teacher Education,* 38(6): 103-15.

Labaree, D.F. (2004) *The trouble with ed schools,* New Haven: Yale University Press.

Labaree, D.F. (2005) 'Progressivism, schools and schools of education: An American romance', *Paedagogica Historica,* 41(1-2): 275-88.

Lagemann, E.C. (2000) *An elusive science: The troubling history of educational research,* Chicago, Chicago University Press.

Laugharne, J. and Baird, A. (June, 2009) 'National conversations in the UK: Using a language-based approach to interpret three key education policy documents (2001–2007) from England, Scotland and Wales,' *Cambridge Journal of Education,* 39(2): 223-40.

Lave, J., and Wenger, E. (1991). *Situated learning: Legitimate peripheral participation,* Cambridge: Cambridge university press.

Law, A. and Mooney, G. (2006) '"We've never had it so good": The 'problem' of the working class in devolved Scotland', *Critical Social Policy,* 26(3): 523-42.

Lawlor, A. (2009) 'The Teaching Council and teacher education', *OIDEAS,* 54: 10-13.

Lawlor, A. (2011) *'Farewell from Áine Lawlor'.* Retrieved from: http://www.teachingcouncil.ie/latest-news/farewell-from-the-director.1121.html

Lawn, M. (2006) 'Soft governance and the learning spaces of Europe', *Comparative European Politics*, 4(2): 272-88.

Lawn, M. and Furlong, J. (2011) 'The disciplines of education: between the ghost and the shadow', in J. Furlong and M. Lawn (eds) *Disciplines of education: Their role in the future of educational research*, London: Routledge, pp 1-12.

LeGrand, J. (2007) *The other invisible hand*, Princeton: University Press.

LeGrand, J. and Bartlett, W. (eds) (1993) *Quasi-markets and social policy*, Houndmills: Macmillan.

Leitch, R. (2009) 'Harnessing the slipstream: Building educational research capacity in Northern Ireland. Size matters', *Journal of Education for Teaching* 35(4): 355-71.

Lewis, H. (2013) 'Welsh government statement - PISA 2012 Statement from the Minister for Education and Skills', 3 December. Retrieved from: http://wales.gov.uk/newsroom/educationandskills/2013/130103pisa/?lang=en

Lingard, B. (2000) 'It is and it isn't: vernacular globalisation, educational policy and restructuring', in Burbules, N. and Torres, C. (eds) *Globalization and education*, New York: Routledge.

Lingard, B. (2006) 'Globalisation, the research imagination and deparochialising the study of education', *Globalisation, Societies and Education*, 4(2): 287-302.

Lingard, B. and Gale, T. (2010) 'Presidential address as pedagogy. Representing and constituting the field of educational research', in T. Gale and B. Lingard (eds) *Educational Research by Association*, Rotterdam: Sense Publishers, pp 1-22.

Lingard, B. and Rawolle, S. (2011) 'New scalar politics: Implications for education policy', *Comparative Education*, 47(4): 489-502.

Lingard, B. and Sellar, S. (2013) 'Policy learning or policy ammunition: Three national responses to Shanghai's performance on PISA 2009', *Professional Educator*, 12 (2): 8-14.

Lingard, B., Martino, W. and Rezai-Rashti, G. (2013) 'Testing regimes, accountabilities and education policy: Commensurate global and national developments', *Journal of Education Policy*, 28(5): 539-556.

Livingston, K. and Colucci-Gray, L. (2006) 'Scottish teachers for a new era: Where should we start from, if not together?', *Education in the North*, 14: 36-37.

Livingston, K. and Hulme, M. (2014) 'Innovations in teacher professional learning in Scotland: moving forward in challenging times', in J. Stephenson and L. Ling (eds) *Challenges to teacher education in difficult economic times: International perspectives*, Routledge: Oxford, pp 197–93.

Livingston, K. and Shiach, L. (2010) 'Co-constructing a new model of teacher education', in A. Campbell and S. Groundwater-Smith (eds) *Connecting inquiry and professional learning in education: International perspectives and practical solutions*, Abingdon: Routledge, pp 83-96.

Lomax, D.E. (ed) (1973) *The education of teachers in Britain*, London: John Wiley.

Long, F., Hall, K., Conway, P. and Murphy, R. (2012) 'Novice teachers as "invisible" learners', *Teachers and Teaching: Theory and Practice*, 18(6): 619-36.

Lortie, D. (1975) *Schoolteacher*. Chicago: University of Chicago Press.

Louis, K. S. and van Velzen, B. (2012) 'Political cultures, education and history – An introduction', in K. S. Louis and B. van Velzen (eds) *Educational policy in an international context: Political culture and its effects*, New York: Palgrave MacMillan, pp 1-4.

Loxley, A., Seery, A. and Walsh, J. (2014) 'Investment in education and the tests of time', *Irish Educational Studies*, 33(2): 173-91.

Lundahl, L., Erixon Arreman, I., Holm, A. and Lundström, U. (2013) 'Educational marketization the Swedish way', *Education Inquiry*, 4(3): 497-517.

Lynch, J. (1979) *The reform of teacher education in the United Kingdom*, Surrey: Society for Research in Higher Education (SRHRE).

Lynch, J. (1984) 'Bradford: a college-college merger' in R. Alexander, M. Craft and J. Lynch (eds) *Change in teacher education: Context and provision since Robbins*, .London: Holt, Rinehart and Winston, pp 215 – 240.

MacBeath, J. (2011) 'Education of teachers: The English experience', *Journal of Education for Teaching*, 37(4): 377-86.

Machin, S., McNally, S. and Wyness, G. (2013) *Education in a devolved Scotland. A quantitative analysis: Report to the Economic and Social Research Council*, London: Centre for Economic Performance, London School of Economics. Retrieved from: http://cep.lse.ac.uk/pubs/download/special/cepsp30.pdf

Mackenzie, R.F. (1970) *State school,* Harmondsworth: Penguin.

MacLure, M. (2001) 'Arguing for yourself: Identity as an organising principle in teachers' jobs and lives' in A. Craft, J. Soler, and H. Burgess (eds) *Teacher development: Exploring our own practice,* London: Sage, pp 167-80.

MacLure, M. (2003) *Discourse in educational and social research,* Buckingham: Open University Press.

Maguire, M., and Weiner, G. (1994) 'The place of women in teacher education: discourses of power', *Educational Review*, 46(2): 121-39.

References

Mahony, P. (2009) 'Should "ought" be taught?', *Teaching and Teacher Education*, 25: 983-89.

Mahony, P. and Hextall, I. (2000) *Reconstructing teaching*, London: Routledge/Falmer.

Mahony P., Menter I. and Hextall I. (2004) 'The emotional impact of Threshold Assessment on teachers in England', *British Education Research Journal*, 30(3): 435-56.

Marker, W. (1994) *The Spider's Web: Policy-making in teacher education in Scotland 1959–81*, Glasgow: Strathclyde University.

Marshall, C. (2013) 'Scotland 'standing still' in schools league table but still beats rest of UK', *The Scotsman*, 3 December, n.pag. Retrieved 8 Dec. 2013 from NewsBank online database (Access World News).

Martens, K., Nagel, A., Windzio, M. and Weymann, A. (eds) (2010) *Transformation of education policy*, Basingstoke: Palgrave Macmillan.

Mattsson, M., Eilertson, T. and Rorrison, D. (eds) (2011) *A practicum turn in teacher education*, Rotterdam: Sense.

Mayer, D., Mitchell, J., Macdonald, D. and Bell, R. (2005) 'Professional standards of teachers: A case study of professional learning', *Asia-Pacific Journal of Teacher Education*, 33(2): 159-79.

Maynard, T., Taylor, C., Waldron, S. Rhys, M., Smith, R., Power, S. and Clement, J. (2013) *Evaluating the Foundation Phase: Policy logic model and programme theory*, Cardiff: Welsh Government.

McAllister, L. (1988) 'The Welsh devolution referendum: Definitely, maybe?,' *Parliamentary Affairs*, 51(2): 149-65.

McCrone, D. (1992) *Understanding Scotland: The sociology of a stateless nation*, London and New York: Routledge.

McCulloch, G. (2011) 'What can higher education offer teacher education?' in SCETT, *In defence of teacher education: A response to the coalition government's white paper for schools (November 2010)*, pp 22-23.

McIntyre, D. (1990a) 'The Oxford internship scheme and the Cambridge analytical framework: Models of partnership in initial teacher education', *Partnership in initial teacher training*, pp 110-27.

McIntyre, D. (1990b) 'Ideas and principles guiding the internship scheme' in P. Benton (ed) *The Oxford internship scheme: Integration and partnership in initial teacher education*, London: Calouste Gulbenkian, pp 17-33.

McIntyre, D. (1995) 'Initial teacher education as practical theorising: A response to Paul Hirst', *British Journal of Educational Studies*, vol 43: 365-83.

McIntyre, D. (2009) 'The difficulties of inclusive pedagogy for initial teacher education and some thoughts on the way forward', *Teaching and Teacher Education*, 25(4): 602-8.

McIntyre, D. and Hagger, H. (1993) 'Teachers' expertise and models of mentoring', in D. McIntyre, H. Hagger, H. and M. Wilkin (eds) *Mentoring: Perspectives on school-based teacher education*, London: Kogan Page, pp 86-102.

McNamara, O. (2010) 'Une approche technique et rationaliste: La formation des enseignants en Angleterre', *Revue Internationale d'Education*, 55: 49-60.

McNamara, O. and Murray, J. (2013) *The School Direct programme and its implications for research-informed teacher education and teacher educators*, York: Higher Education Academy.

McNamara, O., Murray, J. and Jones, M. (eds) (2013) *Workplace learning in teacher education, professional learning and development in schools and higher education*, Volume 10, Dordrecht: Springer.

McNicholl, J. and Blake, A. (2013) 'Transforming teacher education, an activity theory analysis', *Journal of Education for Teaching*, 39(3): 281-300.

McPherson, C. and Raab, C. (1988) *Governing education*, Edinburgh: University Press.

Menter, I. (2011a) 'Teacher education research – past, present, future', *Research Intelligence* 116: 11-13.

Menter, I. (2011b) 'Four 'academic sub-tribes', but one territory? Teacher educators and teacher education in Scotland', *Journal of Education for Teaching*, 37(3): 293-308.

Menter, I., Muschamp, Y., Nicholls, P. and Ozga, J. with Pollard, A. (1997) *Work and identity in the primary school: A post-Fordist analysis*, Buckingham: Open University Press.

Menter I., Mahony P. and Hextall I. (2004) 'Ne'er the twain shall meet? The modernisation of the teaching workforce in Scotland and England', *Journal of Education Policy*, 19(2): 195-214.

Menter, I., Brisard, E. and Smith, I. (2006) *Convergence or divergence? Initial Teacher Education in Scotland and England*, Edinburgh: Dunedin Academic Press.

Menter, I., Hulme, M., Elliot, D. and Lewin, J. (2010a) *Literature review on teacher education in the 21st century*, Edinburgh: The Scottish Government.

Menter, I., Hulme, M., Murray, J., Campbell, A., Hextall, I., Jones, M., Mahony, P. Procter, R. and Wall, K. (2010b) 'Teacher education research in the UK: The state of the art', *Revue Suisse des sciences de l'education*, 32(1): 121-42.

Meyer, H. and Benavot, A. (2013) *PISA, power and policy: The emergence of global educational governance*, Oxford: Symposium Books.

Mincu, M. (2013) 'Teacher quality and school improvement', *Research and teacher education: The BERA-RSA Inquiry*. Retrieved from: http://www.bera.ac.uk/wp-content/uploads/2013/12/BERA-Paper-6-Teacher-Quality-and-School-Improvement.pdf

Moon, J. A. (2004) *A handbook of reflective and experiential learning: Theory and practice*, Hove: Psychology Press.

Montgomery, A. and Smith, A. (2006) 'Teacher education in Northern Ireland: Policy variations since devolution', *Scottish Educational Review*, 37(Special): 46-58.

Moran, A. (1998) 'The Northern Ireland professional growth challenge: Towards an integrated model of teacher education', *Teacher Development: An International Journal of Teachers' Professional Development*, 2(3): 455-65.

Moran, A., Abbott, L. and Clarke, L. (2009) 'Re-conceptualizing partnerships across the teacher education continuum', *Teaching and Teacher Education*, 25(7): 951-58.

Morley, L. (2003) *Quality and power in higher education*, Buckingham: OUP.

Mourshed, M., Chijioke, C. and Barber, M. (2010) *How the world's most improved school systems keep getting better*, London: McKinsey and Company.

Mulcahy, C and McSharry, M. (2012) 'The changing face of teacher education in Ireland: A major overhaul or a cosmetic review?' *Educational Research eJournal*, 1(2): 91-103.

Murray, J. (2002) 'Between the chalkface and the ivory towers? A study of the professionalism of teacher educators working on primary initial teacher education courses in the English education system', *Collected Original Resources in Education* 26(3): 1-530.

Murray, J. (2007) 'Countering insularity in teacher education. Academic work on pre-service courses in nursing, social work and teacher education', *Journal of Education for Teaching* 33(3): 271-91.

Murray, J. (2014) 'Teacher educators' constructions of professionalism: Change and diversity in teacher education', *Asia Pacific Journal of Teacher Education*, 42(1): 7-21.

Murray, J., Campbell, A., Hextall, I., Hulme, M., Jones, M., Mahony, P. Jones, M., Mahony, P., Menter, I., Procter, R. and Wall, K. (2009) 'Research and teacher education in the UK: Building capacity', *Teaching and Teacher Education*, 25(7): 944-950.

Murray, J., Jones, M., McNamara, O. and Stanley, G. (2012) 'Institutional re-orientation attempts and their effects on academics in teacher education: A case study from England', in R. Adamson, J. Nixon and F. Su (eds) *The reorientation of higher education: Compliance and defiance*. Dordrecht: Springer, pp 82-104.

Musset, P. (2010) *Initial teacher education and containing training policies on comparative perspective. Current practices on OECD Countries and a literature review on potential effects*. OECD working paper No 48, Paris: OCED Publishing.

Mutton, T. and Butcher, J. (2008) 'We will take them from anywhere': Schools working within multiple initial teacher training partnerships, *Journal of Education for Teaching: International research and pedagogy*, 34(1): 45-62.

Nagel, A. (2010) 'Comparing education policy networks', in K. Martens, A. Nagel, M. Windzio, and A. Weymann (eds) *Transformation of education policy*, Basingstoke: Palgrave Macmillan, pp 199-226.

National Assembly for Wales (2001) *The learning country*, Cardiff: National Assembly for Wales.

NCTL (National College for Teaching and Leadership) (2014a) *Teaching schools: National research and development network*. Retrieved from: https://www.gov.uk/the-national-research-and-development-network

NCTL (2014b) *Message from Charlie Taylor* (online), London: NCTL. Retrieved from: https://forms.ncsl.org.uk/mediastore/image2/CTletter-new2.pdf

NCTQ (National Council on Teacher Quality) (2013) *Teacher preparation review*, Washington, DC: NCTQ.

Neill, A.S. (1962) *Summerhill: A radical approach to education*, London: Victor Gollancz.

Nelson, J. and O'Beirne, C. (2014) *Using evidence in the classroom: What works and why?*, Slough: NFER.

Newman, J. (2000) 'Beyond the new public management? Modernizing public services', in J. Clarke, S. Gewirtz, and E. McLaughlin (eds) *New managerialism, new welfare?*, London: Sage.

Nic Craith, D. (2014) *The Teaching Council: An emerging policy player*, Paper presented at the Educational Studies Association of Ireland Annual Conference, 11 April.

NITEC (Northern Ireland Teacher Education Committee) and CEPD (Committee for Early Professional Development) (1998) *Teacher education partnership handbook: Integrating and managing partnership-based teacher education in Northern Ireland*, Bangor: Department of Education Retrieved from: http://www.deni.gov.uk/teacher_education_partnership_handbook-3.pdf

Noah, H. and Eckstein, M. (1969) *Toward a science of comparative education*, London: Macmillan.

Northern Ireland Council for Integrated Education (NICIE). Retrieved from: http://www.nicie.org

Nóvoa, A. and Yariv-Mashal, T. (2003) 'Comparative research in education: A mode of governance or a historical journey?', *Comparative Education*, 39(4): 423-38.

Oancea, A. (2010) *The BERA/UCET review of the impacts of RAE 2008 on education research in UK higher education institutions*, London: BERA and UCET.

Ochs, K. (2006) 'Cross-national policy borrowing and educational innovation', *Oxford Review of Education*, 32(5): 599-619.

OECD (Organisation for Economic Co-operation and Development) (1991) *Review of national policies for education: Ireland*, Paris: OECD.

OECD (2005) *Teachers matter: Attracting, developing and retaining effective teachers*, Paris: OECD.

OECD (2007) *Review of the quality and equity of education outcomes in Scotland, diagnostic report*, Paris: OECD.

OECD (2009) *PISA 2009 Results: What students know and can do: Student performance reading, mathematics and science*, vol 1, Paris: OECD. Retrieved from: http://www.oecd.org/pisa/pisaproducts/pisa2009.

OECD (2011a) *Building a high quality teaching profession: Lessons from around the world*, Paris: OECD Publishing.

OECD (2011b) *Lessons from PISA for the United States, Strong performers and successful reformers in education*, Paris: OECD Publishing.

OECD (2012) *Equity and quality in education. Supporting disadvantaged students and schools*, Paris: OECD. Retrieved from: http://dx.doi.org/10.1787/9789264130852-en

OECD (2014) *Improving schools in Wales: An OECD perspective.* Paris: OECD. Retrieved from: http://www.oecd.org/edu/Improving-schools-in-Wales.pdf

Ofsted (2010) *The annual report of Her Majesty's Chief Inspector of Education, Children's Services and Skills 2009/10*, London: The Stationery Office.

Ofsted (2015) *School inspection handbook*, Manchester: Ofsted. Retrieved from: https://www.gov.uk/government/uploads/system/uploads/attachment_data/file/391531/School_inspection_handbook.pdf

O'Hear, A. (1988) *Who teaches the teachers?*, London: Social Affairs Unit.

O'Keeffe, D. (1990) *The wayward elite*, London: Adam Smith Institute.

Osborne, R., Cormack, R., and Gallagher, A. (1993) *After the reforms: Education and policy in Northern Ireland*, Aldershot: Avebury.

Osler, D. (2005) *Policy review of teacher education in Northern Ireland*, Report commissioned by Department of Education (NI) and Department for Employment and Learning (NI). Retrieved from: http://www.deni.gov.uk/osler_report.pdf

O'Sullivan, D. (2005) *Cultural politics and Irish education since the 1950s: Policy, paradigms and power*, Dublin: IPA.

Ozga, J. (2005) 'Modernising the education workforce: A perspective from Scotland', *Educational Review*, 57(2): 207-19.

Ozga, J. (2012) 'Comparison as a governing technology: The case of PISA', *Research Intelligence*, 119: 18-19.

Ozga, J., Dahler-Larsen, P., Simola, H. and Segerholm, C. (2011) *Fabricating quality in education: Data and governance in Europe*, London: Routledge.

Paine, L. and Zeichner, K. (2012) 'The local and the global in reforming teaching and teacher education', *Comparative Education Review*, 56(4):569-83.

Parkinson, J. (2011). 'The rugged landscape of teacher education in Wales', in J. Murray and J. Wishart (eds) *Teacher education in transition: the changing landscape across the UK*, Bristol: The Higher Education Academy/ESCalate, pp 19-27.

Paterson, L. (2003) *Scottish education in the twentieth century*, Edinburgh: Edinburgh University Press.

Paterson, L. (2011) 'The end of BEd, beginning of broad university education', *Times Educational Supplement Scotland*, 4 March, pp 35-36.

Paterson, L. (2014) 'Competitive opportunity and liberal culture: The significance of Scottish education in the twentieth century', *British Journal of Educational Research*, 40(2): 397-416.

Peal, R. (2014) *Progressively worse: The burden of bad ideas in British schools*, London: Civitas.

Peters, R.S. (1963) 'Comments', in J. Walton and J. L. Kuethe (eds) *The discipline of education*, Madison, WI: University of Wisconsin Press, pp 17-22.

Phillips, D. (2006) 'Investigating policy attraction in education', *Oxford Review of Education*, 32(5): 551-59.

Philpott, C. (2014) *Theories of professional learning,* Northwich: Critical Publishing.

Pickard, W. and Dobie, J. (2003) *The political context of education after devolution,* Edinburgh: Dunedin.

Pilley, J. (1958) 'Teacher training in Scotland', *Higher Education Quarterly,* 12(3): 223-344.

Plunkett, D. (1984) 'Southampton: Pressures and initiatives in a university department of education' in R. Alexander, M. Craft, and J. Lynch (eds) *Change in teacher education. Context and provision since Robbins,* London, Holt, Rinehart and Winston, pp 332-41.

Pollard, A. (2014) *REF 2014: What does it mean for education and educational research?* Retrieved from: https://www.bera.ac.uk/promoting-educational-research/issues/ref2014

Pollard, A. and Collins, J. (2005) *Reflective teaching,* London: Bloomsbury Publishing.

Pollard, A. and Oancea, A. (2010) *Unlocking learning? Towards evidence-informed policy and practice in education.* Final report of the UK Strategic Forum for Research in Education, London: SFRE.

Popkewitz, T.S (ed) (1987) *Critical studies in teacher education: Its folklore, theory and practice,* London: Falmer.

Popkewitz, T.S. (ed) (2005) *Inventing the modern self and John Dewey. Modernities and the traveling of pragmatism in education,* New York: Palgrave Macmillan.

Popkewitz, T.S. (2006) 'The idea of science as planning was not planned' in R. Hofstetter and B. Schneuwly (eds) *Passion, fusion, tension. New education and educational sciences. End 19th–middle 20th century,* Berne: Peter Lang, pp 143-67.

Popkewitz, T.S. (2013a) 'Styles of reason: Historicism, historicising and the history of education', in T.S. Popkewitz (ed) *Rethinking the history of education: Transnational perspectives on its questions, methods and knowledge,* New York: Palgrave Macmillan, pp 1-26.

Popkewitz, T.S. (2013b) 'The sociology of education as the history of the present: Fabrication, difference and abjection', *Discourse: Studies in the Cultural Politics of Education,* 34(3):439-56.

Popkewitz, T.S., Lindblad, S. and Strandberg, J. (1999) *Review and research on education governance and social integration and exclusion,* Uppsala: Uppsala University Press.

Pratt, J. (1997) *The polytechnic experiment,* Milton Keynes: Society for Research into Higher Education and Open University Press.

Pring, R. (2007) *John Dewey,* London: Continuum.

PWC and DfES (PriceWaterhouseCoopers and Department for Education and Skills) (2007) *Independent study into school leadership: Main report*, Nottingham: DfES.

Quinn, R. (2012) 'The future development of education in Ireland', *Studies: An Irish Quarterly Review*, Summer 2012, 101(402): 1-3.

Raffe, D. (2004) 'How distinctive is Scottish education? Five perspectives on distinctiveness', *Scottish Affairs*, 49: 50-72.

Raffe, D. (2011) Policy borrowing or policy learning? How (not) to improve education systems. CES Briefing, 57. Retrieved from: http://www.ces.ed.ac.uk/PDF%20Files/Brief057.pdf

Raffe, D., Howieson, C., Croxford, L. and Martin, C. (1999) 'Comparing England, Scotland, Wales and Northern Ireland: The case for 'home internationals' in comparative research', *Comparative Education*, 35(1): 9-25.

Rees, G. (2007) 'The impacts of parliamentary devolution on education policy in Wales', *Welsh Journal of Education*, 14(1): 8-20.

Rees, G. and Power, S. (2007) 'Educational research and the restructuring of the state: The impacts of parliamentary devolution in Wales', *European Educational Research Journal*, 6(1): 87-100.

Reid, J. (2011) 'A practice turn for teacher education?', *Asia-Pacific Journal of Teacher Education*, 39(3): 293-310.

Reid, K. (2011) 'Changes to educational policy and management in Wales: Facing the "cuts" and new strategic challenges', *Educational Review*, 63(4): 439-53.

Richardson, V. (1994) 'Conducting research on practice', *Educational Researcher*, 23(5): 5-10.

Riddell, S., Raffe, D., Croxford, L., Weedon, E. and Minty, S. (2013) *Widening access to higher education: Scotland in UK comparative context. Pre-event briefing*, 8 October 2013, Retrieved from: http://www.esrc.ac.uk/_images/Briefing_TT2_widening%20access_tcm8-28589.pdf

Rizvi, F. and Lingard, B. (2010) *Globalizing education policy*, London: Routledge.

Robbins, L. (1963) *Higher Education: Report of the Committee appointed by the Prime Minister under the chairmanship of Lord Robbins, 1961–63*. Cmnd 2154, London: HMSO.

Robertson, S. (2000) *A class act: Changing teachers' work, globalisation and the state*, London: Falmer.

Robertson, S.L. (2012) 'Placing teachers in global governance agendas', *Comparative Education Review*, 56(4): 584-607.

Robertson, S.L. (2013) 'Teachers' work, de-nationalisation and transformations in the field of symbolic control: A comparative account', in T. Seddon, T. and J.S. Levin (eds) *Educators, professionalism and politics. Global transitions, national spaces and professional projects*, London: Routledge, pp 77-96.

Robinson, W. (2000) 'History of education in the new millennium, Retrospect and prospect in teacher training', in R. Aldrich and D. Crook (eds) *History of education into the twenty-first century*, London, University of London, pp 50-62.

Ross, J.A. and Bruce, C.D. (2012) 'Evaluating the impact of collaborative action research on teachers: a quantitative approach', *Teacher Development*, 16(4): 537-61.

Russell, M. (2013) 'From good to great: Building equity and success in Scottish education', speech delivered by the Education Secretary, University of Glasgow, 27 March. Retrieved from: http://www.scotland.gov.uk/News/Speeches/school-attainment-27032013

Rust, V. (2000) 'Education policy studies and comparative education', in R. Alexander, M. Osborn and D. Phillips (eds) *Learning from comparing. New directions in comparative educational research, volume two: Policy, professionals and development*, Oxford: Symposium, pp 13-40.

Rutten, K., Mottart, A. and Soetaert, R. (2010) 'The rhetorical construction of the nation in education: the case of Flanders', *Journal of Curriculum Studies*, 42(6): 775-90.

Ryan, M. and Bourke, T. (2013) 'The teacher as reflexive professional: Making visible the excluded discourse in teacher standards', *Discourse: Studies in the Cultural Politics of Education,* 34(3): 411-23.

Sachs, J. (2001) 'Teacher professional identity: Competing discourses, competing outcomes', *Journal of Education Policy,* 16(2): 149-61.

Sachs, J. (2003a) 'Teacher professional standards: controlling or developing teaching?' *Teachers and Teaching: Theory and Practice,* 9(2): 175-86.

Sachs, J. (2003b) *The activist teaching profession*, Buckingham: Open University Press.

Sahlberg, P. (2011a) *Finnish lessons: What can the world learn from educational change in Finland?,* New York: Teachers College Press.

Sahlberg, P. (2011b) 'The fourth way of Finland', *Journal of Educational Change,* 12(2): 173-84.

Sahlberg, P. (2012) 'How GERM is infecting schools around the world', *The Washington Post*, 29 June. Retrieved from: http://pasisahlberg.com/text-test/

Sahlberg, P., Munn, P. and Furlong, J. (2012) *Report of the international review panel on the structure of initial teacher education provision in Ireland: Review conducted on behalf of the Department of Education and Skills*, Dublin: Department of Education and Skills. Retrieved from: https://www.education.ie/en/Press-Events/Press-Releases/2012-Press-Releases/Report-of-the-International-Review-Panel-on-the-Structure-of-Initial-Teacher-Education-Provision-in-Ireland.pdf

Scheerens, J. (ed) (2010) *Teachers' professional development: Europe in international comparison*, European Union: Luxembourg. Retrieved from: http://ec.europa.eu/education/school-education/doc/talis/report_en.pdf

Schleicher, A. (2012) (ed) *Preparing teachers and developing school leaders for the 21st century: Lessons from around the world*, Paris: OECD Publishing. Retrieved from: http://www.oecd.org/dataoecd/4/35/49850576.pdf

Schön, D.A. (1983) *The reflective practitioner: How professionals think in action* (Vol. 5126), NY: Basic Books.

Schön, D.A. (1987) *Educating the reflective practitioner: Toward a new design for teaching and learning in the professions*, San Francisco: Wiley.

Schwinn, T. (2012) 'Globalisation and regional variety: Problems of theorisation', *Comparative Education*, 48(4): 525-43.

Scott, D. (2000) *Reading educational research and policy*, London: Routledge Falmer.

Scottish Executive (2001) *Report of the first stage review of initial teacher education*, Edinburgh: Deloitte and Touche.

Scottish Executive (2005) *Review of initial teacher education, Stage 2, Report of the review group*, Edinburgh: Scottish Executive.

Scottish Government (2008) *The Early Years Framework*, Edinburgh: Scottish Government.

Scottish Government (2011) *Advancing professionalism in teaching*, Edinburgh: Scottish Government.

Scottish Government National Statistics (2013) *Public sector employment in Scotland statistics for the 2nd Quarter 2013*. Retrieved from: http://www.scotland.gov.uk/Resource/0043/00433702.pdf

SED (Scottish Education Department) (1977) *Training teachers from 1977 onwards*, Edinburgh: Scottish Office.

SED (1985) *Future strategy for higher education in Scotland*, Report of the Scottish Tertiary Education Advisory Council (STEAC), Cm 9676, Edinburgh: HMSO.

Seddon, T. (2014) 'Renewing sociology of education? Knowledge spaces, situated enactments and sociological practice in a world on the move', *European Educational Research Journal*, 13(1): 9–12.

Seddon, T. and Levin, J.S. (eds) (2013) *Educators, Professionalism and Politics. Global Transitions, National Spaces and Professional Projects*, London: Routledge.

SEED (Scottish Executive Education Department) (2002) *Standard for Chartered Teacher*, Edinburgh: Scottish Executive Education Department.

SEED (2007) *OECD review of the quality and equity of education outcomes in Scotland: Diagnostic report*, OECD. Retrieved from: http://dx.doi.org/10.1787/148012367602.

Seidel, T., and Shavelson, R. J. (2007) 'Teaching effectiveness research in the past decade: The role of theory and research design in disentangling meta-analysis results', *Review of Educational Research*, 77(4): 454-99.

Selleck, R. (1968) *The new education: The English background 1870-1914*, London: Pitman and Sons Ltd.

Shaw, K. (1984) 'Exeter: From college of education to university' in R. Alexander, M. Craft, and J. Lynch (eds) *Change in teacher education. Context and provision since Robbins*, London, Holt, Rinehart and Winston, pp 203-14.

Shewbridge, C., Hulshof, M., Nusche, D. and Staehr, L.S. (2014) *OECD reviews of evaluation and assessment in education: Northern Ireland*, United Kingdom: OECD Publishing.

Shulman, L. (1987) 'Knowledge and teaching: Foundations of the new reform', *Harvard Educational Review*, 57(1): 1-22.

Shulman, L. S. (1986) 'Those who understand: Knowledge growth in teaching', *Educational Researcher*, 4-14.

Sikes, P. (2006) 'Working in a new university: In the shadow of the RAE?', *Studies in Higher Education*, 31(5): 555-68.

Siraj-Blatchford, I., Milton, E., Sylva, K., Laugharne, J. and Charles, F. (2007) 'Developing the Foundation Phase for 3–7-year-olds in Wales', *Welsh Journal of Education*, 14(1): 43-68.

Smeyers, P. and Depaepe, M. (2010) *The educationalisation of social problems*, Dordrecht: Springer.

Smith, I. (2011) 'Re-visiting the Donaldson Review of Teacher Education: Is creative innovation secured?', *Scottish Educational Review*, 43(2): 17-38.

Smith, J. (2012) 'Initial Teacher Education in Ireland: transformation in the policy context', in Waldron, F., Smith, J. Gitzpatrick, M. and Dooley, T. (2012) *Re-imagining Initial Teacher Education: Perspectives on transformation*. Dublin: The Liffey Press.

Smith, M. (1949) *And madly teach*, Chicago: Henry Regnery Company.

Smithers, A., Robinson, J. and Coughlin, M.D. (2013) *The good teacher training guide 2013*, Centre for Education and Employment Research: University of Buckingham.

Smyth, J., Dow, A., Hattam, R. and Shacklock, G. (1999) *Teachers' work in a globalising economy*, London: Routledge/Falmer.

Sobe, N.W. (2013a) 'Entanglement and transnationalism in the history of American education', in T.S. Popkewitz (ed) *Rethinking the history of education. Transnational perspectives on its questions, methods and knowledge*, New York: Palgrave Macmillan, pp 93-107.

Sobe, N.W. (2013b) 'Teacher professionalisation and the globalisation of schooling', in T. Seddon and J.S. Levin (eds) *Educators, professionalism and politics: Global transitions, national spaces and professional projects*, London: Routledge, pp 42-54.

Sockett, H. (2008) 'The moral and epistemic purposes of teacher education', in M. Cochran-Smith, S. Feiman-Nemser, D. McIntyre, and K. Demers (eds) *Handbook of research on teacher education: Enduring questions in changing contexts*, NY: Routledge, pp 45-65.

SOEID (Scottish Office Education and Industry Department) (1993) *Guidelines for teacher training courses*, Edinburgh: SOEID.

SOEID (1998) *Proposals for developing a framework for continuing professional development for the teaching profession in Scotland*, Edinburgh: SOEID.

Stanley, G. E. and Stronach, I. (2013) 'Raising and doubling standards in professional discourse: A critical bid', *Journal of Education Policy*, 28(3): 291-305.

Steiner-Khamsi, G. (ed) (2004) *The global politics of educational borrowing and lending*, New York: Teachers College Press.

Steiner-Khamsi, G. and Florian, W. (eds) (2012) *World yearbook of education 2012: Policy borrowing and lending in education*, London: Routledge.

Stenhouse, L. (1975) *An introduction to curriculum research and development*, Oxford: Heinemann.

Sterman, J. (2000) *Business dynamics: Systems thinking and modelling for a complex world*, Boston, MA: McGraw-Hill.

Stevens, D. (2010) 'A Freirean critique of the competence model of teacher education, focusing on standards for qualified teacher status in England', *Journal of Education for Teaching*, 36(2): 187-96.

Stewart, D., Atkinson, C., Denholm, J. (2005) *Mapping social science research provision in the higher education sector in Scotland*, Edinburgh: Scottish Executive Social Research.

Storey, A. (2007) 'Cultural shifts in teaching: New workforce, new professionalism?', *The Curriculum Journal*, 18(3), 253-70.

References

Stromquist, N. (2002) *Education in a globalized world: The connectivity of economic power, technology and knowledge,* Boulder: Rowman and Littlefield.

Stronach, I. (2010) *Globalizing education, educating the local,* London: Routledge.

Stronach I., Corbin, B., McNamara, O., Stark, S., and Warne, T. (2002) 'Towards an uncertain politics of professionalism: Teacher and nurse identities in flux', *Journal of Education Policy,* 27(2): 109-38.

Stuart, J.S., and Tatto, M.T. (2000) 'Designs for initial teacher preparation programs: An international view', *International Journal of Educational Research,* 33(5): 493-514.

Sutherland, Sir S. (1997) 'Report 10 – Teacher education and training: a study' (the Sutherland Report) in National Committee of Inquiry into Higher Education, *Higher Education in the Learning Society, Report of the National Committee,* Norwich: HMSO.

Tabberer, R. (2013) *A review of initial teacher training in Wales.* Retrieved from: http://wales.gov.uk/docs/dcells/publications/131007-review-of-initial-teacher-training-in-wales-en.pdf

Tatto, M.T. (ed) (2007) *Reforming teaching globally,* Didcot: Symposium Books.

Tatto, M.T. (2013) *The role of research in international policy and practice in teacher education. The BERA–RSA inquiry.* Retrieved from: http://www.bera.ac.uk/wp-content/uploads/2014/02/BERA-Paper-2-International-Policy-and-Practice-in-Teacher-Education.pdf

Tatto, M.T. and Plank, D.N. (2007) 'The dynamics of global teaching reform', in M.T. Tatto (ed) *Reforming teaching globally,* Oxford: Symposium Books, pp 267-77.

Tatto, M.T., Peck, R., Schwille, J., Bankov, K., Senk, S. L., Rodriguez, M., Ingvarson, L., Reckase. M. and Rowley, G. (2012) *Policy, practice, and readiness to teach primary and secondary mathematics in 17 countries: Findings from the IEA teacher education and development study in mathematics (TEDS-MM),* Amsterdam: International Association for the Evaluation of Educational Achievement.

Taylor, C. (2013) 'Towards a school-led education system', Keynote to the North of England education conference, 18 January.

Taylor, S., Rizvi, F., Lingard, Bo. and Henry, M. (1997) *Educational policy and the politics of change,* London: Routledge.

Taylor, W. (1971) 'The future of teacher training', *Education and Training,* August, 258-59.

Taylor, W. (1983) *Teacher education: Achievements, shortcomings and perspectives,* Paper presented at The John Adams Memorial Lecture, London: The Institute of Education.

Taylor, W. (1984) *The national context, 1972–82* in R. Alexander, M. Craft, M., and J. Lynch (eds) *Change in teacher education: Context and provision since Robbins*, London: Holt, Rinehart and Winston, pp 16–30.

Teaching Council (2007a) *The Teaching Council Annual Report 2006/07*, Maynooth: Teaching Council. Retrieved from: http://www.teachingcouncil.ie/en/Publications/Annual-Reports/Annual-Report-2006-2007.pdf

Teaching Council (2007b) *Codes of professional conduct for teachers*, Maynooth: Teaching Council. Retrieved from: http://www.tui.ie/teaching/teaching-council.1701.html.

Teaching Council (2011a) *Initial teacher education: Criteria and guidelines for programme providers*, Maynooth: Teaching Council.

Teaching Council (2011b) *Initial teacher education: Strategy for the review and professional accreditation of existing programmes*, Maynooth: Teaching Council.

Teaching Council (2011c) *Draft code of professional conduct for teachers* (2nd edn), Maynooth: Teaching Council.

Teaching Council (2011d) *Completed reviews of existing teacher education programmes*. Retrieved from: http://www.teachingcouncil.ie/en/Teacher-Education/Initial-Teacher-Education/Review-and-Professional-Accreditation-of-Existing-Programmes-of-ITE/Completed-Reviews/Completed-Reviews.html

Teaching Council (2012) *Code of professional conduct for teachers*, Maynooth: Teaching Council.

Teaching Council (2013) *Guidelines on school placement*, Maynooth: Teaching Council. Retrieved from: http://www.teachingcouncil.ie/_fileupload/Teacher%20Education/School%20Placement/School%20Placement%20Guidelines.pdf

The Daily Telegraph (2013) Retrieved from: http://www.telegraph.co.uk/education/9987974/The-glamour-ofgrammar-an-object-lesson.html

Timperley, H. (2008) *Teacher professional learning and development*. Educational practices series-18, Geneva: UNESCO International Bureau of Education.

Timperley, H. (2013) 'Learning to practise. A paper for discussion'. University of Auckland. Retrieved from: http://www.educationcounts.govt.nz/__data/assets/pdf_file/0014/120146/Learning-To-Practise.pdf

Toloudis, N. (2010) 'Pedagogical conferences and stillborn professionalism among nineteenth century instituteurs, 1830–1848', *Paedagogica Historica,* 46(5): 585-99.

References

Tomlinson, S. (2001) *Education in a post-welfare society*, Buckingham: Open University.

Townsend, T. (2011a) 'Introduction', *Journal of Education for Teaching*, 37(4): 373-375.

Townsend, T. (2011b) 'Searching high and low, searching east and west: Looking for trust in teacher education', *Journal of Education for Teaching*, 37(4): 483-500.

Trace, A.S. (1978) *What Ivan knows that Johnny doesn't*, Westport, CT: Greenwood Press.

Training Development Agency for Schools (TDA) (2009) *The national framework for masters in teaching and learning*, London: TDA.

Tripp, D. (1994) 'Teachers' lives, critical incidents, and professional practice', *Qualitative Studies in Education*, 7(1): 65-76.

Tröhler, D. (2013) *Pestalozzi and the educationalization of the World*, Basingstoke: Palgrave Macmillan.

Truxaw, M. P. et al (2011) 'A stance toward enquiry: An investigation of preservice teachers' confidence regarding educational enquiry', *Teacher Education Quarterly*, 38(4): 69-95.

UCET (University Council for the Education of Teachers) (2014) *UCET annual report 2014*, London: UCET.

Universities UK (2014) *The impact of Initial Teacher Training reforms on English Higher Education Institutions*, London: UUK. Retrieved from: http://www.universitiesuk.ac.uk/highereducation/Pages/ImpactOfITTreforms.aspx#.VKz7SE0qVdg

US Department of Education (2014) 'Teacher preparation issues: a proposed rule by the Education Department on 12/03/2014'. Retrieved from: https://www.federalregister.gov/articles/2014/12/03/2014-28218/teacher-preparation-issues

van Dijk, T.A. (2001a) 'Critical discourse analysis', in D. Schriffen, D. Tannen and H. E. Hamilton (eds) *The handbook of critical discourse analysis*, Malden, MA: Blackwell, pp 352-71.

van Dijk, T.A. (2001b) 'Multidisciplinary CDA: A plea for diversity', in R. Wodak and M. Meyer (eds) *Methods of critical discourse analysis*, London: Sage, pp 95-120.

WAG (Welsh Assembly Government) (2003) *Iaith Pawb: A national action plan for a bilingual Wales*. Cardiff: WAG.

Walford Davies, H. (1923) *The transactions of the Honourable Society of Cymmrodorion Session 1921–22*, London: Honourable Society of Cymmrodorion, pp 1-9.

Walford Davies, H. (1969) *The transactions of the Honourable Society of Cymmrodorion Session 1921–22*, first edition, London: Honourable Society of Cymmrodorion, pp 1-9.

Walker, M. Jeffes, J., Hart, R., Lord, P. and Kinder, K. (2010) *Making the links between teachers' professional standards, induction, performance management and continuing professional development*, London: Department for Education.

Wall, K., Campbell, A., Hextall, I., Hulme, M., Jones, M., Mahony, P., Menter, I., Murray, J. and Procter, R. (2011) 'The TEG bibliography: Having knowledge and using it – next steps?' in I. Menter and J. Murray (eds) *Developing research in teacher education*, London: Routledge, pp 127-38.

Wallace, M. (1993) 'Discourse of derision: The role of the mass media within the education policy process', *Journal of Education Policy*, 8(4): 321-37.

Walton, J. and Kuethe, J.L. (eds) (1963) *The discipline of education*, Madison, Wisconsin: University of Wisconsin Press.

Watson, C. and Fox, A. (2015) 'Professional re-accreditation: Constructing educational policy for career-long professional learning', *Journal of Education Policy*, 30(1): 132-44.

Weisburg, D., Sexton, S., Mulhern, J. and Keeling, D. (2009) *The widget effect: Our national failure to acknowledge and act on differences in teacher effectiveness*. Brooklyn: New Teacher Project. Retrieved from: http://widgeteffect.org/downloads/TheWidgetEffect.pdf

Welsh Government, (2011) *Revised professional standards for education practitioners in Wales*, Cardiff: Welsh Government.

Welsh Government (2013) *Requirements for initial school teacher training courses at higher education institutions in Wales* (Circular 129/2013). Retrieved from: http://dera.ioe.ac.uk/19181/1/140109-requirements-for-initial-school-teacher-training-courses-at-higher-education-institutions-in-wales-en.pdf

Whitty, G. (2008) 'Changing modes of teacher professionalism: traditional, managerial, collaborative and democratic', in B. Cunningham (ed), *Exploring professionalism,* London: Institute of Education, University of London, pp 28-49.

Whitty, G. (2014) 'Recent developments in teacher training and their consequences for the 'University Project' in education', *Oxford Review of Education* 4(4): 466-81.

Whitty, G. and Menter, I. (1989) 'Lessons of Thatcherism: education policy in England and Wales 1979–88', *Journal of Law and Society*, 16(1): 46-64.

Whitty, G., Donoghue, M., Christie, D., Kirk, G., Menter, I., McNamara, O., Moss, G., Oancea, A., Rogers, C. and Thomson, P. (2012) *Prospects for the future of educational research*, London: BERA and UCET.

Widdowson, H.G. (1995) 'Discourse analysis: A critical view', *Language and Literature,* 4(3): 157-72.

Wilford, R. (2010) 'Northern Ireland: The politics of constraint', *Parliamentary Affairs*, 63(1): 134–155.

Williams, C.H. (2013) 'Ysgolion Cymraeg: An act of faith in the future of Wales' in H. S. Thomas and C.H. Williams (eds) *Parents, personalities and power: Welsh-medium schools in south-east Wales,* Cardiff: University of Wales Press, pp 1-24.

Williams, R. (1961) *The long revolution*, Harmondsworth: Pelican.

Winch, C., Oancea, A. and Orchard, J. (2013) 'The contribution of educational research to teachers' professional learning – Philosophical understandings', The BERA-RSA inquiry. Retrieved from: http://www.bera.ac.uk/wp-content/uploads/2014/02/BERA-Paper-3-Philosophical-reflections.pdf

Windzio, M., Martens, K. and Nagel, A. (2010) 'Education policy, globalisation and the changing nation state: Accelerating and retarding conditions', in K. Martens, A. Nagel, M. Windzio and A. Weymann (eds) *Transformation of education policy*, Basingstoke: Palgrave Macmillan, pp 261-76.

World Bank (2013) *What matters most for teacher policies: A framework paper*. SABER Working Paper Series, No 4, April 2013. Retrieved from: http://siteresources.worldbank.org/EDUCATION/Resources/278200-1290520949227/7575842-1365797649219/Framework_SABER-Teachers_Apr.13.pdf

Young, M. (ed) (1971) *Knowledge and control: New directions in the sociology of education,* London: Collier-McMillan.

Young, T. (2014) *Prisoners of the blob: Why most education experts are wrong about nearly everything,* London: Civitas.

Young, M. and Lambert, D. with Roberts, C. and Roberts, M. (2014) *Knowledge and the future school,* London: Bloomsbury.

Zeichner, K. (2009) *Teacher education and the struggle for social justice,* London: Routledge.

Zeichner, K. (2011) 'Rethinking the connections between campus based courses and field experiences in college and university based teacher education', in J. Millwater, L. Ehrich and D. Beutel (eds) *Practical experiences in professional education: A transdisciplinary approach,* Brisbane: Post Pressed, pp 37–60.

Zeichner, K. and Bier, M. (2014) 'The turn toward practice and clinical experience in U.S. teacher education', in K-H. Arnold, A. Gröschner, and T. Hascher (eds) *Schulpraktika in der Lehrbildung. Theoretische Grundlagen, Konzeptionen, Prozesse und Effekte,* Münster: Waxmann, pp 103-26.

Index

Note: page numbers in italic type refer to Figures; those in bold type refer to Tables.

11+ examination: abolition of in Northern Ireland 79
'3 Is' model of teacher education: Northern Ireland 32, 80, 85–6
RoI (Republic of Ireland) 129

A

AACTE (American Association of Colleges for Teacher Education) 71
Abbott, A. 38, 49–50
academic drift 185–6
academic sub-tribes of teacher education 38, 51–2, 100, 103, 197
Academies programme, England 59
accountability 143, 146–7, 176, 225, 228
accountability turn in teacher education policy xii
see also standards
action research 166
activist model of teaching profession 28, 152, 189
Adam Smith Institute 8
ADES (Association of Directors of Education), Scotland 99
Advance Skills Teacher standard, England 33
Advisory Council on Education in Scotland 99
AERS (Applied Educational Research Scheme), Scotland 195
Aldrich, R. 50–1
Alexander, R. 4–5, 57, 58, 60, 63, 64, 67, 70, 179, 209, 210, 232
Andrews, Leighton 40, 41, 119–20
area learning communities, Northern Ireland 78
Arnott, M. 95

Aspiring to Excellence: Final report of the International Review Panel on the Structure of Initial Teacher Education in Northern Ireland (2014, DEL: Sahlberg review) 83–4, 88, 205–6, 211
Australia 46, 188

B

Bailyn, Bernard 51
Baumfield, V. 166
Beauchamp, Gary 109–24, 162, 169, 220
Becher, T. 184
BEd (Bachelor of Education) qualification 6
Northern Ireland 81
RoI (Republic of Ireland) 127, 133–4, 140
Scotland 104
benchmarking, in international performance indicators 40
BERA (British Educational Research Association) 14, 15, 30, 31–2, 34–5, 63, 71, 86, 96, 163, 170, 176, 177, 192, 211, 229, 231
Bier, M. 215
bildung 25
Birmingham, England; 'Trojan horse' plot 228
Bologna Process 134, 162, 190, 220, 230
Borko, H. 171, 175
Bourke, T. 145
Brennan, C. 198
Brisard, E. 209
Bruce, C.D. 166
Bruner, Jerome 25
Bryce, T. 93

279

Burton, N. 166
business capital model of teaching 53

C

Cameron, David 223
Cardiff University, Wales 118, 121
Carroll, J.B. 51
Carter review of initial teacher training (DfE) 16, 73, 192, 211, 221
Carter, Andrew 16
CASS (Curriculum Advisory and Support Service), Northern Ireland 85, 86
CATE (Council for Accreditation of Teacher Education) 8, 60
CBI (Confederation of British Industry) 41
CCEA (Council for the Curriculum, Examinations and Assessment), Northern Ireland 78
CDA (critical discourse analysis) 149
Centre for Policy Studies 8
children's services, integration with education 29
Childs, A. 71
Chilver Review Group, Northern Ireland 82
Christie Commission on the Future Delivery of Public Services (Scotland) 94, 95
CICE (Church of Ireland College of Education), RoI (Republic of Ireland) 135
civil servants: role in Northern Ireland's education policy 77
Civitas 52
Claparède, Édouarde 48
Clarke, Kenneth 8
Clarke, Linda 75–89
Clarke, M. 145, 146
clinical practice in teacher education 31–2, 188, 211–12
clinical reasoning 72
CNAA (Council for National Academic Awards) 30, 63, 100
Coalition government (Conservative/ Liberal Democrat), UK: education policy 45, 59, 64, 162–3, 204–5
Cochran-Smith, Marilyn 12, 166, 174, 210, x–xvi
collaborative professionalism 148, 156, 159
College of Teaching, England 35
colleges of education 6, 67

Northern Ireland 81, 82–3
RoI (Republic of Ireland) 127–8, 135–7, 138–9, *139*
Scotland 96, 98–100, **101–2**
see also HEIs (higher education institutions)
Conway, P.F. 188
Coolahan, J. 128, 130
Cordingley, P. 166
COSLA (Convention of Scottish Local Authorities) 99
counter-terrorism strategies 228
CPD (continuing professional development) in teacher education 32–3, 166
Northern Ireland 81, 85, 87–8
and partnerships 210, 213
Scotland 107–8
Wales 192
Crafts, M. 57, 58, 60, 63, 64, 67, 70
Crawford College, RoI (Republic of Ireland) 136
crisis model of teacher education 44–7
Cromien, S. 130
CT (Chartered Teacher Scheme), Scotland 32, 162
Curriculum for Excellence, Scotland 94

D

Darling-Hammond, L. 12, 44, 144, 146
data, greater use of by teachers 34
Daugherty, R. 118
Davidson, Jane 115–18
Davies, S.M.B. 118
Davies, Walford 122
DCU (Dublin City University) Incorporation, RoI (Republic of Ireland) 135, 136
DE (Department of Education), Northern Ireland 76–7, 80, 83, 87
Decroly, Ovide 48
DEL (Department for Employment and Learning), Northern Ireland 76–7, 80, 83
Aspiring to Excellence: Final report of the International Review Panel on the Structure of Initial Teacher Education in Northern Ireland (2014) (Sahlberg review) 83–4, 88, 205–6, 211
DEL: *Study of the teacher education infrastructure in Northern Ireland* (Grant Thornton, 2013) 75, 82, 83
democratic professionalism 148, 153, 223

Index

Densmore, K. 148
Depaepe, M. 48
Department for Education and Skills, Wales 121
DES (Department of Education and Skills), RoI (Republic of Ireland) 127, 128, 130
DES, England:
  Initial teacher training: approval of courses. (Circular 24/89) 61
  Initial teacher training: approval of courses. (Circular 3/84) 8, 57, 60
  Teaching Quality. White Paper. (1983) 7–8
Dewey, John 25, 27, 48, 166
DfE (Department for Education):
  Carter review of initial teacher training 73, 192, 211, 221
  EBT (evidence-based teaching) 34
  The importance of teaching. White Paper 10, 45–6
  Initial teacher training (secondary phase) (Circular 9/92) 61–2, 202, 208
  The initial training of primary school teachers: New criteria for course approval (Circular 14/93) 61–2, 202, 208
  and research 169
  Teachers' standards (2013) 150–1, 158
DfEE:
  Teachers: Meeting the challenge of change. Green Paper 9
  Teaching: high status, high standards. 9
Dickson, D. 166
dispositions 22
Donaldson, Graham:
  Donaldson Report 2011 10, 15, 24–5, 26, 32, 33, 96, 98, 103, 104, 105, 106, 154, 191, 207, 211
  review of curriculum in Wales 122–3
Drakeford, M. 114
Duncan, Arne 45–6

E

early years education, Wales 116
Early Years Framework, Scotland 94
EBITT (employment-based initial teacher training) 58
EBT (evidence-based teaching) 34, 165, 232
  see also research; teacher as researcher
Economic and Social Research Council: Teaching and Learning Research Programme 14

ECTS (European Credit Transfer and Accumulation System) 134, 190
Education Act 1944 112
Education and Skills Authority, Northern Ireland 79
Education Authority, Northern Ireland 79
Education Reform (NI) Order 1989 79
Education Reform Act 1988 (England and Wales) 7, 79
Education Scotland 97–8
education studies, as an academic discipline
  see also universities
Educational Studies Association of Ireland 128
Edwards A. 113
effective teacher 27
EIS (Educational Institute of Scotland) 97
ELBs (Education and Library Boards), Northern Ireland 79, 205
  CASS (Curriculum Advisory and Support Service) 85, 86
Ellis, V. 197–8
England:
  College of Teaching 35
  counter-terrorism strategy 228
  education reform 7–8, 10–11
  General Teaching Council 23, 64, 157
  Masters in Teaching and Learning qualification 20, 33, 162, 163, 192–3, 221
  partnerships 61–2, 64–5, 203–5, 208–9, 214, 220
  PGCE (Post Graduate Certificate of Education) qualification 192, 221
  PISA (Programme for International Student Assessment), OECD 42, 222–3
  reflective teaching 27
  religion and education 64
  research 162, 163, 176, 194, 195, 222, 229
  resistance to Ofsted inspections 29
  standards 9, 21–2, 21–4, 32, 33, 150–1, 157, 158, 163, 176, 225
  teacher education policy 9–10, 15–16, 45, 52, 57–60, 57–74, 72–4, 180, 184–5, 186, 227
  divergence in 219, 221
  government intervention 60–3
  institutional changes 67–9
  practice turn in 187, 188, 220

281

relationship between theory and practice 70–2
stakeholder power, shifts in 63–7
university/research turn in 192–3, 221, xiv–xv
  teacher educators 198
  teacher shortages 81
enquiring teacher 28
Equality and Human Rights Commission 109
'equity as access' discourse xvi
equity turn in teacher education policy xv–xvi
ESRC (Economic and Social Research Council): TLRP (Teaching and Learning Research Programme) 118, 195
Estyn (Her Majesty's Chief Inspector of Education and Training in Wales) 111
ethical education 229
ETI (Education and Training Inspectorate), Northern Ireland 77, 80
EWC (Education Workforce Council), Wales 111
Expert Teacher standard, England 33

F

Fairclough, N. 149
Farry, Stephen 84
Ferrière, Adolphe 48
Finland 31, 33, 81, 164, 188, 191, 231
Foundation Phase, Wales 116
Free Schools 59
Freire, Paolo 26, 48
Fries, K. 12
Froebel College, RoI (Republic of Ireland) 135
Froebel, F. 25
Fullan, M. 35–6
Furlong, John 15, 27, 73, 78, 114, 121, 122, 135, 168, 176, 177, 181, 183, 204, 208, 211, 221, 232
Further and Higher Education (Scotland) Act 1992 100
Fyne, Christopher 46

G

Gale, T. 148, 229
Gardner, P. 118
Gavin, C. 131

GCSE (General Certificates for Secondary Education) qualifications, Northern Ireland review of 78
gender, and power relations 183
general professional knowledge 22
General Teaching Councils 23–4, 35, 64, 157–8
  England 23, 64, 157
  see also GTCNI (General Teaching Council for Northern Ireland); GTCS (General Teaching Council for Scotland); GTCW (General Teaching Council for Wales); Teaching Council, RoI (Republic of Ireland)
GERM (global educational reform movement) 13–14, 40
Getting it Right for Every Child (Scotland) 94
Gilroy, P. 118, 193
Glasgow West Teacher Education Initiative, Scotland 212
globalisation 145, 159–60, 227
  and teacher education policy 11–14, 41
Goodwin, A.L. 147
Gove, Michael 9–10, 15–16, 23, 26, 42, 46, 169, 186
governing bodies of schools, in Wales 119
Grant Thornton report: *DEL: Study of the teacher education infrastructure in Northern Ireland* 75, 82, 83
Grossman, P. 174
Groundwater-Smith, S. 187
GTCNI (General Teaching Council for Northern Ireland) 80, 82, 87–8, 176
  Teaching: The reflective profession (2007) 87, 151–3, 158, 160
GTCS (General Teaching Council for Scotland) 23, 96, 97, 103, 105, 107, 132, 157, 207
  The standard for career-long professional learning: Supporting the development of teacher professional learning (2012) (SCLPL) 107, 154, 155, 156, 158–9
  The standards for leadership and management: Supporting leadership and management development (2012) (SfLs) 154, 155, 156, 158–9
  The standards for registration: Mandatory requirements for registration with the General Teaching Council for Scotland (2012) (SfRs) 154, 155, 156, 158–9

GTCW (General Teaching Council for Wales) 111, 119, 157
GTP (Graduate Teacher Programme), Wales 111–12
Guimond, S. 159

H

Hagger, H. 71, 210, 215
Hall, Katja 41
Hargreaves, A. 35–6, 53–4
Hargreaves, David 30
HEA (Higher Education Authority), RoI (Republic of Ireland) 134
healthcare services, integration with education 29
HEFCW (Higher Education Funding Council for Wales) 111, 119, 121
HEIs (higher education institutions) 58, 61–3, 67–9, 179–82, 198–9
  changes in, 1984-2014 182–4, 185–96
  changing employment practices in 231
  conceptualisation of 182–5
  Northern Ireland 81, 82–3, 84, 85–7, 88
  RoI (Republic of Ireland) 126, 127–8, 135–7
  Scotland 96, 98–100, **101–2**, 103
  and teacher educators' work and identities 197–8
  university/research turn in teacher education policy 190–3, xiv–xv
  Wales 111–12, 116–17, 119–20, 121, 123
  see also colleges of education; partnerships; universities
Hibernia College 9, 131, 135, 139, *139*, 184, 224
Higher Diploma in Education, RoI (Republic of Ireland) 126, 128
Higher Education Wales 119
Hillgate Group 8
HMI (Her Majesty's Inspectorate) 63–4
Hofsterrer, R. 47, 48
Horlacher, R. 48
hub teaching schools, Scotland 207
Hulme, Moira 37–54, 91–108, 162, 219–33, xv
Humes, W. 93
Hutt, Jane 124n3
Hyland, A. 183

I

identity of teachers 29
IHEs (institutes of higher education) 67
  see also HEIs (higher education institutions)
IME (Irish Medium Education), Northern Ireland 81
Importance of teaching, The. White Paper 10, 45–6
Ingvarson, L. 146
Initial teacher training (secondary phase) (Circular 9/92, DfE) 61–2, 202, 208
Initial teacher training: approval of courses. (Circular 24/89, DES) 61
Initial teacher training: approval of courses. (Circular 3/84, DES) 8, 57, 60
Initial training of primary school teachers: New criteria for course approval (Circular 14/93, DfE) 61–2, 202, 208
integrated education movement, Northern Ireland 78, 79
ITE (initial teacher education) *see* teacher education
ITT (initial teacher training) *see* teacher education

J

James Report, 1972 32, 70
Jephcote, Martin 109–24
Jessop, B. 41
Joseph, Keith 7–8
judgment in practice 72

K

Keating, M. 227
Kennedy, Aileen 91–108, 143–60, xv
Kessels, J.P. 167
Kirk, G. 99
knowledge requirements of teachers 22–3
Korthagen, F.A. 167

L

Labaree, D.F. 52
Labour Party, Wales 114–15
Law, A. 94
leadership, educational 35
league tables 7
  abolition in Northern Ireland 79
learning support assistants 29
Leitch, R. 177

Levasseur, Pierre Émile 43
Levin, J.S. 54
Lewis, Huw 41–2, 120–1
Lieberman, A. 12
Limerick Institute of Technology, RoI (Republic of Ireland) 136
Lingard, B. 229
literacy teaching 9, 61
local education authorities; stakeholder power of in England 64
localisation, and teacher education policy 11–14, 41
London Institute of Education 167
Louis, K.S. 160
Lynch, J. 57, 58, 60, 63, 64, 67, 70
Lyte, S.L. 166

M

MacBeath, J. 65, 164
MacLure, M. 149
Magennis, Geraldine 75–89
Mahony, P. 229
managerial professionalism 148, 151, 156, 157, 158, 223
Mary Immaculate College, RoI (Republic of Ireland) 136
Masters level qualifications in teaching 20, 31, 33, 162, 167, 190–2, 220–1
　Masters in Educational Practice (MEP) qualification, Wales 20, 33, 120, 162, 191–2, 221
　Masters in Teaching (London Institute of Education) 167
　Masters in Teaching and Learning qualification, England 20, 33, 162, 163, 192–3, 221
　Northern Ireland 81, 88, 221
　RoI (Republic of Ireland) 134, 220, 221
　Scotland 105
Maynooth University, RoI (Republic of Ireland) 135
McCormac review (*Advancing professionalism in teaching*: 2011: Scottish Government) 98
McGuinness, Martin 79
McIntyre, D. 31, 71, 210, 214, 215
McKinsey & Co. 13
McNamara, O. 62, 70–1, 118, 193
MDI (Mater Dei Institute), RoI (Republic of Ireland) 135
Menter, Ian 3–17, 19–36, 100, 170, 173, 197, 219–33, xii
Mentor Teacher Initiative, Scotland 207

mentoring 65
　quality of 215–16
meta-cognition 173
Mincu, M. 166
Montessori, M. 25
Montgomery, A. 77
MOOCS (Massive Open Online Courses) 230
Mooney, G. 94
Moore, A. 145, 146
Moran, A. 205
Moray House Project, Scotland 207
Morgan, Rhodri 115
MOTE (Modes of Teacher Education) project (England and Wales) 202–3, 204, 211
Munn, Pamela 135
Murray, Jean 57–74, 179–99, 197, 219–33, xiii
Mutton, Trevor 57–74, 201–16

N

National College for School Leadership 35
National College of Art and Design, RoI (Republic of Ireland) 128
National Council on Teacher Quality 44
National Performance Framework, Scotland 95
nation states 41
NCTL (National College for Teaching and Leadership) 34, 46, 60
NEC (National Education Convention), RoI (Republic of Ireland) 129
Nelson, J. 170
neoliberalism 114
　and education policy 3, 5, 7–8, 40, xii
Netherlands 191
New Education 48–9
New Labour government 5, 9, 35, 114, 115, 162
new technology, impact on teachers 29, 34, 230–1
NISE (National Institute for Studies in Education), RoI (Republic of Ireland) 136
NITEC (Northern Ireland Teacher Education Committee) 77, 85
NIU Maynooth, RoI (Republic of Ireland) 135
Northern Ireland:
　colleges of education 81, 82–3

Index

CPD (continuing professional development) in teacher education 81, 85, 87–8
education policy 78–9
devolution of 5
HEIs (higher education institutions) 81, 82–3, 84, 85–7, 88
Masters level qualifications in teaching 81, 88, 221
partnerships 80, 84, 85–7, 205–6
PGCE (Post Graduate Certificate of Education) qualification 81, 82, 191, 221
religion and education 76, 78, 79
research 162, 175–6, 177, 194, 195
standards 151–3, 158, 159, 160, 162, 223, 225
teacher education policy 9, 75–6, 78–80, 82–4, 88–9, 180, 184, 185–6, 211
'3 I's' model 32, 80, 85–6
continuing teacher education 32
convergence in 219–20
Furlong review 78
institutional arrangements 80–2
key features 76–8
practice turn in 189–90
and professionalism 84, 87–8
quality of candidates 81–2
universities 81, 82, 83, 84, 85–7, 88
university/research turn in 191, 221, xiv
Norway 191
NPM (New Public Management) 34
NPP (National Partnership Project), England 204
NQT survey 65–6

O

O'Beirne, C. 170
O'Doherty, Teresa 125–40, 219–33
OECD (Organisation for Economic Co-operation and Development) 39, 53, 144, 164, 176–7
International Summit on the Teaching Profession (2013) 40
Review of the quality and equity of education outcomes in Scotland, diagnostic report (2007) 95
and RoI (Republic of Ireland) education policy 126–7, 129
Teachers Matter: Attracting, developing and retaining effective teachers. (2005) 222, xv

see also PISA (Programme for International Student Assessment)
Ofsted (Office for Standards in Education) 7, 29, 64, 204, 228
Osler, D. 205
Oxford Internship Scheme 71, 167–8, 211–12
Ozga, J. 95

P

parental choice 7, 79
partnerships 16, 201–3, 216, 220
and CPD (continuing professional development) in teacher education 210, 213
England 61–2, 64–5, 203–5, 208–9, 214, 220
Northern Ireland 80, 84, 85–7, 205–6
as a pedagogical concept 209–12
as a policy issue 202–9
quality of mentoring in 215–16
RoI (Republic of Ireland) 206
Scotland 105–7, **106**, 207
as a teacher education practice 212–16
Wales 203–4, 208
Paterson, Lindsay 104
PCK (pedagogical content knowledge) 22–3, 165, 168
Peiser, Gillian 161–78
performativity 146
Pestalozzi, J.H. 25, 48
PGCE (Post Graduate Certificate of Education) qualification 6, 8, 58, 62, 68, 70, 73
England 192, 221
Northern Ireland 81, 82, 191, 221
Open University courses 81
PGDE (Professional Graduate Diploma in Education) 104
Piaget, Jean 25, 48
PISA (Programme for International Student Assessment), OECD 10, 40
England 42, 222–3
RoI (Republic of Ireland) 41, 133, 140, 222, 223
Scotland 41
Wales 41–2, 119, 121, 222
Plaid Cymru 114–15
Plank, D.N. 11–12, 44
policy analysis:
Scott's nine continua for 149–50
of standards documents 150–60
policy borrowing 39–43
policy transfer 39, 41

in Northern Ireland 75
policy turn in teacher education policy 12, 23, xi–xii
policy-borrowing 13
political intervention in teacher education policy 7–11
Pollard, Andrew 195, 196
Popkewitz, T.S. 47–8
Portugal 191
Power, S. 118
practical theorising 31, 72, 214
practical turn in teacher education policy 31, 46–7, xiii
practice
see also theory and practice
practice turn in teacher education policy 31, 187–90, 220, xiii–xiv
practicum turn in teacher education policy 46–7, 187–8, 210, xiii
practitioner enquiry 165–6, 168, 171
Prevent Strategy, England 228
professional capital 35–6, 53–4
Professional Update (Scotland) 107–8
professionalism 29, 147–8, 226
  collaborative 148, 156, 159
  democratic 148, 153, 223
  managerial 148, 151, 156, 157, 158, 223
  and teacher educators 197–198197
  traditional 148, 154
progressive education 26, 45
proportional representation, in Scotland 91–2
PRSD (performance review and staff development), Northern Ireland 87–8
psychology: influence on educational theory 25
public sector employment, Scotland 93
pupils, stakeholder power of in England 66

Q

QTS (qualified teacher status):
  England 21, 58, 73
  Wales 111
QUB (Queen's University, Belfast), Northern Ireland 81, 82, 83
Quinn, Ruairí 133, 140, 223

R

RAE (Research Assessment Exercise) 117, 118, 170, 177, 193–5
RCTs (randomised controlled trials) 169
Reading Association of Ireland 128
Rees, G. 118
REF (Research Excellence Framework) 100, 169–70, 177, 193, 195, 196, 226–7
  Wales 118
reflective practice 19, 145, 166–7, 168, 172
reflective teacher 27
religion and education 20
  England 64
  Northern Ireland 76, 78, 79
  RoI (Republic of Ireland) 126, 135–7
research 16, 31, 52, 161–2, 175–8, 221–2, 232
  audit and evaluation of
    RAE (Research Assessment Exercise) 118, 170, 177, 193–195117
    REF (Research Excellence Framework) 100, 169–70, 177, 193, 195, 196, 226–7
  capacity-building 194–5
  forms of 166–7
  HEIs' role in 30–1, 182–3, 193–6
  policy context of 162–3
  practitioner enquiry 165–6
  RoI (Republic of Ireland) 137–8, 161, 177, 195–6, 229
  Scotland 162, 175–6, 189, 194, 195, 229
  in teacher education 161, 163–71, 231
  on teacher education 161, 171–5, 231
  Wales 117–18, 121, 123
  see also EBT (evidence-based teaching); universities
research literacy 34–5, 163–4, 175, 190, 196, 229
Review of initial teacher training in Wales (Tabberer) 15, 42, 117, 120–1, 122, 191–2, 208, 221
Review of Initial Teacher Training Provision in Wales: A report to the Welsh Assembly Government (Furlong) 15, 116–17, 121, 122, 177, 184, 186, 208, 211, 221
Review of the quality and equity of education outcomes in Scotland, diagnostic report (2007) (OECD) 95
Revised professional standards for education practitioners in Wales (Welsh Government) 156–7, 158, 159
Richardson, V. 166

Index

Robbins Report 1963 57, 67, 96
Robertson, S.L. 227
RoI (Republic of Ireland):
  'Celtic Tiger' economy 130, 182
  colleges of education 127–8, 135–7, 138–9, *139*
  economic recession 133, 134, 182
  HEIs (higher education institutions) 126, 127–8, 135–7
  Masters level qualifications in teaching 134, 220, 221
  partnerships 206
  PISA (Programme for International Student Assessment) 41, 133, 140, 222, 223
  religion and education 126, 135–7
  research 177, 195–6, 229
  standards 153–4, 158, 223
  teacher education policy 9, 15–16, 45, 125, 180, 184, 185–6, 188
    1965-1975 period 125–8
    1991-2006 period 129–31
    challenges and opportunities in 137–40, *139*
    convergence in 219–20
    divergence in 221
    practice turn in 190
    quality of candidates 81
    Sahlberg review 15, 88, 135, 136, 137, 140, 184, 206, 211
    structural coherence agenda 134–7
  teacher oversupply in 138–40, *139*
  Teaching Council 24, 129, 131–4, 137–8, 190, 206
    Code of professional conduct for teachers (2012) 153–4, 158, 159, 190
  TEG (Teacher Education Group) 15
  universities 126, 127, 128, 135–7, 138, *139*
  university/research turn in 190–1, 221, xiv
Ross, J.A. 166
RSA (Royal Society of Arts) 15, 31–2, 34–5, 63, 71, 86, 96, 163, 170, 176, 177, 192, 211, 229, 231
Ryan, M. 145

S

Sachs, J. 28, 145, 148, 203
Sahlberg, Pasi 13–14, 15, 83, 88, 143, 205–6, 211
  review of RoI (Republic of Ireland) teacher education policy 15, 88, 135, 136, 137, 140, 184, 206, 211

SCEL (Scottish College for Educational Leadership), Scotland 35
Schneuwly, B. 47, 48
Schön, D.A. 27, 166–7
School Direct, England 9–10, 46, 58, 59, 69, 70, 73, 185, 187, 198, 204–5, 209, 220, 224
school effectiveness movement 26
schools:
  and counter-terrorism strategies 228
  see also partnerships
Schwinn, T. 160
SCITT (school-centred initial teacher training), England 9, 58, 185
SCLPL *(The standard for career-long professional learning: Supporting the development of teacher professional learning)* (2012), GTCS 107, 154, 155, 156
SCoTENS (Standing Conference on Teacher Education, North and South) 15, 77–8, 195
Scotland:
  colleges of education 96, 98–100, **101–2**
  CPD (continuing professional development) in teacher education 107–8
  CT (Chartered Teacher Scheme) 32, 162
  devolution of education policy 5
  equity turn in teacher education policy xv
  HEIs (higher education institutions) 96, 98–100, **101–2**, 103
  independence movement 92, 230
  Masters level qualifications in teaching 33, 105
  partnerships 105–7, **106**, 207
  PISA (Programme for International Student Assessment) 41
  proportional representation 91–2
  public sector employment 93
  research 162, 175–6, 189, 194, 195, 229
  SCEL (Scottish College for Educational Leadership) 35
  standards 22, 23, 32, 107, 154–6, 158–9, 162, 189, 223, 225, 226
  teacher education policy 9, 45, 97–8, 108, 180, 184, 185, 186
    accreditation and validation of ITE 103–5
    convergence in 219–20
    divergence in 221

287

Donaldson Report 2011 10, 15, 24–5, 32, 33, 96, 98, 103, 104, 105, 106, 191, 207, 211, 221
  overview of recent developments 95–7
  practice turn in 189
  public policy context 91–5
  teacher educators 197, 198
  TIS (Teacher Induction Scheme) 32
  universities 96, 98–100, **101–2,** 103
  university/research turn in 98–100, **101–2,** 103, 191, 221, xiv
Scott, D. 149–50
Scottish Government 91–2, 93–4
  Advancing professionalism in teaching (2011: McCormac review) 98
  see also Scotland; teacher education policy
Scottish myth 92–3, 104, 108
Scottish Teachers for a New Era programme 212
Seddon, T. 54
SEED (Scottish Executive Education Department) 92
Seidel, T. 165
SENCo (Special Educational Needs Coordinator) standard, England 33
SfLs *(The standards for leadership and management: Supporting leadership and management development)* (2012) GTCS 154, 155, 156
SfRs *(The standards for registration: Mandatory requirements for registration with the General Teaching Council for Scotland)* (2012), GTCS 154, 155, 156
Shannon Consortium Partnership, RoI (Republic of Ireland) 136
Shavelson, R.J. 165
Shulman, L. 22–3
Singapore 164, 231
Sion Hill college, RoI (Republic of Ireland) 128
Siraj-Blatchford, I. 116
Smeyers, P. 48
Smith, A. 77
SMSC (spiritual, moral, social and cultural) education 228
SNP (Scottish National Party) 92, 95, 115
Sobe, N.W. 41, 42
social justice 224
social services, integration with education 29

sociology, influence on educational theory 25–6
soft governance 39
SPD (St Patrick's College, Drumcondra) 135
St Angela's College, RoI (Republic of Ireland) 128, 136
St Mary's College, Northern Ireland 81, 82, 83
stakeholders: shift in power of in England 63–7
Standard for career-long professional learning: Supporting the development of teacher professional learning (2012) (GTCS) 107, 154, 155, 156, 158–9
Standard for Chartered Teacher, Scotland 32
Standard for Full Registration, Scotland 32
Standard for Initial Teacher Education, Scotland 32
standards 16, 22–3, 27, 143–5, 160, 220, 223–4, 225–6, xii–xiii
  definition and purpose of 145–7
  England 9, 21–2, 21–4, 32, 33, 150–1, 157, 158, 163, 176, 225
  Northern Ireland 151–3, 158, 159, 160, 162, 223, 225
  and professionalism 147–8
  and research 162, 169
  RoI (Republic of Ireland) 153–4, 158, 223
  Scotland 22, 23, 32, 107, 154–6, 158–9, 162, 189, 223, 225, 226
  Wales 156–7, 158, 159, 162, 189, 223, 225
  see also accountability
Standards for leadership and management: Supporting leadership and management development (2012) (GTCS) 154, 155, 156, 158–9
Standards for registration: Mandatory requirements for registration with the General Teaching Council for Scotland (2012) (GTCS) 154, 155, 156, 158–9
Stanley, G.E. 145
STEAC (Scottish Tertiary Education Advisory Council) 99
Stenhouse, L. 28
Sterman, J. 159
Stevens, D. 147
Stirling University, Scotland 98, 100
Storey, A. 146

Index

Stranmillis College, Northern Ireland 81, 82, 83
Stronach, I. 145
student teachers, stakeholder power of in England 65–6
subject knowledge 22
Summerhill School 26
systematic synthetic phonics (literacy teaching) 9, 61

T

Tabberer, Ralph 15, 42, 117, 120–1, 208, 221
TALIS (Teaching and Learning International Survey) 10
Tatto, M.T. 11–12, 44, 164, 173–4
Taylor, W. 179
Teach First, England 9, 13, 46, 59, 185
Teach for America 9, 13, 59
teacher as researcher 28, 34
   RoI (Republic of Ireland) 137–8
   see also EBT (evidence-based teaching)
teacher education:
   'crisis' model of 44–7, 51
   academic drift in 185–6
   academic sub-tribes of 38, 51–2, 100, 103, 197
   clinical practice in 31–2, 188, 211–12
   competencies-based 21
   evidence base for 173–5
   and higher education 16, 58, 61–3, 67–9, 179–82, 198–9
   changes in, 1984-2014 185–96
   conceptualisation of 182–5
   teacher educators' work and identities 197–8
   historical overview 5–6, 20–1
   location of 3–4
   regulation of 20–4
   routes into 9–10, 58–60, 65–6
   standards-based 21–4
teacher education institutions:
   US 44
   see also colleges of education; HEIs (higher education institutions); universities
teacher education policy 37–8, 53–4
   accountability turn in xii–xiii
   comparative perspective 39–43
   convergence in 219–21
   divergence in 221–2, 228
   ecological perspective on 49–52
   equity turn in xv–xvi
   future directions of 230–3
   global dimension 11–14
   historical development of 47–9
   policy turn in 12, 23, xi–xii
   political intervention in 7–11
   practice turn in 31, 46–7, 187–90, xiii–xiv
   significance of 4–7
   social embeddedness of 42–3
   travelling policy 38, 53–4
   university/research turn in 190–3, xiv–xv
   and values 3
   see also individual country case studies
teachers:
   changing role of 19
   effective teacher 27
   enquiring teacher 28
   greater use of data by 34
   impact of new technology on 29, 34, 230–1
   knowledge requirements of 22–3
   learning and knowledge development 171–3
   reflective teacher 27
   religious requirements 20
   transformative teacher 28
   see also professionalism
Teachers Matter: Attracting, developing and retaining effective teachers. (2005) (OECD) 222, xv
Teachers: Meeting the challenge of change. Green Paper (DfEE) 9
Teachers' standards (DfE) 150–1, 158
teaching assistants 29
Teaching Council, RoI (Republic of Ireland) 24, 129, 131–4, 137–8, 206
   Code of professional conduct for teachers (2012) 153–4, 158, 159, 190
teaching profession:
   'business capital' and 'professional capital' models of 53–4
   'crisis' model of 44–7, 51
   'new professionalism' in 33–6
   activist model of 28, 152, 189
   concepts of professionalism in 47
   development of 24–6
   four models of 26–8
   and integration of children's services with education 29
   media portrayals of 52
   pressure on 11
   social status of 231
Teaching Quality. White Paper. (DES) 7–8

Teaching Scotland's Future: A report of the review of teacher education in Scotland see Donaldson Report 2011; Donaldson, Graham
Teaching: high status, high standards. (DfEE) 9
Teaching: The reflective profession (GTCNI) 87, 151–3, 158, 160
TEG (Teacher Education Group) 4, 14–16, x
TERN (Teacher Education Research Network), England 195
theory and practice 25–6, 187–8, 211
  integration of 167–8
  new conceptualisations of 70–2
  theorising practice 31
  'theory-practice gap' in teacher education xiii
Thomond College of Education, RoI (Republic of Ireland) 128
TIS (Teacher Induction Scheme), Scotland 32
TLRP (Teaching and Learning Research Programme), ESRC (Economic and Social Research Council) 118, 195
Toloudis, N. 47
Townsend, T. 13, 23
traditional professionalism 148, 154
transformative teacher 28
Trojan horse plot 228
Troops into Teaching 59
Trowler, P. 184
Truxor, M.P. 166
TTA (Teacher Training Agency), England 21, 60, 61, 204

U

UCET (Universities' Council for the Education of Teachers) 14, 15
UCETNI (Universities' Council for the Education of Teachers Northern Ireland) 77
UGC (University Grants Committee) 99
Ulster University, Northern Ireland 81, 82, 83
UNESCO (United Nations Educational, Scientific and Cultural Organisation) 39
universities:
  decline of influence in teacher education in England 60–3
  Northern Ireland 81, 82, 83, 84, 85–7, 88
  RoI (Republic of Ireland) 126, 127, 128, 135–7, 138, *139*
  role in teacher education 10, 19–20, 30–2, 50–2, 60–3, 67–9
  and school-led ITE (Initial teacher education) 59, 69
  Scotland 96, 98–100, **101–2**, 103
  university/research turn in teacher education policy 190–3, xiv–xv
  Wales 111–12, 116–17, 119–20, 121, 123
  see also HEIs (higher education institutions); partnerships; research
University College Cork, RoI (Republic of Ireland) 136
University of Glasgow 168
University of Limerick, RoI (Republic of Ireland) 136
US:
  measuring teacher effectiveness 40
  teacher education policy 12
  accountability turn in xii
  equity turn in xv–xvi
  historical perspective 44
  policy turn in xi–xii
  practice turn in xiii–xiv
  university/research turn in xv

V

values:
  and teacher education policy 3
  values education 228–9
van Velzen, B. 160
Vygotsky, Lev 25

W

Wales:
  country profile 109–10
  CPD (continuing professional development) in teacher education 192
  devolution of education policy 5
  devolution referendum 113–14
  Donaldson's curriculum review 122–3
  Education Reform Act 1988 7
  HEIs (higher education institutions) 111–12, 116–17, 119–20, 121, 123
  Masters in Educational Practice (MEP) qualification 20, 33, 120, 162, 191–2, 221
  OECD report 176–7

partnerships 203–4, 208
PISA (Programme for International Student Assessment) 41–2, 119, 121, 222
political environment and devolution 112–15
research 117–18, 121, 123, 162, 194–5
standards 156–7, 158, 159, 162, 189, 223, 225
teacher education policy 9, 15–16, 45, 52, 109–12, **110,** 111–12, **112,** 115–17, 119–20, 121–3, 122–3, 184, 185, 186, 189
 convergence in 219–20
 divergence in 221
 Furlong review 15, 116–17, 121, 122, 177, 184, 186, 208, 211, 221
 under Huw Lewis 120–1
 under Jane Davidson 115–18
 under Leighton Andrews 119–20
 Tabberer Review 15, 42, 117, 120–1, 122, 191–2, 208, 221
 universities 111–12, 116–17, 119–20, 121, 123
 university/research turn in 191–2, 221, xiv
Walker, M. 147
Wallace, M. 52
Walton, J. 51
Welsh Government 114
 Revised professional standards for education practitioners in Wales (2011) 156–7, 158, 159
Welsh language 110, 113
Welsh Liberal Democrats 115
Welsh-medium education 110, 113
WERN (Welsh Educational Research Network) 118, 194–5
Whitty, G. 7, 15, 59–60, 73, 148, 149, 150, 151, 159, 226
Winch, C. 34–5, 163
WISERD (Welsh Institute for Social and Economic Research, Data and Methods) 121
Wodehouse, Helen 45
Woodhead, Chris 30
workplace learning 70–1
World Bank 39, 53
World Health Organisation 39

Y

Ysgolion Cymraeg (Welsh-medium education) 110, 113

Z

Zeichner, K. 215